The Crime of Maldevelopment

T0383111

This book explores the causal relationship between the deregulation of international economic interests and the forms of violence that prevail in a large part of the Global South. More specifically, this book tells the story of how transnational corporations benefiting from increasing deregulation of their international economic interests, account for severe harm, the unrelenting violation of human rights, and maldevelopment in Latin America. Dependent on the structural deficiencies of the Latin American region, this book tests the examples of the extractive industries and multinational expansionism and the link between deregulated economies at the international level and the damaging local effects that increase what is here called maldevelopment.

Introducing the conceptual category of maldevelopment to criminology, the author makes recommendations for further research and outlines a network of possible mechanisms for its prevention and sanction – and for the work of reparation and construction toward the satisfaction of the needs of the victim or victimizable populations. This provocative and original text will be essential reading for those concerned with white-collar crime and crimes of the powerful, and for researchers in criminology, sociology, law, political science, development studies and international political economy.

María Laura Böhm is an Argentine-German lawyer at the University of Buenos Aires and a criminologist at both the National University of Lomas de Zamora in Argentina and the University of Hamburg in Germany. She obtained her PhD in Social Sciences from the University of Hamburg (with the support of a scholarship from the Konrad Adenauer Foundation) and was Post-Doc Researcher (with a grant from the Alexander von Humboldt Foundation) at Georg-August-Universität Göttingen. Starting in 2015, she became a fulltime DAAD (German Academic Exchange Service) Long-Term Guest Professor at the Law School of the University of Buenos Aires. Her main research interests are the link between criminogenic conditions, economy, transnational corporations and human rights in Latin America, violence and maldevelopment and criminal and security policies.

Crimes of the Powerful

Gregg Barak, *Eastern Michigan University, USA*
Penny Green, *Queen Mary University of London, UK*
Tony Ward, *Northumbria University, UK*

Crimes of the Powerful encompasses the harmful, injurious and victimizing behaviors perpetrated by privately or publicly operated businesses, corporations and organizations as well as the state mediated administrative, legalistic and political responses to these crimes.

The series draws attention to the commonalities of the theories, practices and controls of the crimes of the powerful. It focuses on the overlapping spheres and interrelated worlds of a wide array of existing and recently developing areas of social, historical and behavioral inquiry into the wrongdoings of multinational organizations, nation–states, stateless regimes, illegal networks, financialization, globalization and securitization.

These examinations of the crimes of the powerful straddle a variety of related disciplines and areas of academic interest, including studies in criminology and criminal justice; law and human rights; conflict, peace and security; economic change, environmental decay, and global sustainability.

Torture as State Crime
A Criminological Analysis of the Transnational Institutional Torturer
Melanie Collard

Natural Resources, Extraction and Indigenous Rights in Latin America
Exploring the Boundaries of Environmental and State-Corporate Crime in Bolivia, Peru and Mexico
Marcela Torres Wong

The Crime of Maldevelopment
Economic Deregulation and Violence in the Global South
María Laura Böhm

For more information about this series, please visit: www.routledge.com/Crimes-of-the-Powerful/book-series/COTP

The Crime of Maldevelopment

Economic Deregulation and Violence in the Global South

María Laura Böhm

Routledge
Taylor & Francis Group

LONDON AND NEW YORK

First published 2019
by Routledge

2 Park Square, Milton Park, Abingdon, Oxfordshire OX14 4RN
52 Vanderbilt Avenue, New York, NY 10017

Routledge is an imprint of the Taylor & Francis Group, an informa business

First issued in paperback 2020

British Library Cataloguing-in-Publication Data
A catalogue record for this book is available from the British Library

Library of Congress Cataloging-in-Publication Data
A catalog record for this book has been requested

ISBN: 978-0-8153-5377-5 (hbk)
ISBN: 978-0-367-48358-6 (pbk)

Typeset in Bembo
by Apex CoVantage, LLC

To all young researchers in all disciplines, who aim to go beyond science, to understand life and to improve lives.

Contents

Acknowledgments   xii
Preface   xiii

Introduction   1

Some introductory concepts 5
Structure of the book 7
Note 9
References 9

PART I   11

1   **The Latin American economy and the political and criminal-
    political context**   13

*The political and economic features of the current Latin American
    context 13*
    Resources, deregulation, neoliberalism and development 17
    The impact at the social domestic level 25
Criminal policy in times of deregulation and neoliberalism 27
Free economy, exclusion and violence 32
    As a kind of conclusion 33
Notes 34
References 35
    Filmography 39

2   **Visible and invisible violence according to Johan Galtung**   40

The interrelationship between physical, structural and cultural violence 42
Invisible structures of violence in Latin America 45
    A historical perspective 45

A simple proposal for analysis 51
   Basic needs 51
   Non-satisfaction 52
   Physical and/or organizational obstacles 53
   Avoidability 54
  Structural and physical violent relationships between local and
   foreign actors 55
The visibilization and action against invisible violence 57
Notes 59
References 60
  Filmography 62

PART II   **63**

**3 Seeing invisible violence – case studies from Mexico, Ecuador,
Chile and Argentina**   **65**

The cases and how they will be presented 66
The Salaverna *and* El Peñasquito *cases in Mexico 68*
   i. The case 68
   ii. Relevance of the specific business area or activity 68
   iii. Cultural violence in the region "before" 70
   iv. Structural violence in the region "before" 71
   v. Business, people and the economic situation in the area "during"
     and "after" 72
   vi. Structural violence in the region "during" and "after" 73
   vii. Physical violence in the region "during" and "after" 76
   viii. Cultural violence in the region "after" 77
The Texaco/Chevron *case in Ecuador 78*
   i. The case 78
   ii. Relevance of the specific business area or activity 78
   iii. Invisible violence in the region "before" (cultural and structural) 79
   iv. Business, people and the economic situation in the area
     "during" and "after" 80
   v. Structural violence in the region "during" and "after" 81
   vi. Physical violence in the region "during" and "after" 84
   vii. Cultural violence in the region "during" and "after" 85
The Ralco *case in Chile 87*
   i. The case 87
   ii. Relevance of the specific business area or activity 88
   iii. Cultural violence in the region "before" 89

      iv. *Structural violence in the region "before" 91*

      v. *Business, people and economic situation in the area "during" and "after" 94*

      vi. *Structural violence in the region "during" and "after" 95*

      vii. *Physical violence in the region "after" 96*

      viii. *Cultural violence in the region "after" 97*

   The MOCASE case in Argentina 99

      i. *The case 99*

      ii. *Relevance of the specific business area or activity 101*

      iii. *Cultural violence in the region 104*

      iv. *Structural violence in the region 105*

      v. *Physical violence until today 107*

      vi. *Cultural violence in the region today 110*

  Violent economy and culture 111

  Notes 113

  References 115

   Filmography 118

4   Linking economy and visible violence – case studies from Guatemala, Brazil, Peru and Honduras   **119**

  The cases and how they will be presented 120

  The Indigenous Women of Lote 8 case in Guatemala 121

   The case 121

   Indigenous women and their especial situation in the face of the mining industry 122

   Physical violence against women who defend human rights 123

   Sexual violence in Lote 8 125

  The Matopiba case in Brazil 127

   The case 127

   The interest of the Matopiba project for economic development 127

   The structural and physical negative impact – water and agro-toxics 130

   Physical violence 131

  The Baguazo case in Peru 133

   The case 133

   The free trade agreement with the USA 133

   Unchecked physical violence 135

   In the aftermath 137

  The Valle de Siria case in Honduras 138

   The case 138

   The promise: regulatory simplification to achieve development 139

   Death in slow motion 140

Traceable economic violence 142

Notes 144

References 145

   Filmography 148

PART III   **149**

5   The vicious circle of deregulated international businesses and violence   **151**

Phases of the vicious circle of violence in the regional long-term
   perspective 153

   Preexisting invisible violence 153

   New forms of invisible violence 154

   New forms of visible violence 157

   Reconfiguration and deepened conditions of invisible
      violence – again 160

   Agrarian production "for export" and unmet needs at home 162

Violence again and again: the sovereign power that is never overcome 165

   Sovereign power, governmentality and biopolitics 166

   Norm and law 168

   Power of life and death 170

   Bare life, exclusion and exception 171

   Economization and internationalization of biopolitics 172

Back to the (sovereign) violence in the Latin American territory 174

   The sovereigns and their protected territories 174

Conclusion 176

Notes 177

References 177

   Filmography 179

6   The crime of maldevelopment as a needed conceptual category of criminology   **180**

Accountability without exceptions 181

Development and maldevelopment 186

Background and horizon of a conceptual category of "crime
   of maldevelopment" in criminology 188

   Criminological background on the part of the Global North 189

      White-collar crime and the criminality of the powerful 190

      Macrocriminality 193

      Mass media studies in criminology 194

    Green criminology 196

    Victimology 198

    Crimes of globalization 200

  Criminological background on the part of the Global South 201

    Lolita Aniyar de Castro and the political engagement of
      criminology 202

    Carlos Elbert and the criminological approach to globalization
      and exclusion 203

    Eugenio Raúl Zaffaroni and mass crimes in authoritarian and
      democratic times 204

  Social harm as a subject of study 205

The crime of maldevelopment 208

A new concept as an incentive to think about old problems with new
  approaches 209

Notes 211

References 211

  Filmography 216

**Approaching the crime of maldevelopment – conclusion
and starting point**   **217**

Guidelines for an approach to the crime of maldevelopment 219

Mechanisms for the approach to the crime of maldevelopment 225

Subverting the submissive attitude of criminal law toward the sovereign 228

A call for discussion, exchange and transformative work 232

Notes 232

References 233

Index   235

Acknowledgments

This book wouldn't be thinkable without the support and inspiration of many people and institutions from its very beginning.

First and foremost, I would like to thank the Post-Doc Scholarship received from the Alexander von Humboldt Foundation for the research project on transnational corporations and human rights violations in Latin America, which was the starting point of this journey in concepts and experiences which have become increasingly broader and deeper from the scientific perspective. I would also like to thank Prof. Dr. Kai Ambos for his support during the first steps of this project as host professor at Georg-August-Universität Göttingen.

Further, I would like to thank all students and participants who have heard some of these ideas in classes and conferences and who have shared comments, questions and criticisms with me. In particular, I want to thank the participants of the Permanent Research Seminar on Corporations and Human Rights that I have been leading since 2015 at the Law School of the University of Buenos Aires; these Wednesday meetings have probably been the best imaginable exchange place for growth in this project. To Leandro Costanzo and Rodrigo Raskovsky, colleagues and friends: I am especially grateful for their indefatigable availability as enthusiastic and accurate critical discussants of my job, for they have imperceptibly helped me give shape to many of the criminological, political, economic and sociological views presented here.

I would also like to thank Gregg Barak for his interest and confidence in this project, and Kate Hunter, who as language proofreader has made of the manuscript a readable text.

At last, but actually in first place, as always, I want to thank Rubén, because this has been possible only because we are together.

Preface

Contrary to what the title of this work might suggest at first glance – at first glance conventionally – the idea of this book is to promote the construction of peace practices, in the hope and even in the conviction that this is possible. It is not intended to demand punishment or raise complaints that simply satisfy the need for justice. Of course, this is important in relation to economic activities and measures of the degree of damage and negative impact that impede the possibilities of satisfying the basic needs of populations in the Global South. This may be important for some, and will also be partially treated in this work. However, the main purpose is another. It is true that to speak of maldevelopment evokes images of injustice, of suffering, of historical conditions of submission and of things badly done. Conditions that lead to this will be explained, but the emphasis will be placed, much more, on the descriptive and explanatory visibility of these conditions, in order to find possibilities to address these conflicts in a cooperative and joint manner. The book, therefore, is aimed both at – to use the traditional terms of the penal system and criminology – offenders and victims, and at those who consider themselves mere witnesses. The book is written with deep dedication and care so that its message can be accessible to a peasant – there will be a version in Spanish – and to an official of the International Monetary Fund; it is made so that its proposals can be taken by a legislator, by a militant for the human rights and by a junior researcher; it is guided by the idea that nonconfrontational but cooperative work between an indigenous community and a mining company with transnational capital is possible. Moreover, the society apparently not involved in these conflicts is addressed here, as are workers in the area of media. Maldevelopment is an issue by and to everyone. The list of people to whom this book is directed is as infinite as the roles that these people – finite – occupy in the different social spaces. Depending on the place, the context and the moment, one person suffering from deficiencies in an area may years later turn out to be an actor in a conflictive situation which generates shortcomings for other people. This book, in that sense, aims to be a timeless and impersonal proposal, addressed to each person in particular, and to our societies in general, with their cultural practices and discourses, with their institutions and regulations, with their economic processes and their geopolitical complexities. To those who identify with the miscellanies of the Global South, and those who do so with the miscellanies of the Global North.

This book gathers the result of many years of academic research in different areas of criminal law, criminology, criminal policy and human rights, in a journey that has generated as much learning in the areas of sociology, economics or anthropology as it has about human interactions, global links and intercultural and international cooperation. Furthermore, an active nonviolent pacifism strongly inspires this book. All this mélange of study, learning and experiences was given in periods of work that had as their main working spaces legal and humanistic faculties of universities from both the Global South (fundamentally Argentina) and the Global North (fundamentally Germany).

Those who investigate these topics from an academic perspective are offered technical information and analysis based on previous studies of criminology and the social sciences; those who approach the subject as students are offered an overview of various realities and theoretical approaches to the current world and alternatives in terms of the professional and personal perspective to be adopted in this regard; to those who come to this work in search of ideas for political, economic and institutional action, the work will confront them with realities often silenced or minimized by law, macroeconomics and international politics; these last readers in particular are asked to read with openness not only ideological and technical, but also with human sensitivity, because this book is written from there, and also appeals to that human fiber that is in the microphysics of all macroprocesses. The economic actors, politicians and in general, the actors who are in positions that allow them to adopt measures which will impact important portions of the world population, may perhaps understand through this reading that every decision embodied in a document has an impact in the everyday life of children, of women, men and the elderly. The life and death of people often depends on the decisions embodied in those documents that you sign. The subsistence of an indigenous culture, access to fresh water by a mother and her children, the personal fulfillment of a young woman who wishes to study and contribute to social life without being violated or discriminated against for trying or the need for a man who clings to the cultivation of his land with his people to feed his community. All these situations can arise or not arise according to the documents that are signed, according to the ideas that inspire them and according to the people who put them in motion, or who constructively refuse them and offer alternatives.

Maldevelopment, thus, is present throughout the entire book and has names, places and dates. For this reason, to those who come from places more directly linked to the mud of the Global South of the world and its shortcomings, this book will surely give them the courage to know that they are not alone in their search for answers and ways of action. This book aims to help them in the recovery of the visibility of their situations. This visibility is missing, although many people suffer this silent violence day after day. This work, in short, is for everyone and aims to provide proposals for constructive dialogue to stop the vicious circles of economic policies and violence, and slowly enable the drawing of virtuous circles in processes that favor the construction of economic, cultural and legal peace in local and global forms.

Introduction

This book is a deep study as a continuation of a prior shorter proposal. It is about the causal relationship between the deregulation of international economic interests and the forms of violence that prevail in a large part of the Global South. More specifically, this book tells the story of how transnational corporations benefiting from increasing deregulation of their international economic interests account for severe harm, the unrelenting violation of human rights and maldevelopment in Latin America. Dependent on the structural deficiencies of the Latin American region, this book tests the examples of the extractive industries and multinational expansionism and the link between deregulated economies at the international level and the damaging effects that increase what is here called maldevelopment. This applies for the whole of Latin America in general and, more specifically, for the deepening of violent living conditions among pauperized populations at the local level in particular.

In the previous study (Böhm 2016), it was explained that Latin American countries have giant social gaps. On the one hand, there are economic and political elites, which have historically been in contact with foreign actors. These elites can offer flexible, protective conditions to foreign economic actors even though these conditions often go against the protection of the rights and interests of the local population. On the other hand, the majority of the population does not have sufficient access to fundamental goods such as food, water, decent housing, education, fair work and leisure activities. Each state has a different way of managing these political, economic, social and legal disparities. Despite the efforts some democratic governments have made to reduce the gap over the last two decades, visible results are still pending. The structural and historical foundations of inequality are present – with nuances – in all Latin American countries. In this context, the presence of transnational corporations and the development of their activities are of particular relevance and impact, because these corporations usually enjoy international prestige and support, whereas their activities have an immediate negative impact on marginalized populations. The set of human rights violations caused by business activities includes the displacement of people as long as this is forced, involuntary or occurs by means of fraud; water and air pollution; the extermination of plant and animal life; labor rights suppression; the expropriation of ancestral indigenous land, and the financing of armed groups involved in international crimes. These serious human rights violations might be of a quite different character depending on the region in question and its environmental, human and institutional conditions.

Economic and powerful actors are not perceived as offenders when harm is seen as the result of "normal" business activities. In cases in which transnational corporations that are economic partners of the host state carry out these activities, the negative impact of the activity is usually perceived as less serious. For this reason, it was explained – and this will be remembered here as well – that white-collar crime, the criminality of the powerful and macrocriminality concepts should, therefore, be considered not only at the domestic level, but also particularly at transnational business levels. The influence on decision-makers, businessmen and corporate policies is equal to or even stronger at the international level, and for this reason the impact of positive and negative consequences of businesses in Latin America reproduces larger forms of structural violence. Given that at the national and international level some parts of the population seem to be *superfluous*, and neither the local nor the international actors are respectful of their rights, and because of the prior situation of marginalization, these *superfluous* people will often not be in any situation to make a strong, timely demand for their rights. The victims, therefore, in their invisibility, inaccessibility and voicelessness, should be considered as not only national victims, but also international victims as well.

Cases presented in that article were emblematic for the criminogenic, socioeconomic and geopolitical conditions that, first, are related to international economic policies and, second, lead to the increase not only in human rights violations by transnational corporate actors, but to the rise of both invisible and visible levels of violence. In the same vein, in this book, not only three, but eight cases will be systematically analyzed in order to make these relationships evident. These cases are following: the mining projects *Salaverna* and *El Peñasquito* (Mexico), the oil extraction unit *Texaco/Chevron* (Ecuador), the hydroelectric dam *Ralco* (Chile), the violence against the peasant movement *MOCASE* (Argentina), the rape of *Indigenous Women of Lote 8* (Guatemala), the *Baguazo* massacre (Peru), the expansion of the agro-industrial frontier *Matopiba* (Brazil) and the mining project *Valle de Siria* (Honduras). The impression that large victim groups are anonymous does not mean that they actually are. Every malnourished child has a name, every displaced indigenous person is an irreplaceable member of an ancestral group and each severely polluted lake is one fewer natural source of water for a specific community. The fact that many harmful business activities are related to natural resources explains why the harm remains invisible, because the environment, plant and animal life do not have the possibility to make a claim, and individuals and communities directly affected are, as seen, primarily indigenous and rural people without sufficient access to proper claim mechanisms. It is interesting that environmental protection is becoming internationally more and more deregulated and reregulated, but the lower standards at the transnational level are often imposed by states lacking natural resources in binational documents when negotiating with states with more natural wealth (like the Latin American states). EU regulations, directives by the World Bank or UN resolutions are just as responsible as the United States, Canada or the European states and their foreign trade policies for the economic impact at the macro *and* micro levels. Thus, the environment, animal and plant life have no voice, but they are affected by the detrimental impact of significantly deregulated businesses on Latin American territories, and this deregulation has an immediate impact on the local population. Even more, it has an immediate impact on the international population as well. As soon as natural resources become scarcer, the violent means for their appropriation will become an even clearer reality. The mass media often remain too calm with respect to the violations of economic, social and cultural fundamental rights, because these are the rights particularly affected by transnational business and corporate actors. It should be considered, however, that the non-informed violation of these rights is precisely the kind of violation that leads to the perpetuation of structurally violent conditions.

Three theses were presented in the aforementioned study, and they can be considered a foundation and trigger for the present book. In Latin America, human rights violations by transnational corporations are a direct consequence of national and international economic policies. Further, criminogenic conditions and damage levels share economic and security logics that are to be considered as a whole and with an integral view. The focus for further research, therefore, should be on insecurity understood as violence in its structural and physical forms.

Following that proposal, this book describes and analyzes in a kind of timeline the regional context and the particular situation of economy, social conditions and violence before, during and after the deregulated development of big businesses occurs as part of the internationalization of multinational corporations in Latin America. The previous situation (before the corporation starts with its activity) presents a "favorable context" for the transnational business. The subsequent situation (with advanced activities by the corporation and after the activity has ceased) shows the structural and physical violence which is promoted by structurally violent contexts.

Before and after the corporate activities take place, visible/direct/physical expressions of violence and invisible/indirect structural and cultural expressions of violence exist. Indirect violence is understood here as a cause and a consequence of historical, political, social, economic, cultural and environmental discrimination suffered by important parts of the population of the Global South. This indirect structural violence is analyzed as interrelated to direct physical violence. These forms of violence cause severe harm to individuals and, in this way, they often do so in violation of fundamental rights: avoidable unemployment, water pollution and the lack of education or loss of a piece of land. These are invisible manifestations of violence and they lead, for example, to protests, illness, death, displacement and street crime, which are visible forms of violence. Rural invisible violence and urban visible violence can be understood together through the analysis of corporate-political partnerships at international and national levels. The "insecurity" in the Latin American streets is in this way to be seen as closely related to the local corporate and political enterprises that are inseparable from the internationalization of economic interests. It is, so to speak, a kind of dystopia: the contrary of the utopian "development" promise. This idea will be explained as a "vicious circle": more structural and cultural violence leads to more physical violence, and in turn, this physical violence leads to more structural and cultural violence, and so on. In this way, the book introduces a new criminological category and explains how it is that the economic, political, social and institutional relations of development may also be considered as a crime of maldevelopment.

The three objectives of the book are (1) the description of political, economic, institutional, social and cultural aspects of the Latin American region that configure the forms in which international businesses are incentivized by states, often to the detriment of the local population; (2) the explanation of the interdependence of structural violence or invisible forms of violence and international economic interests, based on concrete cases, and; (3) the proposal of a conceptual category which could be used as a framework for the design of mechanisms of accountability, reparation and reintegration of the conflictive situations on short-, middle- and long-term processes and violence dynamics.

The attention is focused on the Latin American situation and from the perspectives of the Global South.

A paradigmatic example of human rights violations in the context of transnational business activities in Latin America is the mining industry and the indulgent international response to harmful exploitation methods that lead to the contamination of water, air, animal and plant life and even serious health problems for workers and local communities. The recent disaster caused by Samarco Mineracão S.A. (a joint venture of Brazilian, British and Australian capital) in Bento Rodrigues, Brazil, is illustrative. In November 2015, the top tier of the Samarco tailings dam complex collapsed, flooding local communities with mine waste, mud and water. The mine waste destroyed a small town of 650 people and affected more than a dozen riverside towns on its way to the Atlantic Ocean 500 kilometers downstream; at least 17 people died. This was an "accident", it was said, although Samarco had been warned of the structural problem with the dam.[1] However, this kind of accident is quite common in the history of the mining industry in Latin America. Moreover, victims such as mine workers and local communities affected by pollution, harsh work conditions and mine waste are the result of five centuries of tolerance and even complicity between local and foreign interests. Apart from the mining industry, the hydrocarbon and energy industries are also typical examples of harmful transnational businesses. They often operate under special regulations (e.g. free trade agreements, or FTA) and are generally accepted as crucial to national progress and development. This discourse, therefore, legitimizes the reduction of individual and collective rights, and even their violation, when respecting the rights of the affected group is perceived as nonprofitable for national and transnational interests.

The object of this book is Latin America in its international relations. This, however, does not neglect the fact that extreme maldevelopment as a complex result of local and global dynamics is present in African and Asian countries as well (Vivekananda 1987; Amin 2011). This study, in this sense, could be thought of as a kind of methodological proposal for a future comparative analysis between regions.

Some introductory concepts

International economic policies are understood here not as hard law normative, but as the "soft" economic pressure exerted by international organizations (WTO, World Bank, OECD, etc.) and by some states (western European countries, United States, Canada, China) on other states and regions in their asymmetrical interaction, which is commonly a cause of structural violence. This pressure is often exerted by the triggering of *deregulative measures*. Economic deregulation or, as some authors call it from other perspectives, reregulation (Silveira Gorski 2014), is given by the relaxing of some areas organized under state control which become more and more distant to the prior organized area and become, thus, more and more distant from the conflicts which could arise in that area; decisions and measures related to an extensive spectrum of variables are left to the private actors: from the negotiation of land recognition and use for extractive purposes to their renunciation, to their own national jurisdiction for the resolution of a conflict with foreign investments, all these economic policies and practices trace a new map of actors, responsibilities and results at the economic and, therefore, the social and individual levels. Under these actors, there are some who are particularly relevant. In this sense, international economic relations can currently be analyzed by means of the concept "hegemon":

> A hegemon is not just the world's most powerful state; it is a state dedicated to creating and nurturing a global free trade system. It does so first by opening its own markets to foreign goods and services, and sending finance and investments overseas, then by enticing others to do the same. Hegemons can also bolster the global economy by setting up international organizations or regimes.
>
> (Nester 2010: 114)

Deregulation and reregulation in the hands of hegemons can lead to an expansive effect of harmful impact in the short, middle, and long term. These forms of harm will be analyzed here as violence, and in particular, as structural violence.

Johan Galtung (1969) describes *structural violence* as the ensemble of any avoidable physical and organizational structures that prevent people from meeting their basic needs or reaching their true potential. Under avoidable organizational structures, for example, we can list corruption practices that obstruct the satisfactory functioning of government offices when individuals demand protection, or of obstacles in the justice system when affected communities demand justice, or the normative and judicial tolerance of predatory or polluting industrial practices that exploit natural resources for the benefit of a few, but at the cost of the affected communities' natural environment or of ancestral populations, and in this way threatening decent lifestyles in those communities. In these examples, the basic needs (human rights!) are health, education, food and water for the affected human beings; they cannot be satisfied because of an *avoidable* bad response from governmental offices or because of an *avoidable* lack of access to clean food and water in their own place and an *avoidable* lack of access to jobs and salaries which could allow people to pay for food and water in other places. The gap between potential and real rights exposes individuals to harsh conditions whose genealogy can be found in centuries of instability, asymmetrical international relations and elite forms of government. These processes lead to increasing political and economic power positions for some, and therefore trigger the improvement of business relationships with geopolitically better positioned partners rather than focusing on better government design for the best possible realization of fundamental rights for the entire (or most of the) local population.

Domestic structural violence, therefore, is related to international structural violence: whereas in some contexts, peace mechanisms lead to lower structural, cultural and physical violence levels, in other contexts (such as the Latin American context), structural violence levels are stimulated by international policies that make local development difficult for the local population. Moreover, this situation is supported by cultural violence (acceptance of foreign standards and resignation with respect to a less favored position of one's own geopolitical position) and can lead to physical violence (death and illness, violent protest, increase in street crime from generally poor socioeconomic conditions, punitive and violent criminal policies, etc.).

Because of the broad and complex context in which violence forms emerge and develop, and because of the high-level, negative impact that this violence means for whole dynamics, deep structures, relationships and current and future life in the region, it was decided to talk here about *maldevelopment* as a conceptual category. This term was very trendy four or five decades ago. Economic and social tendencies have since silenced it. Given that the reality has not changed in a good direction, it may be time to recover the idea and use it in the current context – and beyond. Maldevelopment is understood as an umbrella concept for underdevelopment, dis-development and overdevelopment (Guha 1987). Here, in particular, it is meant for cases in which the promise of development is part of public policies and programs, and these are carried out with support – or at least without strong opposition – from the public, but are not correctly or sufficiently done and fundamental needs remain unmet. And here we talk about maldevelopment, on the other hand, also in cases in which the idea of thinking with parameters of development – in the Western and Nordic way – is exactly the opposite idea to the worldview of a specific group or culture upon whom this development would be imposed. In the last case, development in the Western-Nordic style often means the infliction of conditions that are by no means legitimated – not even in the hope of the group, because the group does not identify with this promise at all. This is maldevelopment in the Global South.

The use of a conceptual category in criminology for the purposes of description and analysis may be useful – this is the main objective here – for the visibilization and accountability strategies which could be devised and designed in order to achieve the responsibilization, reparation and reintegration of actors and conflicts in a constructive economic, cultural and institutional coexistence. In this sense, the crime of maldevelopment should be seen neither as only a crime of the powerful, nor as only a macrocriminality case, nor as only white-collar crime, nor as only a specific form of global crime or environmental crime. The crime of maldevelopment as a conceptual category in criminology is here presented as a broad field of reflexion and intervention; it is addressed at high-level functionaries as well as low-level agents of states and corporations, and civil society and the mass media too. There are responsible actors at all levels and in the different moments of each conflict and historical step in the region. The crime of maldevelopment as a conceptual category in criminology integrates in this first presentation of the idea old and new criminological fields, making them useful analytical tools for the understanding and intervention in the current Latin American region.

Structure of the book

Part I of the book comprises Chapters 1 and 2. Here, the geopolitical conditions and the current economic and political situation in Latin America are presented, and the utility of the violence concept for the analysis of this reality is explained. Thus, Chapter 1 is about the economic and political context. It explains international and regional economic policies as a criminogenic context for the abuse of the economic, social and cultural fundamental rights of the local Latin American population. The geopolitical situation is exposed as the context that defines regulatory dependencies and economic deregulation (e.g. free trade agreements). In the same vein, the impact of this context on the life of the local population is described. The causal relationship between international economic policies on the one hand, and regional and local economic interests and institutions in Latin America on the other, is analyzed along with the interdependence between host states and transnational and multinational corporations. Chapter 2 is about visible and invisible violence in Latin America and explores the concept and reality of violence in its different expressions. Johan Galtung's approach on structural, cultural and physical violence is taken as a starting point for the development of the concept of violence denoted in this book. Thereafter, the use of violence concepts as tools for the analysis and measure of the economic, social, institutional and political life in the Latin America region is explained as well. These concepts are linked, finally, to main state foreign and local actors in their relationships with the main private foreign and local actors.

Part II of the book is constituted by Chapters 3 and 4. Both are dedicated to the presentation and study of cases, cases which illustrate in a paradigmatic way the relationship between deregulated transnational economies and violence in Latin America. Chapter 3 is focused on structural and cultural violence, especially before big deregulated business starts. This chapter gives details about the reality of structurally invisible violence and the vulnerability of marginalized populations as a facilitating factor for the running of deregulated exploration and exploitation of natural resources in large-scale projects (mining sector, agricultural sector, hydrocarbons sector and clean energies sector) as well as its impact on indigenous people, farmers, rural communities and small cities and villages. The institutional abandonment by the State, along with the indifference on the part of civil society, are presented as central factors facilitating the economic advantage enjoyed by the transnational and multinational corporations to the detriment of the structural and cultural living conditions of the local population. The chapter is developed on the basis of specific selected cases from Mexico, Ecuador, Chile and Argentina. Chapter 4, for its part, makes evident through the selected cases that the deepening of economic and social breaches during the running of deregulated exploration and exploitation of natural resources at a large scale (mining sector, agricultural sector, hydrocarbons sector and clean energies sector) can lead to severe cases of physical violence – in the process and aftermath of the development of big projects. With this aim in mind, what are identified here are, on the one hand, cases of physical "insecurity" related to the criminalization and repression of activists and leaders by the state as well as by private security firms and, on the other hand, the increase of ordinary violent crimes on the part of individuals as a consequence of the deepening of structural and cultural violence in these areas. Whereas Chapter 3 has a more systematic presentation and aims to makes invisible violence visible, the cases in Chapter 4 are told as violent physical situations which have to be seen, however, as visible cathartic moments along a permanent continuum of invisible oppressive living conditions. The selected cases are from Guatemala, Peru, Brazil and Honduras.

Part III of the book, then, is dedicated to Chapters 5 and 6. Chapter 5 is about the vicious circle of deregulated international businesses and violence and describes and explains the "vicious circle" of structural violence, institutional fragility, internationally deregulated economic interests, harm and rights violations, which lead to the deepening of structural violence (that leads to deeper fragility, to more opportunities for easier economic benefits for international actors and to subsequent harm production and rights violations, restarting the circle again and again in this way). These unlimited processes are clarified on the basis of the cases described in Chapters 3 and 4 as well as at regional long-term level, and explain the need of a different criminological conceptual category for the explanation of them as well as for first drafts of accountability mechanisms and intervention. Last, Chapter 6 explains the crime of maldevelopment as a needed conceptual category of criminology. Given that the vicious circle has its basis in structurally international and local avoidable conditions, it is possible to assert the liability of political, economic and social actors in terms of the severe negative impact of their interrelated activities. The chapter lays out, explains and analytically organizes criminological antecedents, purposes and ways of possible forms of understanding of responsibility oriented to the reparation of harms and to the reintegration of actors and social bonds in a constructive way.

In a brief Conclusion, the crime of maldevelopment and some ideas for further research are offered for its use in open discussions, normative adjustments and practical transformative needs and actions.

Note

1 See the note "Entenda o acidente de Mariana e suas consequências para o meio ambiente" on the official site on the case: www.brasil.gov.br/meio-ambiente/2015/12/entenda-o-acidente-de-mariana-e-suas-consequencias-para-o-meio-ambiente; the report on the discussion about "crime or accident?", in Schreiber (2015); and the current dispute on the amount of the harm in Parreiras (2018).

References

Amin, Samir. 2011 (2nd ed.). *Maldevelopment: Anatomy of a Global Failure*, Cape Town et al.: Pambazuca.

Böhm, María Laura. 2016. "Transnational Corporations, Human Rights Violations and Structural Violence in Latin America: A Criminological Approach". *Kriminologisches Journal: Sonderheft Lateinamerika* 4, 272–293.

Galtung, Johan. 1969. "Violence, Peace, and Peace Research". *Journal of Peace Research* 6 (3), 167–191.

Guha, Amalendu. 1987. "Development Alternative and Social Alternative". In: *Premises and Process of Maldevelopment*, Stockholm: Bethany Books, 3–29.

Nester, William R. 2010. *Globalization, Wealth, and Power in the Twenty-First Century*, London: Palgrave Macmillan.

Parreiras, Mateus. 2018. "Promotores proíbem FGV de medir danos causados pela tragédia de Mariana para Samarco". *Em.com.br*. January 26. www.em.com.br/app/noticia/gerais/2018/01/26/interna_gerais,933744/promotores-proibem-fgv-de-medir-danos-no-rio-doce-para-samarco.shtml

Schreiber, Mariana. 2015. "Desastre em Mariana foi acidente ou crime? 'É precipitado avaliar', diz ministro". *BBC*. November 11. www.bbc.com/portuguese/noticias/2015/11/151110_ministro_mariana_ms

Silveira Gorski, Héctor. 2014. "Por un espacio público no estatal. Contra la hegemonía neoliberal y el declive de la democracia". In: Rivera Beiras, I. (ed.). *Delitos de los Estados, de los Mercados y daño social*, Barcelona: Anthropos, 99–112.

Vivekananda, Franklin (ed.). 1987. *Premises and Process of Maldevelopment*. Stockholm: Bethany Books.

Part I

Chapter 1

The Latin American economy and the political and criminal-political context

In this chapter, the economic and political context of Latin American relations with the rest of the world and with the actors and circumstances within their own states is presented. The aim is to explain the framework in which the transnational economic interests and their groups and corporations are acting and what kind of impact these relationships actually have at the local Latin American level. In the first part of the chapter, therefore, a rather economic perspective with an emphasis on international relationships is explained. The role of the international needs and markets will be discussed here, as will the emergence and relevance of economic policies at the international level and how the concepts of development, deregulation and neoliberalism are understood in this book. The second part will focus on the tension between the growing economic freedoms on the one hand and the increasing use of harsh and punitive criminal policies as a way of neutralizing or at least controlling individuals and populations excluded from the economic promise of development and wealth on the other. The domestic and international levels, in this sense, present quite similar dynamics.

The political and economic features of the current Latin American context

Talking about Latin America today and the impact of international economic policies in this region implies, among many other difficulties, accepting the challenge that it is necessary to consider the whole range of connections, interests and nationally and economically powerful actors that are on stage. The map exceeds by far the historical interrelations between Latin America and Europe, and the more recent, but not unproblematic, communications of Latin America with the United States of America. These two main actors remain central. The international scenario, however, when talking about international economic policies, today includes at least China, Russia and India as growing global players. Thus, the way in which policies are now carried out requires new perspectives and vocabulary as well. All this, of course, should be considered when the talk is about Latin America.

For example, whereas one author explains the "Easternisation" of global policies (Rachman 2016) as a kind of shift that we should take into account, another explains that global economic and political games are played more and more under the logic of "connections" and not any more under the logic of "territories" (Khanna 2016). Let me go a bit deeper into these ideas and their significance for Latin America.

In his book, Rachman made a compact presentation of colonization and economic power over centuries, and in this way, he explains the initiation of international economic relationships that continue today:

> The global balance of power began to tip with the great European voyages of exploration of the 1490s. In 1492, Christopher Columbus, a Genoese explorer employed by the Spanish crown, crossed the Atlantic. In 1498, Vasco da Gama, a Portuguese explorer, reached India. It was the Portuguese and Spanish who began the process of transforming the relationship between Europe and the rest of the world. Over the succeeding centuries, Europe's edge in military, seafaring and industrial technology allowed other European nations to build global empires. Russia expanded eastwards across Asia, all the way to the Pacific Ocean. The Dutch built an empire that reached as far as Indonesia. France's colonies extended from Indochina to West Africa and the Caribbean. Britain gained control of India in the eighteenth century and led the "scramble for Africa" in the nineteenth century. By the early twentieth century, the British Empire alone covered almost a quarter of the world's land area. The global domination of the "white races" was almost total. [. . .] [T]he emergence of the United States as the world's pre-eminent power, in the aftermath of the Second World War, prolonged the hegemony of the West. [. . .] These centuries of European and American dominance were based on economic might. [. . .] It is economic might that allows nations to generate the military, diplomatic and technological resources that translate into international political power. But, over the past fifty years, the West's dominance of the global economy has steadily eroded.
>
> (Rachman 2016: 4 ss.)

Latin America, in different ways, remains interconnected with the colonialist perspective of Europe and the United States. In this sense, the shift toward eastern areas, even when it is growing, is still not yet of great significance – at least not in the sense that it could change the structural conditions and practices that are limited to the first international economic powers in the region. China needs more and more soy and minerals, for example, to feed people and provide raw materials for high-tech industries, and thus, Latin America is experiencing the contact and influence of more and more Chinese capital in its territories. However, the Chinese cultural presence and pressure remain secondary. In other words, even if the United States and Europe no longer play the central role they played in Latin America over the last five centuries and especially in the last decades of the twentieth century, they are still more present than other internationally powerful actors, and the traces of their presence reach far, in time and space, into both the past and the future.

At the international level, indeed, the same thing happened

> because the relationship between economic and political power is not straightforward. When China became the world's largest economy it did not also automatically become the world's most powerful country. On the contrary, the US retained a military, diplomatic and institutional edge that continued to justify its title as the "hyperpower".
>
> (Rachman 2016: 9)

And, of course, I would add, that with respect to (but not only) Latin America, this extends to Europe too. And, for the whole world, both powers remain significant because of their more or less democratic and libertarian promises. From this perspective, thus, the

> West's institutional advantage has led to a continuing American and European dominance of international finance and law – which, in turn, translates into a form of political power. Access to Western financial markets, educational institutions and courts still matters to the whole world.
>
> (Rachman 2016: 15; similarly Guha &
> Vivekananda 1987)

Hence, in this interrelationship between Latin America and Europe, and Latin America and the United States, the kinds of interests at stake have changed very little across centuries. Latin America, historically, has provided Europe with raw material and natural resources (Galeano 1984; Altvater 2011). It was gold, silver, corn and cacao in the past, and it is wheat, soy, palm oil and nickel in the present. The United States has found cheap labor and oil and, of course, sugarcane, bananas and cotton. In the past, this all took place through colonial systems, and after the region became more and more politically independent, the goods and financial transfers became more and more sophisticated (Guha 1987; Guha & Vivekananda 1987). In this context, it is interesting to think about the differences among the foreign actors interested in the region:[1] "At least initially, slavery and colonialism were acts of enterprising individuals and companies; governments entered later, often with softening effect" (Galtung 1996: 49). Since then, there have been military interventions in many cases, new corporate interventions in many others or simply diplomatic and free market relationships, in the rest.[2]

This change, however, does not necessarily mean a better situation. As it was said, "While military warfare is a regular threat, tug-of-war is a perpetual reality – to be won by economic master planning rather than military doctrine" (Khanna 2016: xvii). Latin America seems to be locked in this perpetual reality:

> The exploitation of nonrenewable natural resources in Latin America is carried out by large consortiums of Canadian and American origin, whose

objective is to have a strategic reserve in 100 different natural resources and minerals in the next 10 years, that is, they act under geopolitical objectives.

(Catalá Leman 2011)

The Latin American territory is huge and rich. The infrastructure in the region, however, has always been and remains insufficient and poor. The best infrastructure has been created with foreign investments aimed at improving the supply channels from internal areas to foreign countries. Harbors, routes, highways, trains and modern business skyscrapers are all physical infrastructures which were constructed by the local population for the improvement of the trade conditions of local goods on their way to the foreign countries' population.[3] And this point, according to current perspectives on global policy, is crucial. China has elevated infrastructure "to the status of a global good", and there is a reason for this, according to some authors: "Geopolitics in a connected world plays out less on the Risk board of territorial conquest and more in the matrix of physical and digital infrastructure" (Khanna 2016: xvii). This idea, however, does not seem to fit to the Latin American region or, better said: old territorial logics are entangled with new infrastructural physical and digital aims. Given that Latin America retains its role as a natural resources provider, the struggles for the domain and property in this huge and rich natural territory is not part of the past, but an everyday nightmare for large parts of the population. Territorial struggles, as will be seen in the next chapters, are part of an ancient power strategy, that of the sovereign, who remains very active in Latin America and the Global South in general. Today, sovereigns are multiple and their thrones are not in the South, but in the North – their loyal feudal lords take care of their territories.

Technological, digital and highly complicated investment rules are far away from the daily problems of the people living *on* the rich territory, the natural resources and fertile pieces of land. Here, Harari's idea takes on a particular relevance:

> Ever since the Cognitive Revolution, Sapiens have thus been living in a dual reality. On the one hand, the objective reality of rivers, trees and lions; and on the other hand, the imagined reality of gods, nations and corporations. As time went by, the imagined reality became ever more powerful, so that today the very survival of rivers, trees and lions depends on the grace of imagined entities such as the United States and Google.
>
> (Harari 2014: 36)

The imagined reality of economic discourse, actors and dynamics is so strong that the objective reality of abundance and richness of huge areas of the world leads these very areas to be the poorest ones.

The representation of more or fewer interconnections between interests and powerful actors around the world is often done with maps, and this is interesting because maps simplify at the same time that they show only what they want to show: green spaces without people living in them, blue areas free of plant or animal life, even underground richness which looks, to the eyes of entrepreneurs, like gold at the surface of a no man's land waiting for good, brave explorers. Maps help to offer the whole world as a commodity for some. It was well said that "what we put on a map has iconic power to shape how people think" and that "we can never know the world without a map, nor definitively represent it with one" (Khanna 2016: xxi).

Thinking and the way of thinking is, no doubt, one of the most powerful means for the practice of power. In the Latin American case, since the first contact with Europe, this has also been a fact:

> This new power relationship is imposed as a consequence of the conformation of a new and first "pattern of world power" from the conquest of America, in which Europe would have a central position gathering under its hegemony to "all forms of control of subjectivity, of culture, and especially of knowledge". In other words, "all the experiences, histories, resources and cultural products, ended up also articulated in a single global cultural order around the European or Western hegemony".
>
> (Quijano 2000: 209, quoted by Rosso &
> Toledo López 2010: 5)

A new form of reading maps and of reading cultural hegemonies, so to speak, consists of looking very carefully at the economic, cultural and legal ideas that guide international, regional and national decisions. For the purpose of this study, the traces of some of these ideas will conduce toward the exposition of concepts like resources, deregulation, neoliberalism and development and their significance in the Latin American context.

Resources, deregulation, neoliberalism and development

The natural resources of the region were for a long time taken by other states with total impunity, then by agreements between countries and later through the financerization of Latin American economies driven by dictatorial regimes inspired and formed in the economic offices of the international North – essentially American (Heredia 2013; Taiana 2013). Today, however, the mechanisms of negotiation, extraction and transport have become sophisticated in every way. From the design or redesign of international regulations at international and interstate levels (EU directives, creation of economic zones, strategic unions, etc.), toward bilateral agreements that regulate investment conditions and specific industrial areas, there are more and more instruments scattered in the global economy which are weaving the networks of an economic matrix from which it is difficult to escape. For example, in the 1980s and 1990s, moved by the intention of political recognition in the international arena, various Latin

American states began to introduce the liberalization of domestic regulations and the dismantling of protection measures for local interests regarding foreign investment and commercial relations on certain industries (Sadir 2009: 73 ss.). The following are particularly relevant: metal mining (especially opencast); hydrocarbons (traditional extraction and fracking); agroindustry (monocultures, chemical packages and genetically modified seeds and cultures); hydroelectric, wind and nuclear power; and infrastructure projects (roads and canals). This was done theoretically under the same conditions of negotiation between the signatory states. In reality, however, it was carried out precisely within the framework of an asymmetrical relationship – in the context of what has been explained with respect to the Latin American context and its geopolitical situation. After the closing of those agreements and the initial enthusiasm regarding the global recognition that signing them implied, the content of those agreements began to weigh in the region. For example, the Latin American states have been systematically brought before the ICSID, in times of extreme economic difficulties. The claims in the arbitration lawsuits had to do with breaches related to the payment of external debt to private actors, with modifications in the conditions of realization of the foreign investments and in an alleged decrease in the protection of specific industrial areas. All this was cause and result – both – of different cycles of economic crises in the Latin American states which were pushed to the verge of bankruptcies and social unrest (Sadir 2009: 80 ss.; Zanatta 2012: 258 ss.; Silveira Gorski 2014).

Deregulation, therefore, is related to the reregulation of some areas through new rules. The term "deregulation", however, expresses with more clarity the idea of less protection and less assistance and social state intervention in favor of the local society. When public services are privatized and the new owners are fundamentally firms with a majority of foreign capital, or when thousands of hectares of fiscal land are taken by the government from state ownership and sold to – or simply given to – foreign private actors or when long-term residents of rural areas are violently expelled because of the arrival of new extractive projects and remain without legal protection or judicial representation, in all these cases, it is possible to talk about deregulation. The possibility of talking about reregulation and not about deregulation is raised by those who understand that there are no spaces left without regulation, but that the presumed "de-" regulation is based only on new regulations that precisely modify the state of the previous order (Silveira Gorski 2014; Gorenstein 2016; Gorenstein & Ortiz 2016). In this work, however, the use of the term deregulation is preferred, given that it emphasizes the idea of relaxation of controls and of state intervention in favor of less normative forms of ordering. These forms are more typical of politics that repose on the initiative of the market and that place blind trust in the balanced relationships among private individuals.

Deregulation at the Latin American level, for example, reduces through free trade agreements the state's action range or possible private claims. These are, therefore, key elements for the understanding of repeated misconduct toward the environment and the people living in that environment. Gorenstein explains:

> If in the period prior to the 1980s, the national states had a significant relative weight in their links with multinationals, since the 1990s the new international regulatory framework introduced changes in the exercise of their functions and imposed limits on their regulatory capacity after the objective of establishing a good investment climate. It should be underlined that this system does not mean a deregulation of markets in which the parties – nations and companies – are equal and have the same capacities to intervene, but it has been about a regrouping of power relations between States and transnational firms, coinciding with the aforementioned process that accompanied the wave of external investments of the period in LAC – Latin America and the Caribbean. The nations of the region approved, through their parliaments, the normative instruments that promoted external investments by incorporating various favorable clauses to transnational corporations [. . .].
>
> (Gorenstein 2016: 20)

Among the different clauses, the author exposes the following: the clause of *national treatment*, which means that foreign investors enjoy similar treatment to local investors. This implies that any treatment differentiated by the origin of the investor can be considered as a discriminatory attitude and generates the possibility for the foreign investor to claim hypothetical damages before international tribunals; the clause of *most favored nation* ensures the investor the possibility of using the conditions set by other treaties that could be more favorable to its own interests; the clause of *protection of prior investments* sets out that the protection of the investments found in these treaties includes investments made prior to their entry into force, and thus extends the rules favoring all external investments, regardless of when they were made; the clause of *stabilization* guarantees external investments the continuity of investment conditions regardless of legislative changes, which crystallizes the relationship eventually established between the nation and the investor – which clearly favors the latter. Last, there is a clause which is of special relevance in terms of possible conflict and even social conflict related to foreign investments. It is the clause about *supranational courts*. According to this clause, a supranational body is authorized to defend the interests of external investors with respect to government actions related to the investments. Even in cases where, in the first instance, it is foreseen that it is possible to appeal to the competent courts of the country in which the external investment is settled, access to an international tribunal is allowed (e.g. the International Centre for Settlement of Investment Disputes – ICSID – or the United Nations Commission on International Trade Law – UNCITRAL) if the local court did not decide on the merits of the dispute after a short period, or if that decision of the court is still pending but the dispute between the parties remains (Gorenstein 2016: 20, see in the same vein, Zabalo 2008; Raskovsky 2017).

Because of the displacement in the possible jurisdiction, which often means the avoidance of domestic processes and the prior exclusion of responsibility on the part of the investor in cases of environmental harm or in relation to the claims made by part of the population, some authors explain this mechanism and the opportunities that it offers to foreign investors as a *neutralization technique*, in the terms of Sykes and Matza. Defined as "discursive mechanisms used by those who violate the law to deny the criminality of their behavior" (Raskovsky 2017: 2), the original five neutralization techniques explained as useful for the understanding of the negative impact of free trade agreements and the arbitral panels, are denial of responsibility, denial of harm, denial of the victim, condemnation of the condemners and appeal to superior loyalties (Raskovsky 2017: 4–5). Investors use these techniques to claim that the host state is not adhering to the agreement when economic crisis puts the state in the situation of giving preference to the rights of the local population to the detriment of the economic benefit of the foreign corporation. In cases in which the company, for example, has caused severe environmental harm, a common argument is that the harm is not so serious or that it was not caused by the company, but by a lack of control or presence on the part of the state. These few sentences make it clear that any responsibility or eventual responsibility has been neglected from the beginning, and there is a poor chance of proving anything different when the discussion is settled before an arbitral panel and not at the domestic level and near the affected area. Affected populations see their rights violated in the whole sense of this word – because of the FTA, they will not usually be supported by their own state, and the state, on its part, will have to follow the process in an external forum. The figures are objective: "Under this new regulatory framework, the nations of LAC have been brought before the International Tribunal of the ICSID for alleged breaches of the clauses of the bilateral investment treaties in 161 cases, 28% of the total global claims in this court" (Gorenstein 2016: 20).

These briefly explained reasons and examples make it evident that some commercial and economic mechanisms are highly risky for the national Latin American economies and, especially, for their people.

The deregulative economic practices, instruments and policies leave fewer and fewer responsibilities in state hands and, at the same time, fewer responsibilities in the hands of private economic actors. On the other hand, development has been promoted at a discursive level but with other names at least since the beginning of the nineteenth century and explicitly formulated in the twentieth century (Tortosa 2011: 39 ss.). It was promoted in Europe, in the United States and in the explanations they offered as justification for intervention in other contexts – as in the Latin American context (Unceta Satrústegui 2009). Deregulation, a practice of the last decades, seems to be the opposite of the idea of progress in regions with deficient democratic institutions and dependent economies (Pompeu 2013). If the state does not support, move on, contribute to and regulate the main areas related to public services and basic needs (education, health, housing, work, environment and others), how can it be expected that these will develop in order to reach the whole population according to minimal basic standards for a dignified individual and social life? If there is not a state in charge with regard to decisions on natural resources or for the protection of its own people in cases of conflict with foreign actors, how can we speak about development? Thousands of documents and papers signed by international and national organisms at the public and private levels declaring the inviolability of human dignity, the need of better human development indexes or the emergency calls regarding fresh water stocks and green areas seem to be highly insufficient – and, sometimes, even to smell of plain hypocrisy – when they are confronted with the depredatory machinery of international and transnational economic business, the "accumulation through dispossession" ("acumulación por desposesión") (Altvater 2011: 34), also called "necrocapitalism" (Banerjee 2008), now more unchecked than ever before, and which are often closely related to the same organisms and actors who signed the aforementioned documents, full of good intentions.

In this sense, the binary problematic that the Inter-American Court of Human Rights has seen and described between the ideal of development at any cost, on the one hand, and violations of human rights, on the other hand, is probably a little more complicated. Development understood as processes aiming at improvements to economic *and* human life in multifactorial understanding and in a transversal perspective of human rights – these are interrelated, and there are no watertight compartments between them – may not be in tension with the protection of human rights. Notwithstanding, the current deregulatory policies and practices that claim to be development are actually running in the opposite direction. Does development mean only economic growth at the macro level? It does not. This has been widely discussed in the international arena and in the Latin American region. The Gini index as well as the Human Development Index are well examples of this (OECD 2011). If development means human development, and if human development is related not only to macroeconomics figures, as fans of the World Bank or the GDP think, so development and respect for human rights and increasingly satisfied basic needs in the region should be achieved and apparent. The problem is probably that the promise of development, the idea of development and the reality of development are different and often counterfactual proposals (Altvater 2011). This has happened in neoliberal, less neoliberal, progressive and less progressive Latin American governments over time. Deregulation seems to be more identifiable with neoliberalism. However, progressive governments which are resistant to neoliberal doctrines have also dealt with decisions on deregulation and economic licenses at the extractive industries level, for example. And this, again, for real development, presents a problem.

The progressive position on environmental issues is very clear in the case of extractivism: in some cases they use state companies or in others they appeal to agreements with foreign corporations. In areas such as hydrocarbons, they have substantially increased their appropriation of wealth, for example by increasing royalties or taxes, but in other cases they are still very low, as in mining. They renege on the International Monetary Fund and distance themselves from the World Bank, but they repeat the eagerness for foreign investment, increasing loans from China, for example, to finance ventures. They fight the political impositions of the North, but use that same discourse to cut social and environmental demands within their own countries.

(Gudynas 2015: 87)

For this reason, the emphasis is placed here not specifically on neoliberal economic programs, but on deregulative policies and, if such is the case, on the special consequences of deregulation when it exists, also, under governments identified with neoliberal policies as well.

Development, therefore, even though it is quite an old concept, should be rethought in this context in order to put it under potential scrutiny.

Seeking sustainable development or, in more local terms, the *Buen Vivir* of the population and improvement of basic living conditions, some governments initiated – in the years before and after the change of century – more state presence and a more integral approach to severe social lacks in individual, social and state needs. In so doing, many "progressive" governments, identified with a social state, started legal and institutional reforms such as nationalization of corporations, reinitiating of national industries, broader access to education and health systems, investments in national research and revision of historic landmarks untouched since the dictatorship period, recognitions of cultural diversity and mechanisms for the recovery of indigenous identities, among many other policies. The programs and promises, of course, have been always more spectacular than they were in their implemented reality. However, the attempt at stopping decades of neoliberal economic privatization and social exclusion was made.

In this context, however, some areas of the economy and some parts of the population have remained, so to say, forgotten or not sufficiently attended to. This was the case of populations living near (or in) areas rich in natural resources. Even the most expressively progressive government could not withstand the temptation (or necessity?) of maintaining quick access to the economic benefits of natural resources in order to have enough cash money to pay for the infrastructural and urgent social needs of the population. Presidents who won elections thanks to the promise of recognition and respect of ancestral cultures and their environment and original lands have broken this promise. Green progressivism has become "brown progressivism" ("*progresismo marrón*"), as it is called by Gudynas (2015), since from the beginning of the twenty-first century, extractive industries have entered their most aggressive period ever. The state acknowledges its role and responsibility, and works for the respect and realization of social rights, but all this comes at the price of the natural resources, the financing source:

> It is true that progressivism increased and extended the state plans to combat poverty, but it did so again and again invoking the need for extractivism as a source of funding. (. . .) The new environmental framework of Ecuador's Constitution, oriented to biocentrism, should lead to the failure to approve many mining or oil projects, however, this is not happening, on the contrary, progressivism reduces controls and environmental requirements to allow the expansion of mining, oil and agro-industries, they limit social mobilizations, reduce participation mechanisms, etc.
>
> (Gudynas 2015: 85–86)

The "financerization of nature" (Bruckmann 2017) or "commodification of nature" (Svampa 2017: 88 s., and similarly, Gudynas 2015 and Gorenstein 2016) is, therefore, a general problem in the Latin American context because it is the connection between international interests and needs, and the real, local existence of richness under the poorly and insufficiently organized socially marginal life of individuals and communities. The high price of land, water, oil, minerals and soil makes of nature a commodity, and makes of people living in the area obstacles to the conversion of nature into money. This conversion, however, should not be confused with development, as has been said. Coming back to the tension seen by the Inter-American Commission of Human Rights, the problem is that certain people benefit most from the projects, measures and deregulation of economic areas, but it is others who suffer the negative impact of these (badly understood) development projects. There is no balance between profit and loss. There is a right to development and a sovereign state able to decide which is the better way to crystallize this right. However,

> the fundamental relevance of this right is in opposition to a reality in which a large part of extractive activities in the countries of the region – mainly mining and hydrocarbons – are carried out on lands and territories historically occupied by indigenous and tribal peoples, which tend to coincide with areas that harbor a lot of natural resources. In addition, according to information available to the IACHR, with alarming frequency, plans and projects for the implementation of roads, canals, dams, hydroelectric dams, ports, tourist complexes, wind farms or similar activities take place in the area of indigenous and tribal lands and territories. In some areas of the continent, land grabbing for livestock and extensive crops or monocultures – such as sugar cane, soybeans and African palm – especially affect indigenous and tribal peoples, their lands and territories.
>
> (IAComHR, Doc 47/15, par. 16)

Those who are better positioned in their political and economic situation are always benefited, and those who are historically suffering the advances of the modern state, its urbanization and technologization are marginalized peasants, rural communities and indigenous cultures. This sounds "common", "natural" and even "logical". However, it is not. This schema of promoted development is violent in various ways. And this violence cannot be accepted. The acceptance of the development rules as they have been outlined until today is a form of violence. It is cultural violence through the legitimization of physical and structural violence. For this reason, some authors suggest that other ways are to be explored (postextractivism, for instance Gudynas 2015; Svampa 2017). The most interesting aspect here is, probably, that these proposals are inspired not only by economic or cultural reasons, but also by institutional and political convictions. If people are not considered as rights holders, and if people are suffering under unsatisfied needs and this situation can be avoided by the state but is not taken into account, it is possible that these people will lose not only the possibility of a better life in terms of food, housing, environment, work or education. Rather, they will suffer from the so-called development imposed by economic and political actors and lose their place as political subjects. Democracies, in this way, are increasingly illusionary. As Maristella Svampa has summed up:

> There is a challenge to think post-extractivism, namely, to develop alternatives to extractive development models: agribusiness, mega–mining, fracking, mega–dams, which, beyond their internal differences, present a common logic; large scale, export orientation, amplification of environmental and socio-sanitary impacts, pre-eminence of large corporate actors and retraction of the borders of democracy.
>
> (Svampa 2017: 102)

Moving a bit beyond the Latin American region, it is worth mentioning some wise words written by Muhammad Yunus when explaining the relevance of collective action among marginalized people in order to make differences and realize rights at a democratic level. This point may show what is to be improved in the Latin American region as well:

> In a Third World country like Bangladesh, democracy allows the poor to take advantage of their greatest asset – their large numbers. But to do so, they must be actively organized. I knew how crucial it was that all Grameen borrowers' voices be heard, and I asked our staff to work during the weeks before the 1991 election to ensure that 100 percent of all adult Grameen family members were registered to vote. I also recommended that each center collectively decide which candidate the members would support and that they parade to the voting booths together as a voting block. Even

if political office seekers did not take them seriously in that election, they would in the future.

(Yunus 1999/2003: 195)

In this sense, at the international and at the national level, dependencies define the lack of development (in an integral sense). They define maldevelopment (similar Tortosa 2011: 42 s., 377). Thus, both international and domestic dependence turns out to be a criminogenic factor that exposes individuals and populations to external decisions without having the most basic tools with which to deal with them. The structural social and economic situation at the domestic level is exacerbated by external conditions because fundamental rights are not only ignored, but also often violated as a result of business activities carried out by transnational actors supported by international policies and local interests.

International and transnational actors probably do not have sufficient interest in the real integral and sustainable development of the Global South:

> The failure of the Doha Round at the last WTO Ministerial Meeting (Nairobi, December 2015) shows, on the one hand, the lack of global consensus to meet the needs of developing countries – since rich countries will maintain subsidy schemes for the agricultural sector; and, on the other, that the strategy pursued by the central countries has been based on the promotion of regional free trade agreements Trans-Pacific Economic Cooperation Agreement-TPP, for its acronym in English – The Transatlantic Trade and Investment Association (TTIP), between the United States and the European Union, and the renewed interest to reactivate the signing of the European Union-Mercosur agreement. These treaties strengthen the weight of large multinational corporations by including defense clauses for foreign investors and the transfer of dispute resolution to international courts.
>
> (Gorenstein 2016: 21)

In this way, structural differences at the domestic level in the Latin American context become more and more involved in asymmetrical relationships that give advantages to the exploration and exploitation of resources by foreign actors, for example, under conditions that are not respectful of the interest of the local population, which remains – often because of the international economic policies – without national protective legislation.

The impact at the social domestic level

The good or bad relationship that exists between international economic requirements and the follow-up that is given to these requirements in domestic Latin American spheres has a first direct impact on internal socioeconomic relations. It can be noticed, in principle, at the structural level, that those states that apply the deregulation formulas of an internationally imposed neoliberal cut tend to move toward an impoverishment of the population not contemplated by macroeconomics, toward the indebtedness of the average population and to the enrichment of the groups with direct contact with foreign investments. On the other hand, the pressure of the international economy is reflected in certain specific economic sectors, and for the purposes of this work, it is of special interest to mention those which are directly linked to natural resources and, therefore, have a direct impact on the rural population near to mining activities, hydroelectric plants or new agro-economic areas. In cases where international proposals or requirements are rejected, on the contrary, there is a real retraction of the economy due to lack of capital flow and external inputs along with a loss of quality – in many cases – in terms of individual rights – for the protectionism and nationalism that usually accompanies these decisions– at the same time as the most urgent basic needs are met through social programs that are not sustainable over time (Gudynas 2015).

The type of relationship that a state maintains with international economies also has a second level of impact, this time in internal social relations and, in principle, physical relations as well. Individuals and groups belonging to the increasingly excluded population groups begin to live in areas of precarious employment and housing, all of which tend to the emergence or aggravation of street crime practices while giving an exercise of right to public demonstration claiming basic rights unsatisfied. In this way, there is an increase in violence in the internal relations of society, and an increase in the use of violence by states, which resort to the penal system to address the former, and to the use of security forces to silence the latter (Altvater 2011; Böhm 2013). In cases in which unaccepted measures lead to the economic and even ideological isolation of a state, it is usual to observe that the state will exercise controls over the population and, in this way, limit the right to private property and expression. The collectives that see their individual rights limited make protests that are frequently suffocated by the state in a repressive manner. Progressive and socially oriented governments, therefore, when they impose their policies to the extreme, often fall into the indiscriminate use of the penal system, the repression of street protest, and a retraction of democratic governance mechanisms. Criminal policy, therefore, presents particular lines, shared at some point by the neoliberal governments in their majority, and even by governments that make use of their security forces to maintain order in society in general, or in particular in the areas of extractive industries regarding the social conflicts they generate (Svampa 2017: 80 ss.).

The Latin American states that today present progressive socialist or socialist governments with a strong restriction of individual rights and of the exercise of democratic values have been constituted and constructed in their political programs on the base of an extreme reaction of protection and defense against the incursions and historical (political, economic and physical power) and current (economic and logistic power) intrusions of international and transnational economic interests. For this reason, they are not representative of the entire region. It is probable that this reality will change should international politics also mutate. On the other hand, the states that have accepted or reaccepted the international economic mandates and have assumed economic deregulation as a means of growth form the majority, and they present realities perpetuated over time that reproduce the long-standing differences, pressures, interventions and violence. For this reason, these cases will be studied here. The entry and pressures of international capital through the activity of transnational corporations and international economic policy in the Latin American context have new facets today, but they are based on historical realities. This is the history of the unsuccessfulness of the opening and welcome that has traditionally been offered to the promise of development, formulated internationally and locally.

Criminal policy in times of deregulation and neoliberalism

The relationship between the economic system, the criminogenic conditions of a given context and the criminal or security policies adopted by a state at a given moment seem, at first glance, not to be directly related to each other. However, as we have explained elsewhere (Böhm 2013) and recall here for this work, we can glimpse the interweaving of institutional and social strands that concern both the legal-criminal scope and the national economic sphere. From a critical-criminological perspective, it is possible to investigate, for example, whether there is a functional and discursive interrelationship between a neoliberal economic system, deregulated and socially expulsive, and a penally punitivist criminal system, that is, a system that increases in size and intensity its field of action, which incorporates increasingly intrusive means for investigation intensifies the sanctions to be imposed and relegates the "resocializing" goal of the penal system in favor of a merely neutralizing purpose of excluded subjects. Given that international deregulation has an impact on both rural and urban spaces, it is appropriate to recall here, even at the level of criminal policy, the gravity that this use of state violence adds to the situation described so far. The focus, then, will be placed in this second part of the chapter on the links in the domestic sphere between economic policy and criminal policy.

In the Global North, mainly in the countries of western Europe and the United States of America (USA), the relationship between neoliberalism and "hard" criminal policies has been made explicit and visible since the 1980s, and thereafter intensified uninterruptedly and theorized in various contexts (Sack 2003, 2004; Garland 2003), especially in relation to the most marginalized sectors of the population (Barry & Leonardsen 2012). Criminal policy has discursively taken on elements that were formerly characteristic of security, and thus the new security policies have merged with criminal policies including internal affairs issues interspersed with issues and means of foreign policy or specific to police states. The criminal-legal aspect of criminal policy has been distorted, and a political-war defense perspective has become more relevant, a perspective that has always been typical of decisions in the field of external security, but is new in the field of the ministries of the interior and justice of the democratic states. The crime (of the excluded) that supposedly threatens the order (of the included) is persecuted as an enemy, and no longer investigated as an infraction, and, on the contrary, noncriminal acts that could be dysfunctional to the neo-liberal economic order are harshly prosecuted.[4] The damages generated by the economic order itself, on the other hand, have remained so far outside the eye of both the penal system and of the discipline that studies its empirical conditions and offers conceptual explanations: criminology.

According to Loïc Wacquant (2001), whom I follow on this point, the essential characteristics of neoliberalism are (1) economic deregulation; (2) the withdrawal of the welfare state, its retraction, and recomposition; (3) the emergence of an expansive, intrusive and proactive criminal apparatus; and (4) the development of a cultural model of individual responsibility which preaches that how each one of us goes in life depends solely on ourselves, and not on the state.[5]

Given that neoliberalism implies greater freedom of action, and that this greater freedom of action implies many disappointments and greater risks, it is necessary to turn to increased measures that ensure free circulation, free supply and demand; measures, in short, to ensure the system. Both money and goods circulate with little economic state intervention, and this circulation should not be impeded – the system would say – by the dispossessed or those excluded from the labor market, or by the nostalgic spirit of a social solidarity model. And this, which undoubtedly rules in the neoliberal orders of the Global North, has its impact on the international dynamics of these orders in their contacts with the Global South, where the possibilities of greater freedom have shown, in general, only their dark face, without the majority of the population perceiving the material advantages promised. The free circulation of money and goods thus demands *strong punitive state intervention* to definitively separate from society those who have nothing (or not to enter into conflict with those areas of the planet that are rich in wealth without participating in it) and endanger the full enjoyment of that long-awaited freedom – at the domestic level and at the level of transnational capital in circulation. In this same sense, it has been said that "the imposition of the [neoliberal] model, necessarily, includes legislative acts leading to the hardening of sentences to 'criminals considered dangerous' (who can be any ordinary citizen), budget cuts in the public penitentiary system and the privatization of penal facilities" (Silva Sernaqué 1998: 47). Those who "get in the way" know the face of the penal system. Those who claim for their rights know the face of the repressive state (Altvater 2011: 55).

While in modernity, politics was seen as the art of governing and its function was illustrated with the image of a ship (the state) that should be steered by politics, in the postmodern era, it starts instead with a "decentralized" policy that is no longer in the condition, and does not aspire, to determine the course of the ship alone. Many other forces of power participate in the task, from the market and its transnational entities, globalized and localized actors and interest groups, among others. Bauman has already explained that the most fruitful privatization was the privatization of human problems and the privatization of the responsibility for their solution, and that the policy has reduced its recognized responsibilities to issues of public security and has declared its withdrawal from the tasks of social administration, and therefore, has actually dissocialized the miseries of society and translated social injustice into individual disability or negligence (Bauman 1995: 319). This idea, thought in local terms, is applicable also to the international scope, because it has left in the hands of the most vulnerable communities the burden and responsibility of overcoming the externalities – for these communities, purely and simply the loss of their basic conditions of subsistence, in many cases – that large investments and transnational ventures generate in their territories (Galtung 1996: 154 ss.). Security in the neoliberalism of the Global North is understood as the physical and economic security of a large part of the population, which is understood to be threatened by potential Muslim terrorists, adolescents, organized crime, immigrants or refugees. In this approach to the criminal issue, there is no in-depth treatment of the social, political or cultural context, not at the domestic level, to say nothing of the international level. Therefore, the punitive logic remains only in the spectrum of criminalization and "security", forgetting that the integrality of social problems requires the design and implementation of security programs understood in comprehensive terms; that is, a security that in its fullness implies nonviolence and, therefore, peace. Comprehensive security policies have nothing to do with the famished concept of security, a loyal servant of practices of intolerance and exclusion and, therefore, like the penal system, submissive to the interests of groups of economic, political and cultural power. Quite to the contrary, the construction of security in the broad, integral sense should be practiced – if we continue with these same given examples – by promoting understanding between nations and religions, through the study and treatment of structural deficiencies and the lack of containment frequent in the adolescent age group, through the reduction of institutional corruption and economic deregulation (main catalysts of what is known as organized crime), through the adoption of integrated and regulated immigration policies or through the revision of legislation and practices around the weapons industry and market, and the participation in armed conflict. All these would be security policies in an integral sense, aimed at the construction of social networks and individual support, and not at combating insecurity. Criminal policies obsessed with security, on the other hand, reduce the problem to its maximum expression, minimizing human needs and desocializing people's actions and conflicts. The subjects and actors protected by these criminal policies are profitable subjects, in the case of natural persons, and extremely profitable entities, in the case of companies: every one counts only as a wealthy or indebted body, employee or taxpayer, in all cases. In these cases, the state understands them as economic and protectable. Those who are not profitable for the state and the markets generate feelings of insecurity. Take the example of levels of incarceration in the United States, where the vast majority of the prison population comprises young, poorly educated men from the lower socioeconomic strata, often afro americans and *latinos*, who would have many opportunities to swell the stratum of the unemployed if they were free. In fact, some authors point out that if people of these characteristics had not been deprived of their freedom, the unemployment index in the United States during the 1990s would have been (in percentage) at least two points higher than it was (Western & Beckett 1999; Campbell 2010: 61).

Everything that threatens the profitability of the state and its economy is interpreted as a threat to the state itself, and against it acts a violent criminal policy which defines and sustains the submissive criminal system that betrays and delivers in the service of the great economic interests, political and cultural (on this submissive criminal system as opposed to a rebel criminal system, see the concluding chapter). In terms of Stenson and Foucault: "Sovereign practices operate in the name of and with the resources of central state authority and law. This is so even where elements of sovereign power, for example, electronic surveillance of offenders, are sub-contracted to commercial corporations" (Stenson 2005: 273).

The undoubtedly very close relationship between the economy, which is fostered and exploited by the techniques of freedom, and the economy that is protected and defended by security techniques, is reflected in political-criminal discourses and practices, at both the domestic and the international level:

> If the integration of the social body cannot be achieved through persuasion, it must ultimately be guaranteed by force. Under these circumstances, we should not be surprised if a reliance on actuarial and self-regulatory technologies for the majority coexists with a reliance on the attempts to dominate with sovereign technologies significant proportions of the population deemed troublesome (Valverde 1996).
>
> (Stenson 1998: 344)[6]

It could be said that as long as freedom is governed by an extremely deregulatory rationale of the basic norms of state and social service and responsibility, it will be difficult to avoid the presence of exclusionary security mechanisms and of a punitivist criminal system. And this, too, of course, in the Global South. For example, in Argentina – which has, since a couple of years ago, been following the extremely orthodox recipes of neoliberalism – social protest is increasingly criminalized when it makes demands for the protection of basic social conditions for workers or for conflicts over land and natural resources – where the state generally resolves to the detriment of peasant and indigenous communities and to the benefit of transnational investors. Moreover, it has increased the presence of security forces in the street in response to the feeling of insecurity generated in areas considered economically vulnerable, and legislative projects that aim to reduce the age of punishability are under discussion. The social dismemberment caused by neoliberal deregulation seems to find in the constant denunciation and persecution of exclusions its only possible reaction (see Rangugni 2011; Sozzo 2016).

This economy, which is a target and a fundamental element of the current neoliberal societies, has to do with the circulation of goods, wealth, individuals and power, and at the same time enables and requires sustained state intervention: "[T]he new economic order requires monopolized, coercive, sovereign state authority to suppress and contain social dislocation and resistance" (Stenson 2005: 268).

In *The Free Economy and the Strong State: The Politics of Thatcherism*, Gamble (1994) summarizes the idea of complementarity that was mentioned earlier, that idea of neoliberal orders based on scarce state economic intervention and a strong punitive state intervention. The author exposes and criticizes the economic ideas of the neoliberal school of Milton Friedman, and points out how for these liberals – in reality, neoliberals – there is an important difference between totalitarian and authoritarian regimes. This distinction is seldom highlighted. Whereas the former – such as German National Socialism or its contemporary Soviet regime – would have limited both individual liberties and the free economy, the latter – Pinochet in Chile, for example – would have reduced only individual liberties, while the economy and economic relations remained without intervention and untouchable. This is why authoritarianism is preferable for these authors whom Gamble analyzes. What, however, these authors deliberately do not say, remarks Gamble, is that a free market economy was also allowed under National Socialism. Authoritarianism is usually associated with military forces which impose limits on freedom through violence – which happens, of course, at the other ideological extreme as well. And it is true that, in most cases, a free economy is not only not limited, but also even promoted. The support of the Argentine, Uruguayan, Bolivian and Chilean dictatorships, to name but a few, on the part of the North American governments, also had these characteristics: a free market and a strong, violent state precisely oriented to avoid any obstacle – communist – of that free market (similarly Regino 2003; Basualdo 2013).

These dictatorships were intended not only to prevent the entry or expansion of communism to the United States – that is, to protect the "security" of a given population – but also to pursue the opening of the market, of the free market, until that moment intervened in and controlled in many Latin American states (Verbitsky & Bohoslavsky 2013).

In a degree of lesser intensity but with a similar logic, the interrelationship between economic and criminal policies analyzed here may be understood as what have been called "authoritarian democracies" (Silva Sernaqué 1998: 44). If the freedom of the economy is understood as a way to promote the vital processes of a certain population, then this free economy will demand protection at the expense of the political and civil liberties that could endanger it. And in the international arena, the protection of this free economy and its transnational actors will be carried forward even at the expense of the generation of structural, cultural and physical violence in the local population in Latin America, in which case, as the region has been sacrificed to the free economy and its growth in the Global North, it seems that it must accept these conditions, surrender and accept its submission (Schvartzer 2002: 89 ss.; Altvater 2011: 42).

Because of the economization of social and international relations – instead of the promotion of cultural relations and cooperation – the economy calls the tune. The free economy must be protected from danger and, if necessary, may even declare a state of emergency (Agamben 2004: 20). In the state of exception, the rules lose "form". In the state of exception, there is no normality, but neither is there abnormality. This is why laws are nothing but a kind of rules, or directives the only points of reference, if they even exist at all. And these rules or directives in force in the state of exception can be defined under the current neoliberalism by the economy itself:

> According to Schmitt, the directive appears because the legislation is subjected to serve the immediate needs of the economy. In Foucault's terms, the law operates more and more as a norm – or as a tactic, as he also puts it. It is no longer an expression of a legislator's will but an expression of life in the sphere of the economy. It is the laws of economy – as well as biology, psychology, sociology – that define the content of the formless norm.
> (Ojakangas 2005: 17)

Carl Schmitt, the jurist who worked for years as Hitler's theorist, is not the only jurist who saw economics as a "legislator". Today, the German criminal law professor Günther Jakobs makes a similar analysis when he understands that the recognition and assumption of the need for a Criminal Law of the Enemy is a fundamental challenge of criminal law science. To avoid the sin of idealism (Jakobs 2005), says this author, it is necessary to recognize that along with traditional criminal law (which he calls the Citizen Criminal Law), it is necessary to establish a system to fight against those who represent a threat to the socio-normative system: "If it [the legal-criminal science] does not want to acknowledge the need for the latter [the right to fight against the enemy], it will be marginalized by society – economically dominated – for lack of effectiveness" (Jakobs 2000: 53/54). This is what he calls a Criminal Law of the Enemy, criticized and denied by his colleagues, but valid under other labels in the daily legislative, judicial, police and political practices of not only Germany, but also many democratic states in the Global North and in the Global South.[7]

Free economy, exclusion and violence

What has been said about the criminalization of the Mapuche people is applicable to almost all those criminalized by national and international neoliberal punitivism – through the penal system in the first case, through coercive measures as well as visible and invisible violence in the second one:

> The only dead in this conflict are the Mapuche, considered by the State as the internal enemy. This is done under the protection of the doctrine of national security that is alive and well, absolutely valid, and gives ideological support to the anti-terrorist legislation. It places the Mapuche on the stage of the enemy criminal law, for putting at risk the development of the neoliberal economic model, which requires land for forestry companies.[8]

Having studied the logic or symbiotic functioning between the strategies of freedom and security strategies, which under the neoliberal model have placed emphasis on the assurance of the deregulated economy and the criminalization of those excluded from this socioeconomic disorder, it remains to be asked whether as long as the deregulative neoliberal model prevails in the spaces of international economic decision-making and in the economic, business and financial nodes that delineate the needs of the free market, an alternative to the model of punitive and exclusionary security policies may be established. The answer is probably negative. These policies have not been restrained by the fundamental principles of the Western rule of law in the domestic sphere (Böhm 2008, 2011b: Chapter 7) and have difficulties with the protection orders for human rights at the national and regional levels. Therefore, the only way to achieve new systems for the control of social conflict consists in the definitive displacement of the neoliberal deregulated model, and in the construction of economic-legal-institutional solidarity orders. The latter, however, is just an advance in political perspective and there is no concrete proposal for a program of action, because the lessons that must be known and drawn for the success of the program are innumerable. This work is devoted to a part of them.

As a kind of conclusion

Consider that even when criminal prohibitions and sanctions are provided *on paper*, in the Latin American context, *in practice*, they are not effective enough in the protection of individual and collective rights from state and transnational corporate harmful practices.[9] In this sense, Latin America can be considered a "frontier" for transnational business (Ebus & Kuijpers 2016: 125), a place where the rules of the corporations' own countries of origin seem to lose validity. The exception, Agamben would say, comes into force. Furthermore, international regulations, international economy and international policies are to be critically considered because they guide practices and discourses that reinforce violence and insecurity in the Latin American context. The link between criminal policies, violent practices and deregulated economies, which is visible at the domestic level, reproduces and expands its logic at the level of international and human rights conflicts as well.

Global relationships determine the terms among transnational corporations, host countries and affected local communities. Therefore, it is possible to say that global relationships determine local relationships as well. In Latin America, from the host country's side, this contextualization means the recognition of the richness in natural resources of the territory as well as the existing social, economic and *(avoidable)* institutional fragility of means for its protection. These factors, when put into relation with the usually stronger geopolitical and economic states whose corporations are involved in the damaging activities, and measured against the corporations' own situations, explain how criminological analysis needs to be complemented with economic elements, especially with a view to international politics. This means that Michalowski's (2009) notion of empire should be considered to acknowledge that there are still hegemonic economic streams that shape international conditions.

Among these conditions, structural differences and the difficulties in respecting fundamental rights are crucial. International conditions, consequently, are closely related to *structural violence* at both the domestic and international levels. This concept explains the link between international and national policies and between economic and social factors. In particular, their bond with visible and invisible forms of violence can be better explained.

To understand these relationships, then, we will deal in depth with what is referred to here with the direct impact at an economic and physical level; that is, we will see the visible and invisible violence configured by these economic relations between the international and the domestic in those states who say they want to belong and comply with the international mandates of "integration" and "belonging" to the global world that promises development.

Possibly, it is necessary to set a new agenda so as not to reduce the work of responding to the imposed development agenda – by more or less violent means. The hegemonic approach is ideal, or even chimerical. If this is added to the poor compliance of all the actors that interrelate in the international and transnational economic and political scenario, this leads only to an increase in all expressions of violence, as we will see, and in that way, to the generation and deepening of maldevelopment.

Notes

1 Regarding foreign interest starting from the first contact between indigenous people and foreign actors, and the impact this has had on the Latin American region, see the film *El abrazo de la serpiente* (2015).

2 Historical reviews on these processes in Latin America and with different perspectives offer Galeano (1984) and Zanatta (2012). See as an example the Argentinean case in the edited book by Horacio Verbitsky and Juan Pablo Bohoslavsky (2013), with special contributions on the relationships between economic, civil, corporate and military actors during the dictatorship from 1976 to 1983. A lucid illustration of the unequal relationship between Europe and Latin America today and the unequal distribution of resources since the "discovery" of America more than five centuries ago can be seen in the film *También la lluvia* (2010).

3 Two novels by two Latin American Nobel Prize Winners, *Cien años de soledad* (1967) by the Colombian writer Gabriel García Márquez, and *El sueño del celta* (2010) by the Peruvian writer Mario Vargas Llosa, show the economic and political side of the social construction of inequality since the slavery times continued to the territorial struggles and land distribution in detriment of the local population nowadays.

4 By way of example, it can be noted that on the occasion of the G8 meeting in the German city of Rostock (June 2, 2007), military "Tornado" aircraft were used to reconnoiter the terrain and prevent possible groupings that could pose a danger to the security of the meeting. The aircraft overflew the demonstrators at very low altitudes and took photographs to identify them. The attribution of responsibilities and "blame" for the adoption of such a measure, which clearly exceeded the powers of those in charge of ensuring the peaceful development of that "civil" summit, remain unclear and investigated. Shortly before that summit was carried out, numerous raids and arrests were made on people who had been under investigation for being suspected of being part of leftist groups and anti-liberal and anti-globalization movements – branded as terrorists. Several of those raids were later considered illegal. See Stolle (2008).

5 In order to deepen this characterization, see Wacquant (2001), an article in which the author explains and updates the analysis that he already explained extensively in his fundamental work, unavoidable when studying this topic, *Las cárceles de la miseria* (2000), a detailed investigation of social exclusion generated by neoliberalism and the consequent criminalization and imprisonment of the excluded, for the direct benefit of the market (think of the privatization of the prison system, of semi-slave work in prison, of tenders for the construction of prisons, with the consequent assemblies and services specialized that are offered exclusively for prisons and custody of prisoners, see on this subject also Campbell 2010: 61). The socioeconomic exclusion and the fear that it generates in the population are the fertile ground for the economic growth of the business with the criminalization of poverty. On the popular punitivism, see Gutiérrez (2011a, 2011b). Especially Colombo (2011) analyzes the political use of fear and insecurities in the urban areas.

6 The article of Mariana Valverde in reference is "Despotism and ethical governance" *Economy and Society* 1996, 23(3): 357–372.

7 On the Enemy Criminal Law in criminological terms, and in English, see Susanne Krasmann, "Enemy Penology", at the online *Oxford Research Encyclopedia* (2018, January).

8 Manifestation of the lawyer Alberto Espinoza (professional of the Foundation of Social Assistance of the Christian Churches [FASIC] and defender of Mapuche social fighters in various trials) during the Seminar on Anti-Terrorist Legislation held on June 24, 2010, at the Alberto Hurtado University. www.rebelion.org/noticia.php?id=108861

9 For a brief description of the normative *(on paper)* possibilities and their obstacles for prosecution at the level of national and international criminal law, see Böhm (2012).

References

Agamben, Giorgio. 2004. *Ausnahmezustand*, Frankfurt a.M.: Suhrkamp.

Altvater, Elmar. 2011. *Los límites del capitalismo. Acumulación, crecimiento y huella ecológica*, Buenos Aires: Mardulce.

Banerjee, Subhabrata Bobby. 2008. "Necrocapitalism". *Organization Studies* 29 (12), 1541–1563.

Barry, Monica/Leonardsen, Dag. 2012. "Inequality and Punitivism in Late Modern Societies: Scandinavian Exceptionalism Revisited". *European Journal of Probation* 4 (2), 46–61.

Basualdo, Eduardo M. 2013. "El legado dictatorial. El nuevo patrón de acumulación de capital, la desindustrialización y el ocaso de los trabajadores". In: Verbitsky, Horacio/Bohoslavsky, Juan Pablo (eds.). *Cuentas pendientes – Los cómplices económicos de la dictadura*, Buenos Aires: Siglo Veintiuno Editores, 81–99.

Bauman, Zygmunt. 1995. *Moderne und Ambivalenz. Das Ende der Eindeutigkeit*, Frankfurt a.M.: Fischer.

Böhm, María Laura. 2008. "Transformaciones en el Estado de(*l*) Derecho". *Cuadernos de Doctrina y Jurisprudencia Penal. Colección Criminología, teoría y praxis* (5/6) (Ad-Hoc), 15–33.

Böhm, María Laura. 2011a. "Endanger Law: War on Risks in German Criminal Law". In: Duttge, Gunnar (ed.). *The Law in the Information and Risk Society*, Göttingen: Göttingen Universitätsverlag, 145–163.

Böhm, María Laura. 2011b. *Der ,Gefährder' und das ,Gefährdungsrecht': Eine rechtssoziologische Analyse am Beispiel der Urteile des Bundesverfassungsgericht über die nachträgliche Sicherungsverwahrung und die akustische Wohnraumüberwachung*, Göttingen: Göttingen Universitätsverlag.

Böhm, María Laura. 2012. "Empresas transnacionales y violación de Derechos Humanos en América Latina – Dificultades para su imputación y juzgamiento". *Boletín Semestral GLIPGö* 4 (June–December), 11–24.

Böhm, María Laura. 2013. "Políticas de Seguridad y Neoliberalismo". In: Fernández Steinko, Armando (ed.). *Delincuencia, Finanzas y Globalización*, Madrid: Centro de Investigaciones Sociológicas.

Bruckmann, Mónica. 2017. "La financiarización de la naturaleza y sus consecuencias geopolíticas". *Revista Diálogos del Sur*. February 13. operamundi.uol.com.br/dialogosdelsur/la-financiarizacion-de-la-naturaleza-y-sus-consecuencias-geopoliticas/13022017/

Campbell, John L. 2010. "Neoliberalism's penal and debtor states. A rejoinder to Loïc Wacquant". *Theoretical Criminology* 14 (1), 59–73.

Catalán Leman, Martín. 2011. "Minería, una paradoja en el desarrollo de Zacatecas". *OCMAL*. December 6. www.ocmal.org/mineria-una-paradoja-en-el-desarrollo-de-zacatecas/

Colombo, Rafael. 2011. "Populismo punitivo y politización de la (in)seguridad urbana en Argentina: programas electorales, políticas públicas y racionalidades de gobierno en tiempos electorales y más allá". In: Gutiérrez, Mariano (ed.). *Populismo punitivo y justicia expresiva*, Buenos Aires: Di Plácido, 183–218.

Ebus, Bram/Kuijpers, Karlijn. 2016. "The State-Corporate Tandem Cycling towards Collision: State-Corporate Harm and the Resource Frontiers of Brazil and Colombia". In: Brisman, Avi/South, Nigel/White, Rob (eds.). *Environmental Crime and Social Conflict: Contemporary and Emerging Issues*, London/New York: Routledge, 125–152.

Galeano, Eduardo. 1984 (39th ed.). *Las venas abiertas de América Latina*, Madrid: Siglo XXI Editores.

Galtung, Johan. 1996. *Peace by Peaceful Means: Peace and Conflict, Development and Civilization*, London: Sage.

Gamble, Andrew. 1994. *The Free Economy and the Strong State: The Politics of Thatcherism*, Basingstoke: Macmillan.

García Márquez, Gabriel. 1967. *Cien años de Soledad*. Buenos Aires: Sudamericana.

Garland, David. 2003. "Die Kultur der 'High-Crimes Societies'. Voraussetzungen einer neuen Politik von 'Law and Order'". *Soziologie der Kriminalität. Kölner Zeitschrift für Soziologie und Sozialpsychologie*, Sonderheft 43/2003, 36–68.

Gorenstein, Silvia. 2016. *Empresas transnacionales en la agricultura y la producción de alimentos en América Latina y el Caribe*, Buenos Aires: Nueva Sociedad/Friedrich Ebert Stiftung.

Gorenstein, Silvia/Ortiz, Ricardo. 2016. "La tierra en disputa. Agricultura, Acumulación y territorio en la Argentina reciente". *RELAER* 1 (2), 1–26.

Gudynas, Eduardo. 2015. *Derechos de la Naturaleza, Ética biocéntrica y políticas ambientales*, Buenos Aires: Tinta Limón.

Guha, Amalendu. 1987. "Development Alternative and Social Alternative". In: *Premises and Process of Maldevelopment*, Stockholm: Bethany Books, 3–29.

Guha, Amalendu/Vivekananda, Franklin. 1987. "Structural Theory of Overdevelopment and Underdevelopment". In: *Premises and Process of Maldevelopment*, Stockholm: Bethany Books, 166–175.

Gutiérrez, Mariano. 2011a. "Trazos para delinear el 'populismo punitivo' en el caso argentino". In: Gutiérrez, Mariano (ed.). *Populismo punitivo y justicia expresiva*, Buenos Aires: Di Plácido, 59–103.

Gutiérrez, Mariano (ed.). 2011b. *Populismo punitivo y justicia expresiva*, Buenos Aires: Di Plácido.

Harari, Yuval Noah. 2014. *Sapiens: A Brief History of Humankind*, London: Penguin Vintage.

Heredia, Mariana. 2013. "Ideas económicas y poder durante la dictadura". In: Verbitsky, Horacio/Bohoslavsky, Juan Pablo (eds.). *Cuentas pendientes – Los cómplices económicos de la dictadura*, Buenos Aires: Siglo XXI, 47–63.

Jakobs, Günther. 2000. "Das Selbstverständnis der Strafrechtswissenschaft vor den Herausforderungen der Gegenwart". In: Eser/Hassemer/Burkhardt (eds.), *Die deutsche Strafrechtswissenschaft vor der Jahrtausendwende – Rückbesinnung und Ausblick*, Munich: Beck, 47–56.

Jakobs, Günther. 2005. Letter by G. Jakobs signed on 2005, February 7, to the students of the course "*Sicherheit und Freiheit IV. Staat und Gesellschaft. Feindstrafrecht und Kriminologie*", coordinated by Prof. Dr. Fritz Sack and Dr. Jürgen Kühling, *Aufbaustudiums Kriminologie*, University of Hamburg.

Khanna, Parag. 2016. *Connectography: Mapping the Global Network Revolution*, Croydon: Weidenfeld & Nicolson.

Michalowski, Raymond. 2009. "Power, Crime and Criminology in the New Imperial Age". *Crime, Law and Social Change* 51, 303–325.

OECD. 2011. "An Overview of Growing Income Inequalities in OECD Countries: Main Findings". In: Organisation for Economic Co-operation and Development. *Divided We Stand. Why Inequality Keeps Rising*, 21–45

Ojakangas, Mika. 2005. "Impossible Dialogue on Bio-Power. Agamben und Foucault". *Foucault Studies* 2 (May), 5–28.

Pompeu, Gina. 2013. "Humanidade ou nacionalidade: Entre a Soberania do Estado, a Proteção Internacional dos Direitos do Homem e a Responsabilidade Social das Empresas e das Universidades". In: Martins Pompeu, Randal/Marques, Carla Susana da E. (eds.). *Responsabilidade Social das Universidades*, Florianopolis: Conceito, 21–38.

Quijano, Aníbal. 2000. "Colonialidad del poder, eurocentrismo y América Latina". In: Lander, Edgard (ed.). *La colonialidad del saber: eurocentrismo y ciencias sociales*. CLACSO/UNESCO. Buenos Aires, 201–246

Rachman, Gideon. 2016. *Easternisation: War and Peace in the Asian Century*, London: Penguin.

Rangugni, Victoria. 2011. "Delito, (In)Seguridad y Redefinición de las Relaciones de Gobierno en la Argentina Neoliberal". In: Gutiérrez, Mariano (ed.). *Populismo punitivo y justicia expresiva*, Buenos Aires: Di Plácido, 367–386.

Raskovsky, Rodrigo. 2017. "Técnicas de neutralización y Arbitraje Internacional de Inversiones". Paper submitted at the *Seminar on Corporations and Humans Rights* at the University of Göttingen, July 20–21.

Regino, Gabriel. 2003. "Globalización, neoliberalismo y control social. ¿Hacia dónde se dirige el derecho penal en México?" *Nómadas* .0. www.ucm.es/info/nomadas/0/gregino.htm

Rosso, Inés/Toledo López, Virginia. 2010. "Proceso de (des-re)territorialización en Santiago del Estero". *Memoria Académica, Special Issue – VI Jornadas de Sociología de la UNLP*, 1–20.

Sack, Fritz. 2003. "Von der Nachfrage- zur Angebotspolitik auf dem Feld der Inneren Sicherheit". In: Dahme, Heinz-Jürgen/Otto, Hans-Uwe/Trube, Achim/Wohlfahrt, Norbert (eds.). *Soziale Arbeit für den aktivierenden Staat*. Opladen: Leske und Budrich, 249–276.

Sack, Fritz. 2004. "Strukturwandel und Kriminalpolitik". Paper presented at XXXIII. *Symposion "Neue Lust auf Strafen"* at the Institut für Konfliktforschung. Verein Deutscher Strafverteidiger, March 27–28.

Sadir, Emir. 2009. *El nuevo topo. Los caminos de la izquierda latinoamericana*, Barcelona: El viejo topo.

Schvartzer, Jorge. 2002. "La larga crisis de la deuda en América Latina". In: López Villafañe, Víctor/Di Masi, Jorge Rafael (eds.). *Del TLCAN als MERCOSUR. Integración y diversidades en América Latina*, México D.F.: Siglo XXI, 59–96.

Silva Sernaqué, Santos Alfonso. 1998. "El neoliberalismo y el Derecho Penal en las sociedades democráticas". *Barco de Papel* 2 (2), 41–59.

Silveira Gorski, Héctor. 2014. "Por un espacio público no estatal. Contra la hegemonía neoliberal y el declive de la democracia". In: Rivera Beiras, Iñaki. (ed.). *Delitos de los Estados, de los Mercados y daño social*, Barcelona: Anthropos, 99–112.

Sozzo, Máximo (ed.). 2016. *Postneoliberalismo y penalidad en América del Sur*, Buenos Aires: CLACSO.

Stenson, Kevin. 1998. "Beyond Histories of the Present". *Economy and Society* 27, 333–352.

Stenson, Kevin. 2005. "Sovereignty, biopolitics and the local government of crime in Britain". *Theoretical Criminology* 9 (3), 265–287.

Stolle, Peer. 2008. "Die aktuellen Terrorismus-Verfahren und ihre Folgen". *Kriminologisches Journal* 40. Jg. (2), 123–136.

Svampa, Maristella. 2017. *Del cambio de época al fin de ciclo. Gobiernos progresistas, extractivismo y movimientos sociales en América Latina*, Buenos Aires: Edhasa.

Taiana, Jorge E. 2013. "La geopolítica internacional de los apoyos económicos". In: Verbitsky, Horacio/Bohoslavsky, Juan Pablo (eds.). *Cuentas pendientes – Los cómplices económicos de la dictadura*, Buenos Aires: Siglo Veintiuno Editores, 65–77.

Tortosa, José María. 2011. *Maldesarrollo y Mal Vivir. Pobreza y violencia a escala mundial*, Quito: Ediciones Abya Yala.

Unceta Satrústegui, Koldo. 2009. "Desarrollo. Subdesarrollo. Maldesarrollo y Postdesarrollo. Una mirada transdisciplinar sobre el debate y sus implicancias". *Carta Latinoamericana. Contribuciones en Desarrollo y Sociedad en América Latina* 7, 1–34.

Valverde, Mariana. 1996. "Despotism and ethical governance". *Economy and Society* 23(3), 357–372.

Vargas Llosa, Mario. 2010. *El sueño del Celta*. Bogotá: Alfaguara.

Verbitsky, Horacio/Bohoslavsky, Juan Pablo (eds.). 2013. *Cuentas pendientes – Los cómplices económicos de la dictadura*, Buenos Aires: Siglo XXI.

Wacquant, Loïc. 2000. *Las cárceles de la miseria*, Buenos Aires: Manantial.

Wacquant, Loïc. 2001. "The Penalisation of Poverty and the Rise of Neo-Liberalism". *European Journal on Criminal Policy and Research* 9, 401–412.

Western, Bruce/Beckett, Katherine. 1999. "How Unregulated Is the U.S. Labor Market? The Penal System as a Labor Market Institution". *American Journal of Sociology* 104 (4), 1030–1060.

Yunus, Muhammad. 1999/2003. *Banker to the Poor: Micro-Lending and the Battle against World Poverty*. New York: Public Affairs.

Zabalo, Patxi. 2008. "Los acuerdos internacionales sobre inversión, otro obstáculo para el desarrollo de América Latina". *Gestión en el Tercer Milenio, Rev. de Investigación de la Facultad de Ciencias Administrativas* 11 (22), 27–39.

Zanatta, Loris. 2012. *Historia de América Latina. De la Colonia al siglo XXI.* Buenos Aires: Siglo XXI.

Filmography

El abrazo de la serpiente. 2015. Dir. Ciro Guerra. Argentina/Venezuela/Colombia.

También la lluvia. 2010. Dir. Icíar Bollaín. Spain/Mexico/France.

Chapter 2

Visible and invisible violence according to Johan Galtung

Issues such as social injustice, failed development, human rights violations or extremely harmful economic practices on a large scale could be better approached, one could think, by disciplines like sociology and political science, international law or economy. This work, as it is known, is a criminological one. And, in this sense, the approach is quite different. It is different not because of the research subject, but because of the perspective which is used to approach it. All four issues mentioned previously are interrelated and, more importantly, share a common denominator: violence. And violence is an issue for criminological thinking, regardless of which kind of violence it could be. In this chapter, therefore, the concept of violence in the special stream of analysis suggested decades ago by Johan Galtung and its potentiality for the study of the Latin American context will be presented.[1] Social injustice as an active (and not only as a passive) concept, failed development as concrete maldevelopment, human rights violations as extreme cases of infliction of harm on human beings and the pervasive negative impact on real communities as a result of international policies pushing for the deregulation of the economy in the region – all these angles of the issues explain why they are being treated by a criminologist. In this sense, the opposition between development and maldevelopment can be understood in these terms:

> "Maldevelopment" tries to refer not to a Good Living that should be sought for people, but to the verification, first, of the failure of the "development" program and, second, to the verification of the Bad Living that can be observed in the functioning of the system and its components, from national States to local communities. If "development" implies a normative element (the desirable, not necessarily the observable), "maldevelopment" contains an empirical (the observable) or even critical (the undesirable) component.
>
> (Tortosa 2011: 41)

The aim is an explanation of these processes and their violence and a reflection on specific mechanisms which could trigger processes in the other direction.

The origin of Galtung's work in structural violence was determined by the international situation of the late 1960s, basically in search of paths that could lay the foundations for the establishment of peace.[2] The context of the Cold War, and of that silent tension, is without a doubt the scope of origin for his ideas. Peace, in some cases, is not peace, but just an absence of physical violence, or "ceasefire" (Galtung 1998b: 1) with respect to the forms of expressive physical violence characteristic of war, but would not properly be an "absence of violence" (Galtung 1969: 167, 168). For this reason, his work is dedicated to understanding violence in its various facets in order to work on overcoming all of them. That said, it is important to indicate that the concept of structural violence developed by Galtung has its original application framework in the study of international relations, that is, in contexts in which the inequalities between central states and peripheral states were studied as the center and the origin of international and local violence.

The concept of violence developed by Galtung may lead to certain reductions and at the same time difficulties due to the breadth of the conceptual areas it encompasses. De Haan has already warned about the conceptualization of violence: "The concept of 'violence' is notoriously difficult to define because as a phenomenon it is multifaceted, socially constructed and highly ambivalent" (de Haan 2008: 28). The adoption and exhaustive use of one approach in this work is because of the general interrelations that it offers with other disciplines, and, specifically, with the development and maldevelopment issue understood as the subject of this book. Because of this, notwithstanding the excellent criticisms of de Haan to authors who define violence "inclusively", here the risk inherent in a "broad definition" (de Haan 2008: 32–33) is taken as the only way, probably, of studying violences in Latin America in an integral approach.[3]

In the case of Galtung, his proposal presents the great value of directing the investigation, even criminological investigations, we could say, to scopes and areas of work on violence which can shed light on relationships not as visible as physical violence, but generally much more damaging (Galtung 1975: 30–31). It is a way of promoting a "more committed social science" Galtung would even say (1975: 41). Or, in terms of Shinkel, it is a matter of advocating a "liquidation" of the concept of violence in order to avoid absolute definitions that try to capture the idea of violence as a whole (Shinkel 2010: 4), and instead have at hand a concept that is useful for understanding reality.

> The fact that a certain violence can be called structural violence means that certain things can be made visible when this violence is considered in relation to a certain differentiation of the social system, things that otherwise are not seen.
>
> (Shinkel 2010: 13)

This is why we adopt this conceptual tool. We understand that although decades have passed since its emergence, it has not yet been sufficiently explored in its explanatory capacity – both comprehensive and precise – for our regional context.

Of course, we accept that

> it is not so important to arrive at anything like *the* definition, or *the* typology – for there are obviously many types of violence. More important is to indicate theoretically significant dimensions of violence that can lead thinking, research and, potentially, action, towards the most important problems.
>
> (Galtung 1969: 168)

This is the main objective of this work.

The interrelationship between physical, structural and cultural violence

According to his definition, "Violence is present when human beings are being influenced so that their actual somatic and mental realizations are below their potential realizations" (Galtung 1969: 168). There are different ways to avoid the realization of these potentialities. For this reason, the concept suggested by Galtung, which has been taken up here, accepts this complexity and the different interrelations between various forms of violence.

At first, it is central to explain that there is a fundamental distinction between personal and direct violence, and structural or indirect violence (Galtung 1998a: 13 ss.). They are, however, entangled:

> We shall refer to the type of violence where there is an actor that commits the violence as personal or direct, and to violence where there is no such actor as structural or indirect. In both cases individuals may be killed or mutilated, hit or hurt in both senses of these words, and manipulated by means of stick or carrot strategies. But whereas in the first case these consequences can be traced back to concrete persons as actors, in the second case this is no longer meaningful. There may not be any person who directly harms another person in the structure. The violence is built into the structure and shows up as unequal power and consequently as unequal life chances.
>
> (Galtung 1969: 171)

The aim here, therefore, is to explain the different expressions of violence and their interdependencies or connections in order to render them visible – both the originally visible as violence and the originally invisible under this concept.

Personal, direct violence corresponds to a narrow concept of violence directly linked to the physical aspect of violence, which could be defined as "somatic incapacitation, or deprivation of health, alone (with killing as the extreme form), at the hands of an actor who intends this to be the consequence" (Galtung 1969: 168). This is the common understanding of the term.

The concept of structural violence, on its part, implies recognizing that violence is what is done in terms not only of directly damaging another, but also of generating conditions that may damage him or her. Understood in this way, that violence is invisible, because it is not recognized as such.

Structural violence can be defined – taking different elements examined by Galtung in his several works and approaches – as the *set of avoidable physical and organizational obstacles that in structural relationships prevent people from meeting their basic needs or reaching their true potential.* These are avoidable obstacles that prevent basic needs from being met.

The third form of violence explained by Galtung is cultural violence. Even in cases in which physical violence is not taking place, structural violence – a latent form of physical violence – can be alive and reinforced by cultural violence. Thus, the ceasefire would continue to be fueled by its latent physical violence by means of the cultural manifestations of violence, what we call cultural violence. It is also important to consider this manifestation:

> By "cultural violence" we mean those aspects of culture, the symbolic sphere of our existence – exemplified by religion and ideology, language and art, empirical science and formal science (logic, mathematics) – that can be used to justify or legitimize direct or structural violence.
>
> (Galtung 1996: 196)

It is then the more or less institutionalized practices and discourses that in various ways legitimize or justify that there are those who suffer structural violence in addition to physical violence: "Cultural violence makes direct and structural violence appear, and even perceived, as charged with reason – or at least not bad" (Galtung 2003: 8). Structural violence would seem to be a *natural reality* to be accepted.

Further, there are cultural aspects in some societies which are especially used in an aggressive way of communications through lack of openness, through the claim of universal values and truths, or through the conviction of being a selected and better culture (Galtung 1990: 63 ss.). These aggressive features may sound inappropriate for current Western cultures. However, as soon as somebody from the Global North meets somebody from the Global South, these pretenses may arise in one or another way. Cultural convictions about the superiority of technological countries, or discriminatory expressions against indigenous cultures, for example, are warnings about the several ways in which violent cultural aspects could exist.

The study of this cultural violence (e.g. through discourse analysis) may bring to light perhaps not strict determinations, but rather "correspondences" (Midré & Flores 2002: 198) between sustaining structural violence over time and schemes of thought and culture. Without this specific search, on the contrary, the various forms of generation or promotion of the various violences would remain hidden.

Cultural violence can be considered along with the idea of social distance, a concept which in communication studies refers to the shared culture between two individuals in their communication and the relationship between them as a sender and as a recipient, and which is defined by their features, both physical or intrinsic features (e.g. age, gender or ethnic group) and social features (e.g. relative power or authority). Two axes define the path of this relationship: the axis of hierarchy and the axis of familiarity. The first will probably define the relationship as either symmetrical or asymmetrical, and the second in terms of the previous knowledge of the individuals among themselves and with the empathy perceived by them (Edeso Natalías 2005: 247 ss.). Cultural violence, one might add, is likely to be established on the basis of the most extreme distant social relations, such as nonreciprocal knowledge among different cultures, non-empathic communications and highly asymmetrical relationships. Think of a mid-level or senior agent in a Canadian corporation that is in contact with women from a Guatemalan indigenous community. Or even more common in everyday life: think of a judge in the capital city or a journalist in a media program who talks to the same women. Cultural violence leads to social distance and vice versa. In this sense, the use of the same concept in sociology refers further in this direction and ends in the interconnection between social distance and violence, which has been specifically analyzed by certain authors (Arteaga Botello & Lara Carmona 2004). Starting probably with Durkheim in 1893 with *The Social Division of Labour*, social distance has been understood as related to non-solidarity and disorganization in a specific context, that is, to the lack of "symbolic" and "spatial" contact (Arteaga Botello & Lara Carmona 2004: 170 ss.). The neutral idea presented before, in the cases of extreme non-empathic communications, therefore, conduces to the same result.

The fundamental problem here is that structural and cultural violence are *invisible* violence. Unlike the violence of murder or robbery, structural and cultural violence are not perceived or considered to be violence, and therefore are neither prevented, nor sanctioned, nor repaired as violence. This explains, perhaps, why "the law is basically silent about structural violence" (Galtung 1998b: 7). That is, deaths caused by hunger, diseases caused by lack of health care, loss of labor by contamination of artisanal harvesting sources, loss of clean space for children to play in: in all these cases, there is no *A* subject at the head of whom to place the responsibility. Structural violence, invisible and therefore ignored as such, perpetuates itself silently and continues to spread its effects – often from century to century. Only when the invisible violence can be translated as a violation of human rights (normatively recognized) can the people affected sometimes have the abstract ability to demand their respect and fulfillment. However, this capacity in the abstract does not generally translate into effective capacity in the cases of those who are precisely marginalized from state attention (Galtung 1994: 83).[4] And this is the case for the great majority of those who suffer structural violence. Organizational structures include, for example, corrupt practices that impede the proper functioning of government offices when individuals require information, barriers in the justice system when affected communities demand justice or the normative and the judicial tolerance of predatory practices or toxic industries, among others. All these forms, however, are very broad, almost diffuse. And they must be specified if they are to explain reality.

All three forms of violence are closely interrelated and beget each other. For this reason, the explanation of violence should be integral in terms of any description of its complexity. Not only "the picture" of a violence episode, but "the film" of this episode should be considered in order to reach a comprehensive understanding of the situation:

> A bully would be seen as the inevitable product of socialization into a violent structure: he is the rebel, systematically untrained in other ways of coping with his conflicts and frustrations because the structure leaves him with no alternatives. That structural violence often breeds structural violence, and personal violence often breeds personal violence nobody would dispute – but the point here would be the cross-breeding between the two. In other words: pure cases are only pure as long as the pre-history of the case or even the structural context are conveniently forgotten.
>
> (Galtung 1969: 178)

That is, all the related actors and situations (inside and outside the photo) that intervene in the previous, contemporary and even future history of a violent situation should be considered as involved actors and explanatory data.

Invisible structures of violence in Latin America

A historical perspective

> Thus, the potential level of realization is that which is possible with a given level of insight and resources. If insight and/or resources are monopolized by a group or class or are used for other purposes, then the actual level falls below the potential level, and violence is present in the system.
>
> (Galtung 1969: 169)

The difference between a potential satisfaction of basic needs and an effective satisfaction is, in short, the measure of structural violence. In the Latin American context, structural violence is embedded in centuries of instability, asymmetrical international relations and forms of elite government aimed at increasing the position of political and economic power for a few and, therefore, in improving commercial relations with partners geopolitically better positioned, for the development of the region, while a large part of the population is often left out of the benefits of that promised development.[5] When on fertile land there are children dying of hunger, or the villagers near natural water sources do not have fresh water to drink, or when indigenous peoples and peasants, former owners of the land, cannot live without interference in decent living conditions according to their basic requirements, we could, in principle, be faced with cases of structural violence. It was said decades ago that "research in the Americas should focus on structural violence, between nations as well as between individuals, (. . .) the manifest structural violence in the Americas (and not only there) already causes an annual toll of nuclear magnitudes" (Galtung 1969: 183).

In Latin America, relations of structural, cultural and physical violence occurred from the very beginning and were accentuated in severity and scope from their first contact with the European Christian world. There are peculiarities of violence common in the region with regard to their ties to the rest of the world (and with subregional differences in the different states) that have been extant since before the state conformations, that is, from those early times of the presence of European states in the region, determining patterns of structural, cultural and physical violence today (Yuralivker 1992).

Marginalization and economic interests are always on the prowl, and land is the nucleus of conflicts (see Chapter 5). This is not a novelty of the twenty-first century. When the Spanish "conquerors" arrived, they occupied the lands with the objective of obtaining their minerals, and indigenous people were transformed into slaves or, if they were lucky enough to be "reduced" to indigenous communities, only semi-enslaved (Martínez Sarasola 2013: 145 ss.). In the same way, at present, territory in possession and with titles of dominion recognized in favor of indigenous communities are very few, and these lands continue to be coveted by the interests of private actors that crave the exploitation not only of the minerals, but also of the land for agricultural use (e.g. soybean crops) or even earlier, for speculation with land prices. Those who are in the area, in a gradual loss of land (although their rights may expand on paper), perform their tasks as *braceros* (peasants who are recognized only as work power because of the strength of their arms – *brazos*). They receive very little in exchange for their labor, and they are the ones who dismantle their own land and clear the forests to leave the land clean for corporations. In this sense, seen in historical perspective, the structural violence seems to jump out at us. The bodies exposed to it, on the other hand, are current and real today. As Karina Kato explains in relation to the expansion of the agrarian frontier in Brazil through the *Matopiba* project (see Chapter 4), and the institutionalization and subsequent deinstitutionalization of said project, which is at the same time result and generator of structural, cultural and physical violence:

> For those who are in the territory the decree does not make so much difference. Many do not even know what Matopiba is. But they live in Matopiba because they see the advance of the productive frontier, they know that the price of land is in an accelerated process of recovery, they are in contact with more and more companies entering the territories, they are expelled or they accompany expulsions of families who are in possession of the land

where they are living but who do not have its title. And they work in conditions analogous to slavery by cleaning up the land for the formation of these enormous farms. All this they feel on the skin.

(Mathias 2017: 18)

Throughout the centuries, states were constituted in superposition and without respecting prior differences that were given at the subregional level (cultures, languages, original civilizations), so political divisions can explain only some differences that can have occurred in certain areas (specific economic and regulatory policies) since these states were formed, but do not reflect the similarities or deep differences that are transversal to these states. The state constitutions come, on the other hand, from the hand of the first bonds forged with the rest of the world as autonomous or even sovereign states (Pompeu 2013). In codes and regulations, it was shown what part of the population had political decision-making power, what part was in control of land and wealth and what would be the rules for the conservation or modification of those basic conditions (Galeano 1984; Halperin Donghi 2010 – Chapters 1 and 2; Zanatta 2012 – Chapter1).

This brief historical reminder acquires a second dimension if we take the idea of "autarchy" thought by Galtung at the international level to assess the importance of the possibility of states regarding supply in vital areas such as food, energy and health (Galtung 1994: 173, 175 ss.), and the parallel is made with the situation of indigenous peoples throughout history and today. The result is almost explicit in terms of the reflected deficiencies and dependency spaces that have been perpetuated. Similar situations of dependency have been raised and data collected from different countries in and outside the Latin American region, such as the Philippines, Turkey and Mexico, and in relation to the development index of the World Bank – among other agencies. The result was the recognition that there are situations of inequality between different portions of the population according to their greater or lesser access to quality natural resources, which can be raised in terms of conflict, violence and insecurity (Baechler 1999: 13 ss., 24 ss.). Thus, what at one time could have been understood in terms of ethno-political conflict (Baechler 1999: 90) eventually became a static dependency situation (Singh 1987; Islam 1987; Altvater 2011).

With the passage of time, there was a strong democratization in the Latin American countries in various waves of more and more openness and recognition of rights, from the beginning of the nineteenth century onwards and, more recently, in the post-dictatorship decades in the region. However, without a doubt, they have not had enough scope to integrate the entire population into their mechanisms and practices. We can see the continuation of the tensions between integration projects (in terms of "liberal inclusion" of a plurality of people, classes, values and practices) and the perspective of the sustainability of notions of citizenship (Karstedt 2009: 210) which show the alienation with respect to the history and culture of our indigenous peoples and peasant and rural communities, which continue to be vulnerable and marginalized. A text with a similar approach, most inspiring for this study in terms of the situation of indigenous peoples, their state of poverty and their links with white society ("*ladina*") is offered by Midré and Flores (2002) in their work on Guatemala with the suggestive title "Élite ladina, políticas públicas y pobreza indígena" ("Ladino elite, public policies and indigenous poverty").

As Rousseau said,

> Under bad governments, this equality is only apparent and illusory: all it does is to keep the pauper in his poverty and the rich man in the position he has usurped. Laws in fact are always useful to those who have possessions and harmful to those who don't; from which it follows that the social state is advantageous to men only when everyone has something and no-one has too much.
>
> (*The Social Contract*, Book 1, Chapter 9, fn 1)

Well, in Latin America, there were few with much, and many with little, and on that basis the national orders were settled, national states were constituted and the social contract was accepted (Pompeu 2013). Think about the promises of development based on orders and foreign economic interests and under the administration of those few who have a lot. It is not episodic that conflicts over land and territory continue to this day. In fact, there have been a few attempts at agrarian reform that were truncated by military coups and civil reactions prepared and financed by local and foreign interests (Svampa 2017; Kay 2003). Ramón Minieri offered a detailed illustration of how land distribution has worked until today in military and democratic times with the example of the millions of hectares that British entrepreneurs and corporations have in Argentinean Patagonia since the nineteenth century (Minieri 2006).

In fact, the military coups and dictatorships were not unusual in the history of the region. They were always linked to economic interests (for an exemplar of this relationship, see Verbitsky & Bohoslavsky 2013). The last ones, which occurred between the 1970s and the 1990s, were in some cases revised as unjust unpopular regimes and are being judged in the courts; in other cases, the historic revision is still pending. In all cases, however, the dictatorships of the right wing in Latin America have had and still have civil partners, cultural helpers and a wide network of foreign actors interested in the restriction of democratic rights at the civil and political level, whereas the economic elite was doing business with the domestic resources and industries (see Chapter 1). The interrelation between structural, cultural and physical violence is evident – think of the hundreds of thousands of people who disappeared in those years, many of whom had been "given" by their foreign employers.[6] This summary about the Brazilian case can be taken as illustrative for the situation in the whole region:

> The dictatorship "outsourced" the deaths and enforced disappearances of at least 1,196 peasants and supporters with landlord financing. The state

omitted, shelved and outsourced the political and social repression in the countryside, executed by *jagunços* [bullies], gunmen, *capangas* [henchmen] and foremen in the service of some farmers, loggers, rural companies, swindlers and lords of mills, chestnut and rubber plantations.

> (Gilney Viana, former coordinator of the Memory and Truth
> Project of the Human Rights Secretariat (SDH) of the
> Presidency of the Republic, in Gilvander Moreira 2017)

And the current perpetuation of those regimes and rights violations through the imposition of economic policies in favor of the conservative elites and to the detriment of the majorities is evident as well. The most recognized politicians and the most established economic groups, the richest names, families and corporations: many of them have been the same since those times (Verbitsky & Bohoslavsky 2013).

Those few actors in the spheres of economic, political and cultural power from before, during and after the periods of explicit state violence were those who set the pace of relations with the transnational economy. In this context, the promise of development has been always intermingled with economic relations, political-institutional order, cultural discrimination, legal preferences and religious traditions that defined a region accustomed to the presence of structurally violent domination practices.

The historical perspective, in this sense, is of enormous relevance. In Latin America, there are no new situations of imbalance, or successions of violence in the hands of different actors. Although there have been centuries of interrelations, advances and setbacks with regard to the economic and political order, with few exceptions at different specific moments in history, decisions have always lain fundamentally in the power of certain groups. The populations that have suffered and continue to suffer from basic deficiencies have been, in general, the same. Although there have been both displacement and demographic changes that mark shifts from the countryside to the city, from the provinces to the capitals, or from the country itself to the neighboring country, the reality is that the populations that have been forced to adopt these measures in seeking to improve their lives have generally presented a multiplicity of needs and deficiencies, cumulative in nature, that have excluded them from the virtues of development. The route, however, has been marked with improvements in some areas, and the shortcomings of the past are not equal to the current shortcomings. In this sense, the efforts and advances made, either on the part of the state, of other actors or of society itself and the affected population, should be considered. Time, which marks long and slow processes in the modifications of cultural violence, moves somewhat more quickly in relation to structural violence and is even faster and can be just a moment in the direct and physical expression of violence. Structural and cultural changes, of course, are almost as invisible as the violence linked to these cultural structures and practices. Therefore, detecting these differences in our context, if any, is crucial in order to avoid inappropriate generalizations.

If structural violence implies that "basic needs are not met due to avoidable obstacles", a relativization is obligatory when, observing the present in contrast to the past, it is noticed that, at times, the phrase requires adjustment and it would be more appropriate to say that basic needs are *still* not met – sometimes some improvements are visible and a quicker way is not possible. It is about integrating the time variable, and the set of actors – the film that should be seen in its entirety instead of the photo – will become more complex and useful.

The basic need for medical attention serves illustratively to explain the idea of potentiality and its realization. Casting an eye on the distribution of resources and decisions in this regard, in short, serves to assess situations of a greater or lesser degree of avoidability in the failure to satisfy basic needs. In this sense, it is interesting to note that, historically, there have been records of these shortcomings and lack of attention from states. If one takes the case of the Argentine state and the province of Formosa, the youngest province and, at the same time, the one with the highest rates of deprivation at present, it can be noticed that in the times when Formosa had not yet become a province, but was still a national territory, its population in general was marginalized from the attention of the central state. In this province, where indigenous and rural populations are now the most affected by structural deficiencies, structural violence already existed in the past, for instance with respect to the lack of health services. That is, cumulative shortcomings are apparent, as well as the biased views of the hegemonic centers that blame the peripheries without offering a serious approach to the problem. In a memoir from the beginning of the twentieth century, which we have found among old material of the Popular Library of Formosa we read this chronicle – it deserves the long quotation:

Deficient medical attention

1903: September 11

On this date, the newspaper La Nación of Buenos Aires published an article where it is mentioned that medical care in Formosa is deficient and there are many cases of death without medical attention. There is a lot of truth in these lines, although our Mayor, with their doctor Dr. Martin Ruiz Moreno, arrives to secluded places, carrying the few medicines that can be purchased with the four *reals* of their miserable budget. The Central Government could go without 60% of the licensing fees from the shops located in the Villa [Formosa] and with that amount it could pay the salary of a doctor and the costs of the medicines. However, the Central Government not only does not desist, but even for the payment of the 40% destined to the Municipality in many of the cases an interminable paperwork must be done; thus, the case was given that the desperation of funds caused that the Municipality raise a denunciation against the Central Government. Unfortunately we live abandoned within our own country. Many Argentines for not looking up do not know us, even the map is against us since Formosa appears where the geographical representation ends. The National Executive forgets our needs, but not the appointment of a Maciel-type commissioner or a devourer of Indians in the style of Bouchard.

(Reproduced in Casals 1966: 261)[7]

From the capital, Buenos Aires, the complaint. In Formosa, on the margin, the shortcomings. More than a 100 years later, this review is a shout. And it is not a question here of justifying deficiencies that correspond to local conditions, but of questioning actors equally involved in the interwoven structure that organizationally continue to hinder the real satisfaction of basic needs, still integral or relatively unsatisfied. And even more so, as is often the case with cultural violence that legitimizes physical and structural violence, they feed off each other. Here, too, as the review from 1903 shows, the structural deficiencies did not ignore the cynical denunciation through hegemonic cultural means (the newspaper *La Nación* continues to be a means of communication that gives voice to the traditional conservative elite sectors in Argentina) or obviate the use of physical violence, perhaps in the figure of Commissioner Maciel, perhaps in that of the "devourer of Indians, Bouchard", as the only means of trying to restrain or cover up the shortcomings generated. This shows repression as the obverse of economic abandonment (see Chapter 1).

A simple proposal for analysis

If the concept of structural violence in its broader sense is deconstructed in its central elements, these become parts of a larger tool for the analysis of reality. In what follows, then, the concepts of *basic needs, non-satisfaction, physical and/or organizational obstacles* and *avoidability* will be presented.

Basic needs

Basic needs refer to those requirements that need to be satisfactorily met by human beings in order first to satisfy their basic need to *live*, and whose non-satisfaction would have "bad consequences" (Galtung 1994: 88): these include the need to eat, to dress, to provide ways to cure diseases and to have sufficient living space, among many others. Because human beings are social and political creatures, these basic needs are extended to those essential needs for the minimum realization of human beings in their life in society: the need for education, for freedom, to practice their rites and maintain their customs, to develop activities, to have a means of subsistence, to be part of the decisions that affect their own existence and vital situation, among others.

As noted, these ancient basic needs could at some point be equated with the idea of fundamental rights as they were developed in modern times (Galtung 1994: 112 ss., 170 ss.). Thus, for example, the basic *need to live* would be the basic need corresponding to the *human right of life*, the basic *need to develop activities that provide for their means of subsistence* would be covered in part by the *human right of decent work and remuneration*. This equation, however, as Galtung himself points out, does not exactly work that way. Speaking of human rights implies, first, that although they are intrinsic to the human being and in theory do not require prior recognition, in practice they have required normative documents to recognize them and provide them with a protective framework; that is, they have an "institutional character" (Galtung 1994: 170) that provides – but also requires – a jurisdictional area of demand. Rights, even if they are so called, do not necessarily guarantee a better position regarding the possibilities of compliance, even in states bound by the rule of law (Böhm 2011). It has already been pointed out that "it is the rule of law that has left so many people without rights" (Rivera Beiras 2014: 262). For this reason, addressing the issue of what needs to be met in terms of basic needs seems to be preferable.[8] If you work on the needs, the evaluation is done directly on the reality, that is, on a lack or damage directly observed and perceived. It is not necessary to wait for such lack or damage to be listed in a document in order to be declaimed and claimed (Galtung 1994: 83 ss.). This would be, in any case, a second step. In a systematic way, Galtung classifies the needs into four groups and their respective negation forms: survival needs (negation: death, mortality), well-being needs (negation: misery, morbidity), identity, meaning needs (negation: alienation) and freedom needs (negation: repression) (Galtung 1996: 197, 2003: 9; for a clear explanation and illustrative table, see Tortosa 2011: 47 ss.).

When speaking of structural violence, then, the first level of evaluation will be whether there are basic needs that are affected in any way. If the degree of affectation is severe, it must be evaluated whether they are directly unsatisfied and negated, and if so, whether that negation is avoidable.

Non-satisfaction

The degree of satisfaction of the basic needs requires an evaluation that, in fact, could be arbitrary or too subjective. And, at a certain point, it is. However, if one takes as a parameter what is minimally necessary to consider that a given need is satisfied, the work becomes less complex. If the realization of the basic need reaches a minimum level that allows the continuity of operation and the fulfillment of the vital and social function that this need comes to cover, it can be said that the basic need has been satisfied. Otherwise, it will be a basic need unsatisfied. If health is what allows human beings to maintain a pace of life adequate to their general requirements and physical activities, for example, it can be said that not having medicine to relieve a cold or earache, circumstantially, does not imply the non-satisfaction of that "health" need, given its lightness and transience. On the contrary, lack of access to means of prevention (or even being exposed to a means that worsens the pathological picture) of lung cancer undoubtedly implies the non-satisfaction of the basic need for access to medical care. In this case, the function that medicinal care must fulfill is to provide the means for the regular continuation of the life of the affected human being. A significant deviation from the vital activity due to a decrease in health quality due to lack of care implies, then, the non-satisfaction of that need.

Such non-satisfaction, however, does not always imply structural violence. For this to be the case, this non-satisfaction of basic needs must be a consequence of the existence of avoidable physical and/or organizational obstacles (Galtung 1969, 1998b).

Physical and/or organizational obstacles

Physical obstacles can generally be perceived with the senses; that is, there is a mechanical impediment to the satisfaction of the basic need in question. Physical barriers include a fence or a wall that prevents access to food or water, a river that separates a population from another population where health and sanitation services exist, an arid land unsuitable for planting or a flooded area that blocks children's way to school. All these are physical obstacles that can mean, if sustained over time, the impediment of satisfying people's basic needs for drinking water, medical attention, sowing their own food or education.

Organizational obstacles, unlike physical ones, cannot easily be perceived with the senses, but require the knowledge and analysis of social and institutional interactions in the space in question. The organization of the mechanisms provided for the satisfaction of needs is usually very complex in today's societies. From the smallest school space to the political design and distribution of state units: all this belongs to the organizational means that, when they do not work properly, can lead to the non-satisfaction of basic needs. The diversion through corruption practices of funds intended for health or education, the projection of agricultural production based on certain forms of cultivation and neglecting others or the unintelligent monitoring of river cleaning activities, to name but a few, would be organizational obstacles that would mean that basic needs for medical care, education, food or access to water were impeded in their implementation. It is, in short, a matter of distribution of resources:

> Resources are unevenly distributed, as when income distributions are heavily skewed, literacy/education unevenly distributed, medical services existent in some districts and for some groups only, and so on. Above all the power to decide over the distribution of resources is unevenly distributed. The situation is aggravated further if the persons low on income are also low on education, low on health, and low on power – as is frequently the case because these rank dimensions tend to be heavily correlated due to the way they are tied together in the social structure.
>
> (Galtung 1969: 171, with more references)

When evaluating the possible presence of structural violence, both types of obstacles must be detected, and they are often interrelated: the physical obstacle that prevents children from going to school in a rural area, for example, may be directly linked to disagreements in the infrastructure and sanitation offices that have to do with the consequences of the rains and the necessary resources to do so. Here, physical and organizational obstacles would be found together, preventing the realization of the basic need to study. In the same sense, the Inter-American Commission on Human Rights reported by the end of 2017 the cumulative geographic, economic, cultural and social obstacles that stand in the way of Latin American people living in poverty and destitution who try to exercise their rights (IACHR 2017).

Avoidability

The concept of avoidability, the fourth level in this proposal of analysis, requires incorporating the ideas of reality and potentiality into the study. Avoidability will arise whenever, in a context that potentially enables the satisfaction of basic needs, these are not met in reality, although the circumstances – potentially – should allow that satisfaction. Reality is what it is, worth the simplicity of this affirmation. This is the current level of realization of a certain need, which would be, for example, the quantity and quality of water and food that is ingested, the medical attention received, or the effective attendance or absence from school. Potentiality, on the other hand, is the maximum level of what can be achieved in a specific temporal-spatial context depending on the level of information and available resources. The assessment of this potentiality, as recognized by Galtung himself, is highly problematic (Galtung 1969: 169), but can be understood, for a first approximation, without major difficulty. Thus, the potential level of realization is that which is possible with a given level of insight and resources. If insight and/or resources are monopolized by a group or class or are used for other purposes, then the actual level falls below the potential level, and violence is present in the system (Galtung 1969: 169).

If in a specific context, in a given time and space, there is a potential possibility that – taking one of the previous examples – the food resource produced is of sufficient nutritional quality and its quantity is also sufficient to cover the food needs of the population of that place at that time, but instead, there are in that time and place members of that population whose nutrition is of lower nutritional quality and in less quantity than necessary, then this reality lies below the potential. Potentially the need for food may be satisfied, but in reality, it is not. This situation is what can be explained as avoidability. You could have enough quality food, but you cannot count on it. It is avoidable that you do not have it. This then leads to the idea that deaths from starvation or diseases caused by malnutrition are equally avoidable.

The idea of structural violence in general, and in particular the aspect of avoidability, is one that makes relevant the great difference that exists between talking about social injustice and talking about structural violence. Social injustice seems to be "the fault" of everyone and nobody at the same time. Structural violence, on the other hand, makes it possible to trace paths of accountability and responsibility. What is important to highlight here is that this tracking must occur in each specific case and in each context in order to avoid unjustifiably distributing responsibilities in spaces that already have difficult-to-handle suffering. As Galtung himself exemplifies when taking the case of tuberculosis: to attribute responsibility for tuberculosis deaths in the nineteenth century would have been nonsense, because in that temporal context, tuberculosis was still an evil for which prevention methods or cure were not known; but if cases of death from tuberculosis occur in the twenty-first century, when treatments are widely known and available, here, yes, those deaths, in principle, are avoidable. In the nineteenth century, the potentiality was not above reality. In the twenty-first century, on the contrary, potentiality is very much above reality; that is, the damage generated by that reality would be avoidable (Galtung 1969: 168).

It is necessary to detect inequality as a form of structural violence (Galtung 1972: 29): "If we accept that the general formula behind structural violence is inequality, above all in the distribution of power, then this can be measured; and inequality seems to have a high survival capacity despite tremendous changes elsewhere" (Galtung 1969: 175). In the case of Latin America (and the Global South in general), inequality in the distribution of power has made an impact for centuries. The proposal is to detect small spaces where we can analyze and tentatively measure their current situation, define the spaces of violence and their previous steps. An approach is necessary that provides guidelines on how to continue with the survey, with the systematization, and especially with an integral way of thinking and acting. This approach allows us to act much more here and beyond what could be criminal, civil or administrative legal responsibility. The objective is to gradually reduce the spaces that allow, time and again, individuals and communities to live and die in the midst of deep, structurally avoidable deficiencies.

Structural and physical violent relationships between local and foreign actors

The conditions explained so far are the current Latin American context in which transnational economic activities are carried out both by national states and international economic actors, who are visible representatives of the economy and international economic policies. That is, it is not new that there is structural, cultural and physical violence in the region. The interesting thing is to assess, in particular, the role that transnational corporations occupy in this framework with conditions of investment and growth favored by the deregulation of the economy in the international order, which promises, on the other hand, conditions that promote regional development. In this way, what could be understood as a positive development ideal (see Chapter 1), if it does not meet essential requirements regarding the sustainability of such development, can very quickly become a form of silent war, a gradual loss of quality and quantity of essential elements in the vital situation of individuals and people.

In his work about a structural theory of imperialism, Galtung explained in a sophisticated but clear way that there are myriad possible combinations between center and periphery, in state relations and also within states; it is common, for example, that the centrally positioned actors in a periphery state will have better relationships (more empathy) with actors in the center states than with their own periphery people in their peripheral states (Galtung 1972: 29). Thus, economic relations with respect to raw materials, or even in general, generate more and more disparities within an actor's own population in a periphery country, whereas in the states of the center, disharmony is not so common. This disharmony in the peripheral nation is related to the unequal distribution of resources and shows that structural violence is not only inside a country, but also is related to the external relationships between different actors of these countries (Galtung 1972: 37, 41 ss.). These explanations may sound a little strange, but they are not. They may be uncommon or not so current terms to explain that elites in the countries of the Global South are more interested in their own relations with actors in the Global North than they are in the people in their own states. It is the social distance, mentioned previously, which explains these violent, non-pacific processes (Arteaga Botello & Lara Carmona 2004: 174).

For this reason, resorting to physical violence seems not to be a problem in many cases. Physical violence is used against the people in the periphery of their own country when it is exercised by the state. The fight against these people is the explanation of physical violence directly related to structural violence.

Invisible violent relationships go hand in hand with physical forms of violence – sometimes to protect investments and sometimes to bring a demanding population under control. In each case, the constellation is different, yet at the same time it is similar to the interaction of visible and invisible violence in all the countries of Latin America. As Bruckmann explained:

> As we have been affirming for some years, the global dispute for natural resources develops multidimensional strategies of access, management and appropriation of these resources at a planetary level that articulates transnational corporations as the main economic operators of this process, militarization policies of the territories, diverse mechanisms of criminalization of protest and popular movements, policies of destabilization of democracies in the region as well as commercial and political instruments aimed at weakening the processes of integration in Latin America.
>
> (Bruckmann 2017)

As at the beginning of the twentieth century in Formosa, direct violence is still used by the state against the marginalized population as a common mechanism (on this use, see Chapter 1). It is useful to recall here that structural violence, in its general concept, can be understood as what is usually called *social injustice* (Galtung 1969: 171). This concept has the advantage that no one can be held accountable for it: it is a historical, economic, cultural and institutional framework of factors that blur to the most remote extremes the identifications between suffering and the ultimate cause of those sufferings, and in that way the concept of social injustice makes the route of transmissions of imputation and responsibility unfeasible. Only visible, physical forms of violence are left in sight of public policies, or rather of criminalizing public policy. Criminal policy "sees" the physical violence that often emerges from invisible cultural and structural violence. Social injustice (structural violence) fueled by and working in conjunction with cultural violence (indifference that legitimates and justifies structural violence) fertilizes spaces and manifestations of physical violence. It is a vicious circle of extreme complexity and multifactoriality.

The visibilization and action against invisible violence

The main question here may be how to make visible the invisible violence, and how to act against it. Three first answers can be found in Galtung, again: form of relation, measure and actor's position in the structure.

Here, *form of relation* refers to Galtung's explanation when describing the different ways in which the violence triangle can be understood:

> Using direct and structural violence as overarching categories or "super-types". "Cultural violence" can now be added as the third super-type and put in the third corner of a (vicious) violence triangle as an image. When the triangle is stood on its "direct" and "structural violence" feet, the image invoked is cultural violence as the legitimizer of both. Standing the triangle on its "direct violence" head yields the image of structural and cultural sources of direct violence. Of course, the triangle always remains a triangle – but the image produced is different, and all six positions (three pointing downward, three upward) invoke somewhat different stories, all worth telling.
>
> (Galtung 1996: 199)

And, with reference to the *measure*, the point is to stress the fact that structural violence can be measured because it is principally a violence based on inequality between resources and power. As mentioned previously: "If we accept that the general formula behind structural violence is inequality, above all in the distribution of power, then this can be measured; and inequality seems to have a high survival capacity despite tremendous changes elsewhere" (Galtung 1969: 175).

The final suggestion is related to the complex schemata that could be constructed depending on the place and the role played by various actors in various systems and structures:

> Most fundamental are the ideas of actor, system, structure, rank and level. Actors seek goals, and are organized in systems in the sense that they interact

with each other. But two actors, e.g. two nations, can usually be seen as interacting in more than one system; they not only cooperate politically, e.g. by trading votes in the UN, but also economically by trading goods, and culturally by trading ideas. The set of all such systems of interaction, for a given set of actors, can then be referred to as a structure. And in a structure an actor may have high rank in one system, low in the next, and then high in the third one; or actors may have either consistently high ranks or consistently low ranks.

(Galtung 1969: 175)

The integral description of the relation among forms of violence, inequality data and actors' positions would probably provide some ideas about the traceability, if it may be called this, of responsibilities and forms of action. The violence stories, which are worth telling, take place all around the world, and here in particular, the stories of some Latin American cases will be told in the following chapters (Chapters 3 and 4).

The basic needs related to food, to preventing and treating health problems, to study at various educational levels, to have a dwelling that protects from bad weather, from external risks and provides shelter and space for the rest and to have individual and social means of subsistence and cultural recognition are all basic needs recognized not only in the documents that Galtung relied on in his study – the Universal Declaration of Human Rights, the Covenant of DESC and DCP (Galtung 1994: 112 ss.), but also in subsequent international and regional documents such as the American Declaration of Human Rights, ILO Convention 169 or the United Nations Declaration on the Rights of Indigenous Peoples, to mention three of the most relevant. There is a range of documents in recognition and declaration of human rights. And this recognition, from one perspective, is excellent. From another, however, it is less so. What is at issue in assessing the existence or nonexistence of structural violence in a particular space-time is to assess the specific situations and put the focus of the study, first, on the distance between the recognition of such rights *on paper*, for example, and the realization of such rights *in practice*, or, in Galtung's terminology, the difference between potentiality and reality in terms of the degree of satisfaction of basic needs in evaluation. If this examination is carried out in legal or jurisdictional terms, the analysis table will be very small. If the view is broadened to address basic needs in a more comprehensive sense – not standardized in human rights documents – the analysis becomes more complex and probably more profitable at the same time. Reality has to be looked at, first, in its level of potentiality, second, in the physical and organizational obstacles that impede the realization of that potentiality, and, third, according to the avoidability of such obstacles and the actors related to them.

From the general idea that the development promised to the region is not really such, it is noticeable that the conditions in which regional economic policy continues to develop are likely, in fact, to continue and even deepen the violence in the region, to the point of generating the opposite of what they pretend to generate: Maldevelopment instead of Development. In this sense, then, it is useful to study in concrete cases these elements set out here in a conceptual and regional manner. If one really sees the deepening of violence and can direct this deepening to the economic activity of transnational corporations and the state measures and practices that contribute to them and which are facilitated by international deregulation, it is worth wondering whether this maldevelopment is not attributable to certain actors (foreigners and locals). This accountability would be useful in terms of improving the possibilities of prevention, punishment and reparation, and if so, it would be important to evaluate it from a criminological perspective if it is not an area of study that deserves special attention and a new conceptual research field. I will come back to this in the next chapters, after presenting eight concrete cases that illustrate what is proposed here.

Notes

1 As an encyclopedic approach to the concept of violence, see Heitmeyer and Hagan (2003), who already in their first chapter explain the difficulties of the work by the pretense of addressing as many concepts of violence as possible, without losing the compiler logic and the use that it must provide. For a critique of the concepts of extensive violence, and advocating a systematic study of concepts of violence that allows defining "mostly agreed" concepts as a basis for analysis, see de Haan (2008), who presents an exhaustive classification and analysis of authors, their proposals and uses of the concept of violence.

2 For an approach to his figure and the relevance of his work, still relatively unattended in our field, despite the analytical and emancipatory force of his proposals, which must be updated and contextualized for their application, see Galtung and Fischer (2013). In this eloquent text, his publications and concepts are exposed and explained, and his life and work are presented and illustrated.

3 I would like to express my gratitude to Prof. Willem de Haan for the exchange and the fruitful discussions that we enjoyed in Buenos Aires in the summer of 2017 on this issue. Our different opinions in many senses were, because of these differences, accurate helpful warnings to my work since then.

4 An explanation and illustration of this dissonance between the recognition of basic needs as fundamental rights, and the difficulties of this institutionalization, in different contexts, can be observed in the Documentary *Los Derechos Humanos Por y Para el Pueblo* (2011).

5 For a case study on Mexico and the Gulf Nahuas indigenous population under maldevelopment conditions, see Chevalier and Buckles (1995). Cases, however, are not exclusive to Latin America. For a specific case study on the Philippines and its conditions and perception of causes of poverty and conflict, see Tuason (2010). Monographic on the African context and with specific cases, see Amin (2011).

6 A great novel on the direct impact of foreign economic interests in an entire country is *Weekend in Guatemala* by Nobel Laureate in Literature Miguel Ángel Asturias (2006).

7 Because of the chronicle style and the antiquity of the text, the original version in Spanish is offered here as well: "Atención médica deficiente. 1903: setiembre 11. En la fecha publica el diario 'La Nación' de Buenos Aires, un artículo donde se menciona que la asistencia médica en Formosa, es deficiente y son muchos los casos que mueren sin atención facultativa. Hay mucho de cierto en estas líneas, aunque nuestros municipales, con su médico Dr. Martín Ruiz Moreno, llegan hasta lugares apartados, llevando las pocas medicinas que pueden

adquirir con los cuatro reales de su miserable presupuesto. El Gobierno Central puede desistir del 60% de las patentes de los comercios ubicados en la Villa y con ese importe costear el sueldo de un médico y los costos de los medicamentos, pero no solamente no desiste, sino que para abonar el 40% destinado a la Municipalidad en muchos de los casos se debe hacer un papeleo interminable y llegó el caso que la desesperación de fondos hizo que la Municipalidad demandara al Gobierno Central. Desgraciadamente vivimos abandonados dentro de nuestro propio país; muchos argentinos por no levantar la vista nos desconocen, hasta el mapa está en contra nuestra al figurar Formosa dentro de la representación geográfica, donde termina el mismo. Olvida el Ejecutivo Nacional nuestras necesidades, no así el nombramiento de un comisario tipo Maciel o un devorador de indios tipo Bouchard".

8   It is the same preference that leads one to choose the study in terms of conflict, harm and violence, when it comes to the spaces that must be addressed by criminology for, as is the case of this piece of research, to deal with the processes of injury of historically invisible rights for the penal system, accustomed to think in terms of crime. See Rivera Beiras (2014), as well as the dialogue between Wayne Morrison, E. Raúl Zaffaroni and Roberto Bergalli that took place in Barcelona and was published in the same year (see Morrison et al. 2014).

References

Altvater, Elmar. 2011. *Los límites del capitalismo. Acumulación, crecimiento y huella ecológica.* Buenos Aires: Mardulce.

Amin, Samir. 2011 (2nd ed.). *Maldevelopment: Anatomy of a Global Failure.* Cape Town et al.: Pambazuca.

Arteaga Botello, Nelson/Lara Carmona, Vanessa L. 2004. "Violencia y distancia social: una revisión". *Papeles de Población* 40 (April/June), CIEAP/UAEM, 169–191.

Asturias, Miguel Ángel. 2006 (2nd ed.). *Week-end en Guatemala.* Buenos Aires: Losada.

Baechler, Günther. 1999. *Violence through Environmental Discrimination: Causes, Rwanda Arena, and Conflict Model.* Social Indicators Research Series. Vol. 2, Dordrecht: Springer-Science+Business Media, B.V.

Böhm, María Laura. 2011. *Der ‚Gefährder' und das ‚Gefährdungsrecht': Eine rechtssoziologische Analyse am Beispiel der Urteile des Bundesverfassungsgericht über die nachträgliche Sicherungsverwahrung und die akustische Wohnraumüberwachung,* Göttingen: Göttingen Universitätsverlag.

Bruckmann, Mónica. 2017. "La financiarización de la naturaleza y sus consecuencias geopolíticas". *Revista Diálogos del Sur.* February 13. operamundi.uol.com.br/dialogosdelsur/la-financiarizacion-de-la-naturaleza-y-sus-consecuencias-geopoliticas/13022017/

Casals, Fernando. 1966. *Formosa. Desde el candil 1879 hasta el alumbrado público de candencia al vacío 1923.* Buenos Aires: Ed. Efemérides Comentadas del Autor.

Chevalier, Jacques M./Buckles, Daniel. 1995. *A Land without Gods: Process Theory, Maldevelopment and The Mexican Nahuas.* London/Atlantic Highlands, NJ: Zed Books.

De Haan, Willem. 2008. "Violence as an Essentially Contested Concept". In: Body-Gendrot, Sophia/Spierenburg, Pieter (eds.). *Violence in Europe,* New York: Springer.

Edeso Natalías, Verónica. 2005. "La distancia social y su importancia en la interacción: propuesta para su estudio en clase de ELE". *ASELE, Actas XVI 2005,* 247–257.

Galeano, Eduardo. 1984 (39th ed.). *Las venas abiertas de América Latina.* Madrid: Siglo XXI.

Galtung, Johan. 1969. "Violence, Peace, and Peace Research". *Journal of Peace Research* 6 (3), 167–191.

Galtung, Johan. 1972. "Eine strukturelle Theorie des Imperialismus". In: Senghaas, D. (ed.). *Imperialismus und strukturelle Gewalt. Analysen über abhängige Reproduktion,* Frankfurt a.M.: Suhrkamp, 29–104.

Galtung, Johan. 1975. *Strukturelle Gewalt, Beiträge zu Friedens- und Konfliktforschung*, Reinbek bei Hamburg: Rowohlt Taschenbuch Verlag.

Galtung, Johan. 1990. "Visionen einer friedlichen Welt". In: Galtung, J./Lutz, D./Röhrich, W. (eds.). *Überleben durch Partnerschaft. Gedanken über eine friedliche Welt*, Opladen: Leske + Budrich, 31–80.

Galtung, Johan. 1994. *Menschenrechte anders gesehen*, Frankfurt a.M.: Suhrkamp.

Galtung, Johan. 1996. *Peace by Peaceful Means: Peace and Conflict, Development and Civilization*, London: Sage.

Galtung, Johan. 1998a. *Tras la violencia, 3R: reconstrucción, reconciliación, resolución. Afrontando los efectos visibles e invisibles de la guerra y la violencia*, Bilbao: Bakeaz/Gernika Gogoratuz.

Galtung, Johan. 1998b. *Violencia, Guerra y su impacto.* http://red.pucp.edu.pe/wp-content/uploads/biblioteca/081020.pdf

Galtung, Johan. 2003. *Violencia Cultural. Documento de trabajo N°14.* Gernika-Lumo: Fundación Gernika Gogoratuz.

Galtung, Johan/Fischer, Dietrich. 2013. *Johan Galtung: Pioneer of Peace Research*, Heidelberg: Springer.

Gilvander Moreira, Frei. 2017. "Concentrar terra para crescer o capital e a violência". *MST*. November 23. www.mst.org.br/2017/11/23/concentrar-terra-para-crescer-o-capital-e-a-violencia.html

Halperin Donghi, Tulio. 2010 (7th ed.). *Historia contemporánea de América Latina*, Buenos Aires: Alianza Editorial.

Heitmeyer, Wilhelm/Hagan, John (eds.). 2003. *International Handbook of Violence Research*, Dordrecht: Springer.

IACHR. 2017. *Informe sobre Pobreza y Derechos Humanos en las Américas*. OEA/Ser.L/V/II.164. Doc. 147. December 5.

Islam, Safiqul. 1987. "On the Controversies of Development and the Conceptual Evaluation of Maldevelopment". In: *Premises and Process of Maldevelopment*. Stockholm: Bethany Books, 71–103.

Karstedt, Susanne. 2009. "Democratization and Violence: European and International Perspectives". In: Body-Gendrot, Sophie/Spierenburg, Pieter (eds.). *Violence in Europe: Historical and Contemporary Perspectives*, New York: Springer, 205–225.

Kay, Cristóbal. 2003. "Estructura agraria y violencia rural en América Latina". *Sociologias*, Porto Alegre 5 (10), 220–248.

Martínez Sarasola, Carlos. 2013 (1st ed.). *Nuestros paisanos los indios. Vida, historia y destino de las comunidades indígenas en Argentina*, Buenos Aires: Del Nuevo Extremo.

Mathias, Maíra. 2017. "Matopiba: na fronteira entre a vida e o capital". *EPSJV/Fiocruz*. September 19. www.epsjv.fiocruz.br/noticias/reportagem/matopiba-na-fronteira-entre-a-vida-e-o-capital

Midré, Georges/Flores, Sergio. 2002. *Élite ladina, políticas públicas y pobreza indígena*, Guatemala: Magna Terra/Instituto de Estudios Interétnicos/Universidad San Carlos de Guatemala.

Minieri, Ramón. 2006. *Ese ajeno sur. Un dominio británico de un millón de hectáreas en la Patagonia*. Viedma: Fondo Editorial Rionegrino.

Morrison, Wayne/Zaffaroni, Eugenio Raúl/Bergalli, Roberto. 2014. "Diálogos sobre criminología, genocidio y daño social con Wayne Morrison, Eugenio Raúl Zaffaroni y Roberto Bergalli". In: Rivera Beiras, Iñaki (ed.). *Delitos de los Estados, de los Mercados y daño social*, Barcelona: Anthropos.

Pompeu, Gina. 2013. "Humanidade ou nacionalidade: Entre a Soberania do Estado, a Proteção Internacional dos Direitos do Homem e a Responsabilidade Social das Empresas e das Universidades". In: Martins Pompeu, Randal/Marques, Carla Susana da E. (eds.). *Responsabilidade Social das Universidades*, Florianopolis: Conceito, 21–38.

Rivera Beiras, Iñaki. 2014. "Retomando el concepto de violencia estructural. La memoria, el daño social y el derecho a la Resistencia como herramientas de trabajo". In: Rivera Beiras, I. (ed.). *Delitos de los Estados, de los Mercados y daño social*, Barcelona: Anthropos.

Shinkel, Willem. 2010. *Aspects of Violence: A Critical Theory*, Basingstoke: Palgrave Macmillan.

Singh, Kullar Harbinder. 1987. "Galtung and Wallterstein on Structural Theory of Imperialism: Roots of Social and Economic Disequilibrium". In: *Premises and Process of Maldevelopment*, Stockholm: Bethany Books, 61–70.

Svampa, Maristella. 2017. *Del cambio de época al fin de ciclo. Gobiernos progresistas, extractivismo y movimientos sociales en América Latina*, Buenos Aires: Edhasa.

Tortosa, José María. 2011. *Maldesarrollo y Mal Vivir. Pobreza y violencia a escala mundial*, Quito: Ediciones Abya Yala.

Tuason, María Teresa. 2010. "Peace Psychology in a Poor World: Conflict Transformation in Response to Poverty". In: Carter, Candice C. (ed.). *Conflict Resolution and Peace Education: Transformations across Disciplines*, New York: Palgrave, 127–155.

Verbitsky, Horacio/Bohoslavsky, Juan Pablo (eds.). 2013. *Cuentas pendientes – Los cómplices económicos de la dictadura*, Buenos Aires: Siglo XXI.

Yuralivker, David. 1992. "América Latina: nuevas perspectivas de desarrollo". In: Asociación Latinoamericana de Organizaciones de Promoción (ed.). *América Latina: opciones estratégicas de desarrollo*. Caracas: Ed. Nueva Sociedad, 99–107.

Zanatta, Loris. 2012. *Historia de América Latina. De la Colonia al siglo XXI*. Buenos Aires: Siglo XXI.

Filmography

Los Derechos Humanos Por y Para el Pueblo: Haciendo Realidad los Derechos Económicos, Sociales y Culturales desde las Bases!, Documentary. Red-DESC. 2011.

Part II

Seeing invisible violence – case studies from Mexico, Ecuador, Chile and Argentina

This chapter describes and systematically relates, from four cases, events that are apparently unrelated to each other and, above all, have little visibility in their interrelations. Different roles that companies can cover in their legal activities are exposed. On the other hand, these companies are presented, fundamentally, as actors representing international economic policies. The companies, and the transnational companies in particular, are the visible expressions and interventions of these international economic policies when they arrive and develop activity in the different local spaces. Thus, it is through the activity of companies that economic deregulation (or reregulation, as it has also been considered by some authors – see Chapter 1) and international policies of liberalization of certain markets due to the increase in global demand (or demand in certain regions) are put into practice. The impact of economic policies, therefore, is channeled by these companies. Their own regulations and internal structures, their form of interaction with state and social actors and the place they occupy in their countries of origin define the type and degree of impact that their presence will have on the area in which they sit. According to the position that their countries of origin occupy in the international geopolitical scenario, the consequences of this impact will be, in turn, more or less considered by local and international actors.

The proposal is to make visible the impact of international economic deregulation through various activities carried out by foreign companies in the Latin American region. Working with specific cases is a plastic way of describing more or less complex events and processes based on legislation, institutions, populations, economic actors, preexisting conditions and relatable and measurable consequences, and this in the before, during and after phases of a specific business activity. A chronological story has its difficulties, and therefore each case is organized according to a conceptual guide and according to the ideas of visible and invisible violence studied in the previous chapter. In this chapter the emphasis, in turn, is placed, as indicated at the beginning, on invisible violence, that is, those manifestations of violence that are not usually considered violence, and that at the same time are related to physical and direct violence recognized as such. The idea is to make visible that non–visible violence. With the visibility of the situation and violence in the *before*, the general reference is to the previous socioeconomic situation of the local population, to criminogenic conditions (facilitating possible harmful situations), to the promise of development linked to that previous situation (work, health, well-being, growth) and the state of greater or lesser cultural violence from the institutions that nurture and spread discourses around identities and societies. The explanation of the forms of violence that take place during the economic activity and after its cessation includes the activities and transformations that can be described in the relations of the local population with each other, in their living conditions and in their links with the state. It is about explaining the life situation of the local population after a start–up period for the activity in question. Ultimately, it is about reflecting the consequences of the arrival of foreign investment and of the launching of a new economic activity encouraged by the state for the sake of national development. In most cases, these are data that touch the current reality of these areas, given that the effects often continue and the impact of transnational economic activity has begun, but has not ended. In this study of the impact of the initiation of the activity, physical violence is also described if it was present in the case.

The analysis is focused on cases chosen among different countries, economic conditions and types of economic activity. In all cases, these are activities with greater or lesser extent and impact in the territory, but they are always linked to a specific population area, about which basic information can be obtained before and after the initiation of the economic or industrial activity. Today, deregulatory economic policies at the international level have their greatest impact in Latin American extractive activities. For this reason, the cases selected here correspond to this sector of the economy. Service, financial and secondary industries are expressly excluded from the present study.

Each of the four cases will be identified respectively, with a brief name that will be used throughout the work in order to simplify the exposition of facts and analysis. This name may refer to the place, the company, or the population involved, according to how the facts are best known in the respective country.

The cases and how they will be presented

The first three cases correspond to specific projects and companies. The emphasis of the analysis is on the type and form of the business activity, the establishment of the company in the location, its interrelation with the local population, and the impact generated by its presence. The fourth case has been selected taking into account state action rather than the action of companies. It refers to situations in which specific economic measures have been adopted with respect to an economic area that in recent decades has been especially promoted in Latin America: agroindustry. Along with the other three aforementioned economic branches (mining, hydrocarbons and energy), this economic area has intensified its relevance over the past two decades with a distinct effect on historically marginalized collectives of the population such as the indigenous, peasants and landless people.

The cases are the following:

1 *Salaverna* and *El Peñasquito* cases, on metal extraction, destruction of villages (geologically and infrastructurally) and population displacement in Mexico;
2 *Texaco/Chevron* case, about oil exploitation, pollution and lack of access to justice due to economic agreements and corruption in Ecuador;
3 *Ralco* case, on the construction of a hydroelectric dam, deforestation, militarization of the area and displacement of the indigenous population in Chile;
4 *MOCASE* case, related to large estates, agroeconomic business and land conflicts and the social changes caused by specific deregulative laws on the part of the national and provincial political power in Argentina.

The exposition will not be outlined in chronological order, but will present a progressive sequence from the least visible case in terms of violence to the most visible one. Advancing through the cases will show an increase in the existence of unmet basic needs and the increased use of physical violence as a recourse. The aim here is to slowly train and open the reader's view and common understanding of economic practices and actors in order to make this view and understanding more complex. The theoretical concepts studied in the prior chapters should become more comprehensible and tangible thanks to this study of cases.

The exposition will follow a similar outline in each case. However, not all aspects will be presented with the same type of information sources or in the same degree of detail. The data gathering was adapted to the particularities of each case and, in particular, according to the availability of information in each country with respect to each corporation and conflict. The objective has always been to obtain as much information as possible at various levels in order to reach the most objectively acceptable exposition and understanding of each case. Each case is different; so are the expositions different as well. Taking these conditions into account and following the theoretical approach presented in earlier chapters, the basic schema for the presentation of the cases is as follows: *i. The case:* the case is described according to the main information about the economic project or political economic measure; *ii. Relevance of the specific business area or activity:* the relevance of the specific business area or activity is depicted, taking into account the national economy in general and the regional economy in particular; *iii. Cultural violence in the region "before":* information about cultural violence in the region before the business activity started or before the political measure was taken is presented through a description of the relationships between local people, economic actors, the public in general and specific biases such as religion, education, culture or mass media discourses and practices; *iv. Structural violence in the region "before":* data are exposed about structural violence in the region before the business activity started or before the political measure was taken and are described by means of an explanation of the interrelationships between state, economic and local civil actors as well as in terms of the grade of satisfaction or non-satisfaction of basic needs on the part of the local population; *v. Business, people and economic situation in the area "during" and "after"*: main information about the business, people and economic situation in the area after the initiation of the business activity or since the adoption of the political economic measure is presented; *vi. Structural violence in the region "during" and "after"*: data are exposed about structural violence in the region after the initiation of the business activity or since the implementation of the political measure; *vii. Physical violence in the region "after"*: the physical violence directly and indirectly related to the business activity or political economic measure in the area is presented through a description of direct, physically violent acts at the individual and collective levels on the part of the local population and civil society (social protests, roadblocks, i.a.), economic actors (e.g. threats and aggression from private security agents) or the state (e.g. illegal detentions, protest repression); and *viii. Cultural violence in the region "after"*: information is presented about cultural violence in the region after the initiation of the business activity or since the adoption of the political economic measure.

To paraphrase Galtung: each case is a story worth telling. This is the aim of the following pages. Every reader – scholar or journalist, politician or student, corporate agent or human rights defender – is invited to approach the reading in this way. More than cases, these pages tell stories about people, about mothers and fathers, children and elderly people. After reading, their living conditions will be a bit closer and more visible to the rest of society and to other societies than they were before.

The *Salaverna* and *El Peñasquito* cases in Mexico

i. The case

The case analyzed here includes two extractive projects, *Mina Frisco-Tayahua* and *Mina Goldcorp-El Peñasquito*, which were developed in the Mazapil municipality of the State of Zacatecas, in Mexico. The Tayahua mine in Salaverna was operated from the 1990s and until 2013 – in a first period – by the Frisco company of Mexican majority capital, and now the activity has been restarted – the second period. The Peñasquito mine has been in operation since 2007 and is operated by the Canadian company Goldcorp. In both cases, the metal exploitation has the objective of extracting gold, silver, zinc, copper and lead. It is noteworthy that these activities are carried out in a Mexican state with a semi-arid climate and, therefore, with a lack of water – a resource essential both for its inhabitants and for mining exploitation.

ii. Relevance of the specific business area or activity

Mining is one of the oldest and most important activities carried out in Zacatecas. Among its main minerals are silver, gold, mercury, iron, zinc, lead, bismuth, antimony, salt, copper, quartz, kaolin, onyx, quartz, cadmium and Wollastonite.

The state's mineral riches were discovered shortly after the arrival of the Spaniards, and some of Mexico's most famous mines date back to 1546. The silver mines are the most important (Alvarado's, for example, where they extracted more than 800 million dollars' worth of silver between 1548 and 1867), to the point that Mexico is the world's leading producer of silver. At present, there are approximately 85 economic units involved in mining activity. As Professor Tetreault explains, the capital invested is, for the most part, Mexican:

> Although the most common belief is that foreign companies have most of this industry in their hands, the reality is that they are Mexican companies, mainly Grupo México, Peñoles and the Mining Company Frisco, those who "exert oligopolistic control over the sector".
>
> (Ollaquindia 2014)

The predominantly Mexican nationality of mining companies, however, does not mean that the activity is carried out independently of the interests of international capital. It should be considered that the financing of projects is usually done by international entities such as the World Bank, the Export-Import Bank of the United States (Eximbank) or the Bank of Commerce of Mexico (Bancomer, purchased in 2000 by BBVA, of Spanish capital) (Valadez Rodríguez 2005). Besides, mining takes place largely for export, with the United States, Japan, Peru, Switzerland, the Dominican Republic and Canada being the main countries to which Mexican mining production is exported (Catalán Leman 2011). Canada, besides, has particular historic ways of imposing its capital, among other forms, through the promotion of neoliberal reforms as regard to its capital in foreign countries and through the direct intervention in administrative mining sectors in Latin America (Tetreault 2013: 194 ss.). On the other hand, especially since the 1960s, the impact and environmental, economic and social risks of mining have increased with the increase of direct foreign investment in the region, which has intensified and expanded in the area since the end of the twentieth century and the beginning of the twenty-first century (Catalán Leman 2011).

In 2015, the State of Zacatecas had 1,579,209 inhabitants over an area of 75,539 km², so it has a population density of 19.73 inhabitants/km². It has 58 municipalities, many of which are directly involved in mining activity. According to the Ministry of Economy, in 2011, the mining production of Zacatecas generated profits of 68 billion pesos, equivalent to 43% of the national value in the sector (Agencia Reforma 2013).

Particularly in the case of *El Peñasquito*, the state's economic interest in the mine has been reflected in regulations that are detrimental to the local population. Goldcorp, supported by the Agrarian Procurator Office and the Ministry of Economy, has monopolized the land owned by the *ejidos*. The *ejidos* are communal parcels of land in rural areas which were granted to groups of people for exploitation; they are considered a success from the Mexican Revolution in terms of redistribution of land. In this case, however, through so-called temporary occupation agreements, these areas have been transferred to companies. These agreements are legal instruments derived from the neoliberal policies of 1992 that allow commercial companies to make agreements with *ejidos* and agrarian communities, to cede the temporary use of land in exchange for payment (Garibay et al. 2014). Between 2006 and 2010, Goldcorp acquired 7,971 hectares of the four ejidos: Cedros, El Vergel, Mazapil and Cerro Gordo.

iii. Cultural violence in the region "before"

Before the beginning of the mining activity, the population of *El Peñasquito* was beyond the attentive eye of the State, that is to say, unprotected. Although mining has always been a relevant activity in the area, large-scale, open-pit mining continues to be a novelty. In this sense, official discourse and action have violated the local people's need for information, understanding and expressing their opinion regarding the changes that could be generated. Culturally, due to its physical and cultural distance from urban society, the local population was confronted with actors and interests with whom it did not find itself on an equal footing or at an equal capacity to carry out a symmetrical dialogue. This was explained as follows:

> The population is poor. Marginalized. Abandoned by neoliberal policies, it was a breeding ground for the arrival of the transnational Goldcorp Peñasquito. The state, municipal authorities, all levels, were accessories to this dispossession. They handled the peasants: You are free. We are in a free and democratic country where you are going to decide whether you do business with the company, and only you. They did not talk to the people about what open-pit mining was, about the implications, they did not tell them it was a mining industry different from the traditional one that had been there in that region for three hundred years, or well, since the arrival of the Spaniards. They were not told that dynamite had to be used, they were not told that cyanide was being used, they were not told that 4,500 hectares would be dismantled at the start. They were not told that to grind a ton of ore a ton of water was needed, in a region where the water is vitally important.
>
> (Lecturer Octavio Vásquez, Universidad Autónoma de Zacatecas)
> (Documentary *Reportaje Minera Peñasquito* 2014, 5'55")

Thus, the state placed itself in the role of intermediary and not of a principally interested party; it was the first to see this false recognition of the autonomy of its people while leaving it in the hands of foreign investment. The only alternatives were either submission to the new conditions or migration as a social manifestation in their networks of families and friends; this is the "culture of migration" of which Salas Luévano speaks (2013: 19). These possibilities seem to mark the only options for this population whose situation has aroused indifference from the rest of society and the state.

iv. Structural violence in the region "before"

The precarious conditions in the satisfaction of basic needs are evident if one observes the strong migratory tendency of Zacatecas, which began its incursion as an expeller of the labor force as far back as the end of the nineteenth century. According to Salas Luévano, since the beginning of the twentieth century, Zacatecas, along with Jalisco, Michoacán and Guanajuato, already constituted an expulsive labor force region (Salas Luévano 2013: 88/89). So, she explains that

> in general terms, it is affirmed that the origin of the Zacatecas exodus is closely linked to the following factors: the current economic paradigm and its state and regional policies that do not have among their priorities the reduction of regional inequalities; the scarcity of employment and income opportunities for the population of the state, which is related to the absence of industrial development, a service sector that barely reaches a significant presence, to which are added the crises that the agricultural and mining activity have faced, and that they have become expellers of a constant labor force, consequently causing unemployment and underemployment of the population in both sectors. Various factors have influenced this migratory process, such as the precariousness and the exclusionary nature of the productive structure of Zacatecas, characterized, among other things, by a limited industrial sector, an agricultural activity that is not very technified or oriented toward family subsistence; an extensive range of livestock industry specialized in raising live cattle and a mining sector *which has almost no impact on employment and the regional economy.*
>
> These characteristics place the state as one of the least capable of generating employment in the country, as indicated in the State Development Plan (1999–2004). It is interesting to note that, *although the Zacatecan economy has had periods of significant expansion, at present it continues to be located as one of the states with the greatest poverty and marginalization in the country.*
>
> (Salas Luévano 2013: 91, italics mine)

The population's basic needs, which were unsatisfied at the start of the mining industries remain unsatisfied, although Zacatecas has been a productive state for some time.

On the other hand, at the structural level, the link between the previous situation of the population and economic conditions prior to the development of these mining activities requires, in this case, that attention be paid to the legal meshes that can be more or less elastic and permissive with respect to certain actors and certain economic activities. In this case,

> Burnes Ortiz explained that the problem has its origin in the liberalization of legislation and dismantling of constitutional norms in the domain of natural resources and the issuance of a new mining law in June 1992 which

simplified the process of granting concessions and has resulted in a negative impact of mining in the current social and ecological fields.

(Catalán Leman 2011)

The law – as in the case of the temporary occupation agreements – facilitates the expansion of transnational economic actors in poor regions.

v. Business, people and the economic situation in the area "during" and "after"

In both the *Salaverna* and *El Peñasquito* cases, the activity of the mines involved the total displacement of the population and the construction of new villages, due to the total destruction of the original ones, because the exploitation of the mine required it. This had an impact not only on the environment and flora and fauna, but also on the living conditions and cultural identity of the peoples who had lived there for centuries.[1] *Nuevo Peñasco* was founded in the first case, and *Nuevo Salaverna* in the second (De la Torre 2015: 104–105).

The case under study is also in a general context of exploitation that generates many returns in areas where the population currently continues to be harmed rather than favored. The situation, and the real impact of mining in general and in Mazapil in particular, is evident in this analysis:

Of every thousand pesos in minerals such as gold, silver and bronze obtained in Zacatecas, only 98 cents remain in the state, according to estimates by the Center for Development Studies of the Autonomous University of Zacatecas (UAZ).

In Zacatecas there are 70 mining projects with foreign investment that exceeds 2,344 million dollars, according to official figures.

There is the largest producing mine in the world, Fresnillo PLC, which in 2008 generated profits of 2 billion dollars, with an annual production of 34 million ounces of silver, which they expect to double by 2018.

Another example is the Peñasquito Mine, located in the semi-arid region, where there are the highest rates of extreme poverty in Zacatecas, which arrived in 2007 with an initial investment of 1,590 million dollars.

Currently, the company extracts 150 thousand tons of open-pit gold per day, which places it in the first place in Latin America and second worldwide.

However, all this wealth is not reflected in municipalities such as Mazapil, Concepción del Oro, Melchor Ocampo and El Salvador, whose budget as a whole does not exceed 250 million pesos a year, and its almost 45 thousand inhabitants dispersed in more than 300 communities lack the most basic services.

(Agencia Reforma 2013)

In the same way, a direct local actor like the Secretary of Economic Development of Mazapil presented an illustration of the case with qualified information:

> We have not had anything from the El Peñasquito mine, although they take out millions of dollars every day, they do not even leave jobs for our people, the majority hire them from outside and the aquifers are running out [. . .] We wanted to propose that the mine support us with a type B hospital to care for the population, opportunities for our children and social welfare projects, but they do not receive us, we cannot close our eyes or generate false expectations, in the long run this will leave us pure contamination.
>
> (Agencia Reforma 2013)

That this claim was spoken by a local politician could raise suspicions regarding his capability and possibility of doing more to protect the population and the resources, on the one hand. On the other hand, however, the studied complexities existing between centers and peripheries (see Chapter 2) and between central states and the elitist way of governing in Latin America (see Chapter 1) could bring some new questions into consideration. The distances between federal states and the states, and between the leaders of the states and agents of the municipalities, are often huge. As in the Formosa case presented earlier (Chapter 2), the internal tensions in the state make it clear that there is not "the" state, but several agents acting in the name of the state and with its faculties, but there is neither an integral program of action, nor any integral common policies, which could be held solely responsible for the negative effects of economic activity. The analysis, therefore, becomes increasingly complicated.

vi. Structural violence in the region "during" and "after"

As has been mentioned, the economic benefit obtained by companies and entrepreneurs

> is not reflected in municipalities such as Mazapil, Concepción del Oro, Melchor Ocampo and El Salvador, whose budget as a whole does not exceed 250 million pesos a year, and its almost 45 thousand inhabitants dispersed in more than 300 communities lack the most basic services.
>
> (Agencia Reforma 2013)

In the specific case of the mine in Salaverna (Tayahua), the impact generated by the mine can be summarized in the description of the hollowing out in the infrastructure and in the population which was linked to the alleged physical danger represented by the mine and the risk of collapse. This has led to the destruction of infrastructure and the displacement of the population: "When we arrive it seems that it is a ghost town, by the silence that dominates; the barking of dogs that roam the street give indications that there may be people in the worn houses of the place" (Belmontes 2016). A collapse that occurred in the mine in 2012 created a geological fault for which there is a risk of another collapse, and this led to the cessation of activity in 2013, as alleged by state agencies. However, the small population that remains in the place (16 families in a village which, before the collapse, was home to more than 80) does not believe in this risk. Rather, the inhabitants feel pressured to leave the place for the interest of the state and of the company in depopulating the territory for the reactivation and expansion of the mining exploitation.

The population remains forgotten. The economic expansion and growth reflected in the local GDP (Zacatecas is one of the states with the highest growth in recent years, reflecting economic growth of 7.5% according to the percentages of annual GDP between 1994 and 2008, and 4.3% between 2005 and 2015), however, have not implied a real reduction in poverty. On the contrary, villages that historically had enjoyed a certain degree of self-sufficiency have become villages in clear decline.

> The scenario of depopulation in the communities of the municipalities of the State are a portrayal of the conversion of formerly prosperous towns now depopulated, where you see the transit of people only in times of patron festivities, when the migrants return, celebrate and live with those who stay, and then return to their daily lives in the United States.
>
> The depopulation that is registered in the municipalities will mean that in the near future, they will be outside the legal focus sustained in the Third Chapter (corresponding to the Creation, Fusion and Suppression of Municipalities), in its Article 124, in point II, which states: "That the territorial surface on which it is intended to constitute is not less than one hundred and fifty square kilometers; point III, That the population in that demarcation be greater than fifteen thousand inhabitants; point IV, That the town chosen as municipal seat has indispensable public services" (Political Constitution of the Free and Sovereign State of Zacatecas, 2005); which implies the possibility of carrying out a redistribution of the municipalities in the interior of the State of Zacatecas.
>
> (Salas Luévano 2013: 97)

The depopulation and the transformation of self-supplied villages into displaced communities lacking in their most basic needs is also explained, and fundamentally so, by the direct negative impact of mining operations. As Guzmán López has concluded in his study, the negative environmental impacts generated by mega-mining in Zacatecas were diverse. Among them, in the first place, it is the territorial dispute and competition with agricultural production areas that stand out, both with regard to access to land – in terms of land area – and with regard to access to water – in terms of volume. Second, soil pollution is caused by millions of tons of solid waste as well as by contamination of ground and surface water sources produced by the various techniques applied in extraction – drilling, milling and leaching. This has led to a reduction in food production. Maize and beans, staple foods, have fallen by more than half in their production in the area of the Peñasquito mine since 2009, due to loss of arable land and loss of soil quality and access to water (Guzmán López 2016: 125). Professor Tetreault's description regarding this basic triad of impact due to environmental pollution, land and water hogging, and therefore the loss of agricultural production spaces, is identical (Godoy 2017).

Added to all this is the impact on "urban" life.

In particular, situations experienced by specific inhabitants should be mentioned at the local level, with respect to the cases studied here. This brings qualitative data in terms of the structural conditions of life that give body to information that otherwise remains a form of theoretical criticism or big data. On education in Salaverna, for example, you can see a testimony that emerges from an interview with Emiliano, a boy who lives in (old) Salaverna:

> In the past, the school was here in the town, but the school was moved to New Salaverna and I cannot see all my friends anymore; in the past, after school, we played all afternoon and we ran, now everything is quiet and gone.
>
> (Belmontes 2016)

This story, although at first glance it appears to be merely sentimental or even childish, is nonetheless a daily tragedy for a child, accompanied by an effective diminution of possibilities in terms of realizing his need for education and social contact with others. As he continues in the note: "*But that has not been the hardest part, he stressed, because now, for those who stayed, attending classes every day is very complicated, because they have to travel about 5 kilometers to reach the school*" (Belmontes 2016). Many children take this route on foot, so those still living in the original town have permission to arrive half an hour late.

Regarding housing, another qualitative illustration is this case of an adult resident, Jesús Montoya Cárdenas, who at the time accepted the transfer offered by the company and said he regretted having given up his house in exchange for one of the new housing units, because the company had not complied with what it had promised years before.

> They told us that if we came here they would give us deeds to the houses, 15 thousand pesos and that they would even provide a party hall. We were going to have everything: church, hospital, school, but what is the use if there are not even teachers for all the children?
>
> (Belmontes 2016)

Although they have already received documents concerning the houses, because they do not know how to read or write, they do not know the exact content of the papers. However, as they explained, "*in the documents that the company distributed, there is no legal security for those who live in the houses in that subdivision, since it specifies that the mining company owns the lots and real estate delivered*". The new location and the new home, to which he agreed when he felt forced by the situation, changed his life completely. Again, this testimony may seem merely sentimental, and yet it is the story of a life and a cultural belonging that has been uprooted by force, as Montoya Cárdenas himself explained with tears in his eyes:

> I'm not used to being locked in, but now I do not even know how to go back up there: when you said you were coming here, at that moment they made holes in the houses and a truck knocked them down.
>
> (Belmontes 2016)

In terms of health, in Mazapil, the municipality where both mining operations are located, there is only one primary care health facility for the 17,000 inhabitants, who are distributed throughout approximately 115 small communities, "the majority with deficiencies of all public services" (Mejía 2015). The shortcomings of the health care system were evident when, on July 29, 2015, a cargo truck (in operation of the Peñasquito mine) was travelling on a road for which it was not authorized. Its brakes failed, and it ran over a group of pilgrims, killing 27. The injured people had to be transported to rooms in different municipalities.

vii. Physical violence in the region "during" and "after"

In terms of direct and visible physical violence, it has been perceived by women in particular. The level of conflict increased after the installation of the mines: "There is a population of workers from other parts who do not have roots in the community. And it begins with the consumption of drugs, alcohol; there are men looking for sex; prostitution occurs" (Godoy 2017). Although the consumption of neither drugs nor alcohol nor sexual services should be considered violent in themselves, they do facilitate a context of aggression and violence when these activities occur suddenly, due to the exogenous population's demand and in clear detriment of the female population. Locally, the potential for physical violence is evident and should be considered.

In another order of problems, the generation of new physical violence has also been noticed by the company, and not only in terms of the conflict that may exist in relation to its workers. The business interest was clear in both Salaverna and Peñasquito, in terms of the need to evict the residents, and this led to threats and acts of violence against the local population when there were refusals and resistance. The company, in the task of eviction, acted with the support of state officials, who were committed to the security of the project (Nieto 2017; Documentary Salaverna 2017).

Physical violence, finally, can also be documented in terms of damages arising from negligence and leading to tragic outcomes. These are directly linked to the mining activity and the lack of sufficient regulation or controls by the state, as was the case with the aforementioned accident, which took place in July 2015, when a truck loaded with sand travelled in violation of the regulations for urban roads. At the time of the accident, the driver was travelling under the authority of El Peñasquito-Goldcorp.

To these specific situations can be added various illegal activities carried out by the company, such as falsification of titles, blackmail in order to obtain land, abuse of power, intimidation and threats (Garibay et al. 2014), which come with the aforementioned pollution, diseases caused by said contamination, the death of livestock and the loss of crops. All this has mobilized the local population, who in various blockades and demonstrations have denounced their suffering and even formed the Common Front of Those Affected by Peñasquito Mining (FCAMP).[2] This last group of acts does not seem to belong to acts of direct or physical violence. Nevertheless, considering the visible and direct physical damage that is caused, it seems relevant for the potential and reality of social conflict (physical, visible) that it entails.

viii. Cultural violence in the region "after"

The negative structural impact due to the effects on the satisfaction of basic needs related to food, health, the environment, housing or education, brings with it negative social and cultural effects which further weaken the possibilities of local resistance. In the first place, the potential for resistance is reduced by the "disarticulation" and "decomposition of the social network" generated, as explained by Professor Tetreault at the Autonomous University of Zacatecas, who counts the social decomposition and vices generated in the interrelation among the new inhabitants (employees of the mine) and the local communities among the consequences of the mine. In particular, here, women bear the brunt of the consequences of the change, both because of the aforementioned migration, and because of difficulties in interacting with new adult men outside the community (Godoy 2017).

The interaction difficulties are, moreover, directly linked to the state's attitude of betrayal in favor of corporate mandates, that is to say, for its intervention in the role of spectator or partial third party – promoter of the investments – and not as a central actor in the generation, management and provision of public service or care and protection of the rights of the local population. State indifference with respect to the population, in this sense, is an eloquent example of social distance (see Chapter 2) (Documentary Salaverna 2017).

These disarticulations and fragilities, along with the state's lack of interest in discourse and practice with respect to the destiny of the population, may have a long-term cultural consequence that has already been predicted by the population of Salaverna: "*If we continue to allow open-cast mines. . . . The village of Mazapil is in danger of extinction, practically*" (Documentary Salaverna 2017: 4'50").

The *Texaco/Chevron* case in Ecuador

i. The case

In 1976, Texaco (later Chevron), in cooperation with the national company Corporación Estatal Petrolera Ecuatoriana (CEPE) – predecessor of the State Company Petróleos del Ecuador (Petroecuador) – formed a consortium for the exploration and production of oil, with CEPE having 62.5% of the consortium, which continued to be managed and operated by Texaco. In 1990, the State entrusted Petroecuador with the administration and operation of the consortium, and Texaco continued to receive dividends. In 1992, at the end of the concession contract, Petroecuador became the owner of 100% of the interest, and Texaco withdrew from the country. Thus, during this period, between 1972 and 1992, the company Chevron built and used pipelines in a technical condition of low quality between Lago Agrio and the Harbor Esmeraldas in the province of Sucumbíos. It was possible to drill for oil only after the government had declared the land "vacant" even though it was owned and inhabited by the local population (Kimerling 1991; Donziger et al. 2010).[3]

ii. Relevance of the specific business area or activity

A description of the oil industry in Esmeraldas requires a brief historical overview. Let's start by recalling that in 1964, in a context of dictatorial government, a concession agreement was established by the Ecuadorian government with Texaco Petroleum Company, a subsidiary of Texaco which was in consortium with Gulf Oil (Lara 2009: 519 ss.; Zanatta 2012: 188; Halperin Dongui 2010: 599 ss., 712 ss.).[4] The concession given by Ecuador had a term of 28 years – it would last until 1992 – for the exploration and joint production in the Ecuadorian East.[5] Since 1964, numerous drilling operations have been carried out in the North Amazon, and in 1967, the first oil was obtained from a well that was called Lago Agrio 1, around which a town began to form that would later become Nueva Loja, capital of the province of Sucumbíos (Ortiz 2011).[6] In 1971, the Hydrocarbons Law and the Constitutive Law of CEPE (Corporación Estatal Petrolera Ecuatoriana) were promulgated and entered into force in 1972.

In this context, in 1972 Texaco-Gulf built the Trans-Ecuadorian Pipeline System (SOTE), for which the most economical technology was used, given that at that time environmental awareness and control standards in Ecuador were practically nonexistent, companies considered its rainforest to be a no man's land, and the few requirements which did exist could easily be circumvented (Haller et al. 2007: 313).

On June 23, 1972, CEPE was created, the entity in charge of developing activities assigned by the Hydrocarbons Law: to explore, industrialize and market other necessary products of petroleum and petrochemical activity. In this way, for the first time, the national government had an instrument that allowed it to manage and control on its own account for the benefit of the country. On the other hand, in 1973 Ecuador joined the Organization of Petroleum Exporting Countries (OPEC) in order to improve its position of power vis-à-vis the importing countries, thus promoting a nationalist policy (Fontaine 2007: 72; Lara 2009: 538). Thus, the national wealth "immediately became the axis of the state economy – and led to the formation of new, small and large companies related to oil activity, the multiplication of jobs but also the proliferation of symptoms and episodes of widespread corruption" (Lara 2009: 539).

iii. Invisible violence in the region "before" (cultural and structural)

It is interesting to note that through various "laws of colonization", large territories ancestrally owned and inhabited by indigenous communities were left in the hands of landowners as simple grazing land or areas for exploitation.

Texaco advertising from the time stated "bringing muscles and machinery to a territory untouched by civilization" (documentary film *Crude* 2009: 21').

As Kimerling wrote, "To the international petroleum industry, the Orient is a remote but booming frontier, where an enterprise can extract high profits with virtually no environmental regulation or oversight" (Kimerling 1994: 201). This can easily be explained through the physical distance between the Lago Agrio population in the rainforest and the capital city, Quito: seven hours by bus, without any state office which could be informed or resorted to in cases of need.

Because of the distances and relative isolation of communities living in the rainforest, cultural identification is anything but simple. The Sucumbíos Court in its First Judgment, for example, made this clear when explaining that 42 individuals had signed the petition against Texaco but that they claimed environmental harm affecting around 30,000 people, whose identity remained indeterminate:

> Those potentially affected by the activities of the Consortium are divided into several diverse human groups, which claim to be united by the fact of being affected by environmental damage without belonging to the same nation, or neighborhood, but are identifiable by sharing affectations from environmental damage.[7]

The relative isolation of the area was explicitly recognized, for example, by the Court, when it was explained that no statistical data about health conditions and health services were available for the province of Sucumbíos by the end of the 1980s.[8] In the time before Texaco arrived, there was even less information. Some aspects, curiously, were defined by contrast. According to an infrastructure study from 1989 to 1990,

> the province of Sucumbíos has the lowest total of all the Amazonian provinces of domiciliary connections to drinking water and also in access to

public taps, which does not mean that the inhabitants of these areas do not consume water, but necessarily implies that *the inhabitants of these provinces have a greater dependence on natural water sources.* (italics mine)[9]

The direct relationship with natural resources and, at the same time, the almost nonexistent contact with the state, left these populations completely exposed to the private economic actors, who – as mentioned earlier – understood the area as empty and simply waiting for their business.

iv. Business, people and the economic situation in the area "during" and "after"

In 1992, the year in which Chevron/Texaco withdrew from Ecuador, and after the presidency of Sixto Durán Ballen, a period of neoliberal reforms began (privatization of public sectors such as telecommunications, hydrocarbons and electricity, liberalization of trade, legal guarantees for foreign investments, increase of loans from the World Bank, among others) (Lara 2009: 582 ss.). In this context, it is worth mentioning the sanction of the Hydrocarbons Law. This law would have caused the state's income from its participation in oil exploitation operations to decrease from 90% to 33% in favor of private companies, given that in some cases the totality of the profits was granted to the corporations (Weber 2008: 74–84), as well as the withdrawal of Ecuador from OPEC, "while, by contrast, the entry of large oil companies was authorized to participate in the commercialization of the gasoline produced in the country" (Lara 2009: 583). In the same year, 1992, Petroecuador commissioned the Canadian consultancy firm HBT Agra Limited to carry out an independent and impartial audit of the Texaco facilities in order to assess the direct and indirect environmental and socioeconomic impact of the Texaco operations. Texaco would be bound by the results (Kimerling 1994: 200). One year later, on August 27, 1993, Ecuador signed a Bilateral Investment Treaty with the United States.

In 1993, also, the civil lawsuit against Texaco was initiated in the United States. It was filed in that country because of the lack of confidence that the plaintiffs had in the Ecuadorian judicial system (see ahead, *point vi.*) (Kimerling 1994: 202). In 1995, through a contract signed with Ecuador's federal government – still under the regime of Sixto Durán Ballen – Texaco assumed responsibility for a third of the environmental liabilities that had been left in the rainforest, and was disconnected from the responsibility of cleaning up the other two-thirds. Under this agreement, between 1995 and 1998, Texaco carried out the remediation work that was pending. When this work had been completed, an agreement was signed with the government and the four municipalities where the consortium operated: Lago Agrio, Shushufindi, La Joya de los Sachas and Francisco de Orellana. Through this agreement, the state was satisfied and freed the company from any future liability or obligation in relation to environmental damage (Ortiz 2011). However, according to what was claimed by the plaintiffs in the *Aguinda v. Texaco* case (see ahead), as well as by different environmental groups and organizations for the protection of human rights, the cleanup had not been carried out properly. According to Texaco – today Chevron – on the other hand, all the required procedures had been completed, with Petroecuador alone being responsible for cleaning up the remaining waste – even though Petroecuador, de facto, had not operated the facilities except in the last year prior to Texaco's withdrawal.

The change in the presidency in 2007 gave a new perspective to the *Texaco/Chevron* case. Whereas before 2007, Ecuadorian regimes friendly to neoliberal and foreign investments neglected the impact of the damaging activities carried out by Chevron, the left-wing, socially oriented regime that assumed the presidency that year paid attention to the victims' demands and publicly stated that foreign actors would not take advantage of the local population in the future.[10] This, however, should not divert attention from Correa's economic policy, which has since shifted toward what Gudynas has called "brown progressivism" (see Chapters 1 and 2). The harshness toward Chevron, mobilized in part as a gesture of rejection of the policies and negotiations of neoliberal governments of the past, has changed over the past years and been replaced with extractive policies and even persecution that local communities, the environment and human rights defenders suffer in areas of mining production and extractions (see ahead, *point vi.*).

v. Structural violence in the region "during" and "after"

The political and economic interrelationships are extremely harmful when the basic function of the state is not fulfilled, and its functionaries act following the mandate of economic actors. The required – and possible – intervention of the state that, manifestly, did not take place, has caused by omission uncountable damaging consequences at various levels. A letter sent from the Governor of Napo to the CEO of Texaco – an engineer – on March 21, 1983, makes the structural weaknesses of the local government evident:

> It is a citizen claim, [oh] Mr. Manager of Texaco, that there is serious damage being caused in the sector of Shushufindi by the pollution of waters, rivers, estuaries and quebradillas, because of the disposal of hydrocarbon waste by workers of the CEPE-TEXACO Consortium (. . .) Because of this, in the most measured way I allow myself to beg you to deign to arbitrate measures to avoid that they continue causing these damages, which – and this will not escape your enlightened criteria- will ultimately become incalculable repercussions for the ecological system and above all for the agricultural sector.[11]

To what extent could it be possible for the population to reach satisfactory levels of health, access to drinking water and sufficient food in the area when the governor himself was asking Texaco for contamination – *please* – to be controlled, softly writing a sort of petition instead of initiating legal action (administrative sanctions had basically been disobeyed) with the immediate effect of halting the activities and for the protection of the local people and environment?

According to the definition of structural violence, access to legal aid and justice are considered as basic social needs. In this respect, the situation for the population in Esmeraldas is – still – bad. Several legal proceedings at different levels and areas have been open since 1992 and until today, they have canceled each other out (civil, criminal and administrative cases initiated both against Texaco/Chevron and against Ecuador). The people, in the meantime, are still waiting for a (re)constructive answer.

In particular, the difficulties in proving causality between contamination and illness have hindered individual criminal proceedings. In 1993, a collective civil suit representing around 30,000 locals was presented under the Alien Tort Claims Act (ATCA) (case *Aguinda v. ChevronTexaco*) and after almost 20 years, the suit was dismissed on grounds of forum non conveniens, that is, because the US forum was considered unsuitable for judging the distant and complex situation in Esmeraldas, and the case was returned to Ecuador. In February 2011, a Lago Agrio Court (Ecuador) ordered Texaco to pay US $18 billion (later reduced to $9.5 billion) for contamination. Because various other claims, charges and procedures within and outside Ecuador are still open, no payment has yet been made to the victims.

Another proceeding was open under the *Racketeer Influenced and Corrupt Organizations Act* (RICO) and here, in March 2014, the US District Court for the Southern District of New York decided that the Ecuadorian judgment had come as the result of fraud and racketeering and was thus unenforceable. Nevertheless, some states have started to enforce the Ecuadorian judgment in their territory and have considered placing an embargo on corporate capital (Kimerling 1991; Donziger et al. 2010).

Furthermore, on August 31, 2011, an Arbitral Tribunal in The Hague issued its arbitration award and established that the Ecuadorian State should pay Chevron/Texaco an approximate value of 96 million dollars, after it had rejected the company's initial claim for 1,605 million dollars. Particularly serious in these awards is that the Court decided that, as a consequence of the judicial delays, it could itself decide on the six demands and take the place of the Ecuadorian judges, completely ignoring its decisions and overstepping its authority.

In 2010 and 2011, Ecuador filed two annulment proceedings (for the awards of jurisdiction and partial liability, and for the final award) which were consolidated into a single proceeding. Ecuador alleged lack of jurisdiction of the Arbitral Tribunal, given that Chevron's six lawsuits (filed between 1991 and 1993) were not covered by the Bilateral Investment Protection Treaty (BIT) signed with the United States, which entered into force in 1997 and cannot be enforced retroactively. At that time, Ecuador argued, Texaco no longer had investments in Ecuador, so the Tribunal would not have jurisdiction to decide on its claims. On May 2, 2012, the District Court of The Hague rejected the claim of nullity filed by Ecuador to the awards issued by the Arbitral Tribunal.

The District Court of The Hague reiterated the arguments of the Arbitral Tribunal and admitted the existence of a supposedly valid arbitration agreement. To this end, it took into account the concession and investment agreement signed between Ecuador and Texaco in 1973 and considered that the effects of this agreement persisted by the time the signed liberation agreements between Ecuador and Texaco were signed in 1995. Thus, Article VI of the BIT was interpreted in isolation from the rest of the agreement and applied retroactively. Today, therefore, there are still various processes pending while the local population waits for an answer.[12] Delays and opposing decisions are the typical effects of arbitral panels and their awards as interpreted and implemented according to the Bilateral and Free Trade Agreements. Here, the use of these instruments as a "technique of neutralization" of responsibility, as Raskovsky (2017) explained (see Chapters 1 and 6), becomes explicit.

Moving to the health issue, it is relevant to mention that running parallel to the bureaucratic and economic struggles, people have continued to suffer from increasing cases of disease while mortality levels have grown continuously. During the 20 years of use, more than 18 billion gallons of toxic waste water were released into the Ecuadorian Amazon River. Contamination of the surrounding area was caused by Texaco's neglect of technical safety standards during the use of the pipelines and after their cessation of activity. And this, as the Court of Sucumbíos stated, had been *avoidable*:

> Texpet omitted the use of available technology (reinjection equipment, steel tanks) and recommended practices (reinjection of formation water) to prevent foreseeable damage. A direct consequence of this omission is the admitted dumping into the Amazonian environment of 15,834 million gallons of formation water, which would foreseeably cause damages that could also be avoided with the implementation of available technology. In the same way, the construction of open-air, uncoated pools could not be considered as a recommended practice for environments where nearby water sources are in danger. The reported contamination was considered dangerous, because the possibility is accepted that the dumping of fluids such as those that Texaco admits, in the name of Texpet, cause harm to agriculture and people's health.[13]

The damage remains today. Expert reports give an account of the numerous damages to the environment and their direct impact on health. Among them, the following summarizes the main ones in an integral, specific way at the same time:

> Direct pollution to the rivers, essential sources of water for most families, is one of the worst problems, since that water is used for cooking, drinking,

bathing, washing clothes and for animals. Pollution has led to the presence of diseases caused by exposure and consumption of water from rivers, causes skin diseases, intestinal and vaginal infections, and in many cases cancer, in women basically of the uterus, ovaries and breast; in general of the throat, stomach, kidney, skin and brain.[14]

The problem is that lack of a healthy environment remains invisible; it is an unperceived non-satisfied need, invisible not only for individuals, but also for the law, as Galtung said, and as the lawyer from Texaco clearly exemplified: *"This is industrial exploitation permitted by law. This is not pollution"* (documentary film *Crude* 2009: 32'). In fact, this is pollution, and the non-satisfactory provision of health services for people exposed to this pollution increases the rates of disease and collective problems because the rural population does not have sufficient access to the two urban hospitals nearest (though still distant) to the oil industrial area (Celi et al. 2009: 45).

In a relevant research study of 2009, the health level in the population of the province Sucumbíos was rated as not very satisfactory. With a health index of 46.2 (under the national index of 57.7) and with high levels of infant mortality (32/1,000) and chronic malnutrition (29.7%), the province has the worst health conditions in Ecuador (Celi et al. 2009: 43). As the authors of this study explain:

> This situation is due to the high levels of oil pollution that the province suffers, and the population must face very complex diseases, before which the health centers have not foreseen forms of control.
>
> So many of the interviewees in this research argue that due to pollution there are also respiratory problems and allergies. Some also claim that many cases of cancer have been observed. (. . .)
>
> On the other hand, while the Participatory Plan of the province (2005–2015) reported two deaths from cancer in 2000, the Ministry of Health registered twenty-seven cases in 2006.
>
> (Celi et al. 2009: 44)

As time goes by, the cases of cancer and death from cancer have increased, given that the disease can take some years to develop as a consequence of excessive exposure to toxic substances, and death is the result of many years of failed or unsatisfactory treatment. Particularly in the provinces with high levels of oil production, like Sucumbíos and Orellana, the figures are quite clear in this regard. After oil production has stopped, in polluted areas, among workers and the local population, cases of cancer can appear even up to 20 years later (Rourke 2010).

vi. Physical violence in the region "during" and "after"

Physical violence related to the oil production in Lago Agrio has similar features to violence in mining areas in general (Svampa 2017). Women are especially affected by the conduct of the new men (workers and company employees) and because of the new household dynamics when the local men start working for the company or, because of the displacement and decline of animals in the area, when the men of the community have to go out and reach distant areas for hunting, fishing or working. Women remain alone in the village, and often, these new dynamics facilitate conditions for the infliction of sexual violence against them (Martínez 2004).

Women and men, further, are often – and this was also the case in Ecuador – involved in demands and protests against the oil facilities, and this opposition is repressed and criminalized by the state. At the time of the initiation of the Chevron exploration and work, there was a dictatorial government in the presidency. This fact explains, on the one hand, the lack of resistance and the submission of the population; on the other hand, it demonstrates in itself the clear presence of physical violence because of the dictatorial menace and conditions on the part of the state.

In the Report of Amnesty International *"Para que Nadie Reclame Nada"* (2012, *So that Nobody Claims More*), information was collected about the use of detention, deprivation of liberty and filing of unfounded charges against protesters from indigenous and peasant communities between 2009 and 2011 in Ecuador. These figures are recent and cannot be directly applied to the resistance in the Chevron case. However, the physical violence inflicted on communities by the state must be considered as a common context. State forces and private forces ensure the development, and in Ecuador, this has been the case until today (Martínez Novo 2017).

Last, poisoning is – no doubt – physical violence: *"They pretend to cheat by saying it was common procedure [. . .]. Poisonous water was thrown into the estuaries"* (documentary film *Crude* 2009: 7'20" ss.).

vii. Cultural violence in the region "during" and "after"

This quotation from the researcher Kimerling is an excellent summation of the non-visible cultural aspects that prevent the satisfaction of basic needs of the local population:

> Ecuador's social reality supercedes the legal guarantees of its Constitution and of international human rights instruments. Racism against indigenous peoples, widespread poverty, and extreme inequality characterize Ecuadorian society. Discrimination against indigenous people and the poor is pervasive, and state and non-state actors routinely violate the constitutional guarantee of equal protection of the law. Political and economic power is concentrated in the hands of a small elite, who effectively exclude the majority of Ecuadorians from meaningful participation in the political system. Secrecy, which characterizes most government decision-making, limits the accountability of public officials.
>
> (Kimerling 1994: 203)

After the proceedings had been opened, Mr. Callejas, the lawyer representing Chevron, said that this was a hydrocarbon industrial area and, therefore, *"nobody should live here"* (documentary film *Crude* 2009: 19'). In this expression, he seems to forget that people had been living in the area *before* the industrial development started. For the company, the local population continues to be seen as an obstacle and not as individuals and communities damaged by the industrial activity. For this reason, corporate representatives can see the harm as externalities (see Chapters 1 and 2).

The distance between this population and the urban areas, of course, intensified the indifference on the part of the public. The externalities of the company – damaging and later killing people through environmental pollution – are still considered to be isolated cases. There is neither empathy nor social proximity between the urban population and the people in Lago Agrio.

The victims' situation and position almost 20 years after Texaco stopped the activity cannot be considered – in any way – satisfactory with regard to the most basic needs. On the contrary, the poor standard of living has consistently remained so over time.[15] Rural areas have not experienced any decline in poverty, as urban areas have. Between 1995 and 2006, national poverty ("pobreza nacional"), according to the measure of Unsatisfied Basic Needs (NBI, in the Spanish abbreviation) decreased from 53.6% to 45.8% of the total population. In urban areas in this period, the proportion of poor people decreased from 29.2% to 24.8%. In rural areas, the figures still showed an extremely high rate, with a slight decrease of poor people from 88.8% to 82.2% (Mocha 2012: 16 ss.). In Lago Agrio, specifically, in 2001, 84.2% of the population were living under conditions of poverty, and among them, 40.1% were living in conditions of *extreme* poverty, one of the highest levels in the country (Celi et al. 2009: 43).

In the meantime, there are not many people living there, because in the general context of discrimination, the situation of the affected peoples in this case generated displacement and population decline, explained partly because of the insufficient possibility of practicing traditional activities which could ensure survival (Celi et al. 2009: 40 ss., 42). It is, as the Sucumbíos Court revealed,[16] cultural damage caused by forced displacement due mainly to the impact suffered by land and rivers, which led to the decline of the species that were used for traditional hunting and fishing. The modification of traditional customs was, therefore, a direct consequence. And this change did not occur in the sense of adaptation to the promised development, but of relocation in a context of continued discrimination and silent violence. According to the Gini coefficient, in Ecuador, inequality did not really change between 1995 (0.43) and 2006 (0.46): even worse, it increased a little bit (Mocha 2012: 34).

The case of women requires especial attention given that they are responsible for food preparation, cleaning and all home-centered work directly related to the need of food, water and a healthy environment for their children. Oil production and all collective dynamics changes brought by the big companies have an immediate impact in the perception and self-perception of women and their role in the community, as it was seen in the Mexican *Salaverna* and *El Peñas-quito* cases as well. Linked to the aforementioned question of physical violence against women, further, they live under cultural pressure as family leaders, a fact which is often forgotten in the violence reports on mining and oil production in rural areas (Martínez 2004).

Last, education for children is insufficient in the oil industrial rural area as well. The district of Lago Agrio counts among the districts with the lowest level of school enrollment – 5.7 years of attendance. Adult illiteracy is high (8.1%), schools are not properly equipped and there are not enough teachers (Celi et al. 2009: 46 ss.).

The best description of how all the types of violence interact in this case probably appears in these words by Celestino Piaguaje, a member of the Secoya folk, who tells us:

> *From year 60 to 69, the Secoya and Siona lived in the villages in a more dignified way. There was no pollution and everything was normal, like our own lives, the people of the jungle. We lived well from hunting and fishing and the environment was very healthy. Then, from the year 70 on, it changed totally, very abruptly. First you could see how the companies arrived, opening the trails in the communities and also the helicopters, they built a heliport and you could see their arrival to our communities of this Amazonian plain. It was seen as temporary work, but then the work of drilling and exploitation of oil was carried out. Hence I say, it seems that it changed life completely, which forced us to look for another way of life, to have another alternative for a good life, because there was no hunting, there was no fishing, so we had to raise cattle in order to live well . . . not to be in search of another form different from the one we had lived of the traditional hunt, and of the fishing.*[17]

The *Ralco* case in Chile

i. The case

In 1997, the company Endesa – of Spanish capital – made public its decision to build the Ralco hydroelectric plant in the Biobío (the name of the valley that is home to the river). Under the protection of Law 19,253, also called the *Indigenous Law*, the Mapuche-Pehuenche people formally opposed the construction of the plant. Given the degree of conflict, the special rapporteur sent by the UN, Rodolfo Stavenhagen, indicated that there was a violation of human rights in the construction of the Ralco hydroelectric plant in Alto Bio Bío. The ARCIS University of Chile also opposed the project and described the situation as a genocide against the Mapuche people. Despite these reports and opinions, construction began in May 2004, following the flooding of the Ralco Valley. The work was completed in 2005. Throughout the construction period and after, the indigenous people (Mapuche-Pehuenche) were displaced from their ancestral land using legal and illegal means such as administrative irregularities and fraudulent practices in terms of signatures and allocation of new living areas.

ii. Relevance of the specific business area or activity

Given that hydroelectric energy is one of the most important sources of energy in Chile (Moraga 2001), the relationship of an energy company with political institutions and interests has great strategic relevance. A favored position in the relationship with the state, in this sense, may have a severely negative impact on the protection of the interests of the population with respect to this central resource, electrical energy, and the even more essential natural resource of water.

Regarding Endesa's prominence not only in the region, but also in the country, and what its presence in the indigenous region implied, it has been said:

> There was a feeling of lack of protection, they felt it was very difficult to fight against the State of Chile and against a transnational company as powerful as Endesa. Even this situation coincides with the arrest of former dictator Augusto Pinochet in London by order of Judge Garzón of Spain and Endesa is of particular importance because Martin Villa, President of Endesa, becomes the interlocutor of the Government of Chile in order to try to convince Garzón in Spain of desisting from the prosecution measure against Augusto Pinochet . . . then Endesa not only has the power of a tremendous transnational, but also has a plus of political power of influence before the Government of Chile . . . so much that Mr. Martín Villa was condecorated.
>
> (documentary film *Apaga y Vámonos* 2005: 36'50")[18]

The fact that the conflict arose in the energy area, and with Endesa as the main actor directly linked to Spanish political power and the most nationalist and conservative ideologies (both in Spain and in Chile), made the dispute a veritable confrontation between David and Goliath, in which, clearly, David did not have the support of those who should have been his main protectors (Kol 2003). The Institute for Indigenous Studies stated at the time:

> We have also learned of the action taken by Endesa before the authorities in order to obtain their approval of the project, even going so far as to undermine the seriousness of the consulting given to CONAMA by institutions like ours in the environmental impact assessment process to achieve this end.
>
> (Namuncura 1999: 144)

In the same sense, Deputy Andrés Palma, in the session of June 12, 1997, said, "Despite the existence of an Indigenous Law and one of environment, in this country ENDESA is still in command" (Namuncura 1999: 148).

iii. Cultural violence in the region "before"

The situation of respect or damage in cultural terms is linked, in this case, to the river directly affected by the construction of the dam. It is about the Biobío, one of the most important rivers in Chile, which originates in the Andes mountain range and empties into the Pacific Ocean. This river has an enormous ecological value, as well as great historical and political importance for the Mapuche people, because it was the natural frontier during Spanish colonization. Between the southern bank of the Biobío and the Chacao canal, progress was impossible and the Spaniards could not reach or subdue this town of the indigenous population. This natural protection of the river has, therefore, also marked an emblem in Mapuche autonomy and identity historically, because it allowed the preservation of tradition, culture and language for a long time (documentary film *Apaga y Vámonos* 2005: 20'; Berger & Katz 1997).

In this case, the families affected by repression are from the communities of Ralco-Lepoy and Quepuca Ralco of the Mapuche-Pehuenche people:

> The population of these communities is about 215 families, totaling about 1,200 people. There are also about 12 settlers' families in the town. Ralco is an indigenous territory that originally experienced various Pehuenche domain processes. Soon it underwent intense military offensives, as a result of the "Campaign of the Desert", carried out by the Argentine military and the "Military Excursion to the Cordillera Araucana" by the Chilean National Guard. Later came the appropriation of lands by Chileans and the sale of plots. Now it is an area affected by business megaprojects.
> (Namuncura 1999: 245; similarly Berger & Katz 1997; Moraga 2001)

The complexity of the tension between the national institutional ideology and the preexisting indigenous worldview and reality, and its implication in this concrete case, are seen in these words:

> That was the test that the democratic government in Chile had to face: constructing the Ralco Plant or maintaining relations and respecting the place where Pehuenches lived together (. . .). There, the State of Chile had to take an option. This is how it was found that it was inclined towards its own interests and its development options to the detriment of the indigenous people.
> (documentary film *Apaga y Vámonos* 2005:, 20'10")

Development, thus, was something opposed to what could be expected from the indigenous position. And development was exactly what the state wanted to achieve (Moraga 2001; Kol 2003).

The lack of empathy, and the abuse of the situation of cultural distance not only between the indigenous population and the government, but also with respect to the company, is evident in the behavior of the business actors, who were able to take advantage of the lack of resources (literacy, legal support, communication) that these indigenous communities suffered in the face of the company. This is how a state observer from CONADI expressed himself:

> Throughout our work in the area, we have witnessed the pressure exerted by Endesa on the Pehuenche families directly affected by the project, through deception – when they are told that if they do not accept the relocation, they will be displaced from their current lands without obtaining any benefit – and from their illicit actions, such as the entry onto indigenous lands of their officials without authorization in order to obtain their consent with respect to this project and the resettlement from their current lands.
>
> (Namuncura 1999: 144, with more references in
> Castro 2014; Rubinstein 2014)

From a legal perspective, these are illegal acts that vitiate any documents. Criminologically speaking, these acts make visible the criminogenic conditions of the facilitation of the violation of rights and the exercise of violence at various levels. The condition, obviously preexisting at the beginning of the construction of the dam, of being "indigenous", placed these communities in a situation of extreme exposure to foreign economic interests, which not only were not properly regulated or controlled by the state, but also were mobilized by the state itself.

The social distance (see Chapter 2) linked to cultural violence has been magnificently explained and its effects have also been mentioned with regard to the concrete relationship with land and money, in these terms:

> What in the mere sight of entrepreneurs and merchants appears as a territory with exchange value, for the indigenous world it has a different connotation. How are these two points of view reconciled on the same subject, which for the powerful is resolved with the free play of supply and demand (seeking, in addition, to invest as little as possible and earning as much as possible), with the indigenous *Mapuchecentric* vision, in the sense that *the earth is "the center of its existence and culture"*?
>
> The non-indigenous common inhabitants do not share ancestral values, do not have their own language (with the exception, of course, of the general language of the country), do not have an ancestral worldview; they are – in a generic sense – ordinary people and for the same, the common citizen will always agree to an advantageous negotiation.
>
> (Namuncura 1999: 170 – author's italics)

If the Pehuenche lands affected by the Ralco Project had to enter the market of supply and demand of land, as essential to building a gigantic dam like Ralco, they would have a financial negotiation value that would be the envy of the wealthy families of this country. And do you know why? *Because without these 638 indigenous hectares, today inhabited by 98 Pehuenche families, you cannot build the dam.* (. . .) The drama of Ralco, for the Pehuenches, is that the owners of the plots are not in the normal sense of citizenship. To be more clear and abrupt, *the difference lies in their status as indigenous.*

(Namuncura 1999: 171 – author's italics)

Hence, the debt that the state has with the indigenous people in cultural and territorial terms is both historical and current at the same time (Urquieta Ch. 2013; Rubinstein 2014).

iv. Structural violence in the region "before"

The situation of cultural violence is directly linked to the structural violence in which these communities live, given that the lack of recognition for their identity and dignity implies indifference and abandonment to their fate regarding their basic needs as well. It is, therefore, a question of communities which, over the course of history, have been vulnerable to the advances of states and nonindigenous society (Rubinstein 2014).

In the visits to the Alto Bío Bío the inspection commission in charge studying the situation before the construction of the dam realized that they were facing a socially vulnerable and legally vulnerable population, composed of simple and humble people, mostly illiterate, with bilingual limitations due to a more intense management of their own ancestral language and with no knowledge about the complex legal implications derived from its sole signature (Berger & Katz 1997; Namuncura 1999). The main figure in the defense and struggle, the elder Nicolasa Quintremán, was the most illustrative example of somebody defending her own rights in a foreign language – in her case, Spanish (Cuentas Ramírez 2014).

These conditions – as usually happens and was also seen in the previous cases – are highlighted by the physical, literal distance between these communities and the offices that could take care of their orders. Neither access to information nor access to preventive measures, nor the recognition of specific authorities for the care and protection of indigenous needs and interests were present prior to the start of the project. In a remote indigenous area, far removed from any urban center, the first news that could be given to CONADI came after a long journey:

At the end of April 1998, several leaders of the Pehuenche Communities based in Ralco Lepoy and Quepuca Ralco traveled to Santiago headed by the "Lonko Mayor", President of the Board of Caciques of Alto Bío, Antolín Curriao. They requested to talk with the Director of CONADI to present a complaint.

It was an exhausting trip from these remote locations to the capital. Going down from Quepuca Ralco to the town of Santa Bárbara, in the winter period, can mean a transit of up to five hours in a local vehicle. Then, you have to go to Los Angeles (another two hours) and board a bus there to the capital (ten to twelve hours). For elderly people, such as the Caciques del Alto Bío Bío, this represents an intense effort.

(Namuncura 1999: 9)

And even then, having arrived at the place, the institutional networks would refuse their services, reinforcing relations and schemes of vulnerability and invisible violence through the withholding of information, attendance and comprehension concerning their – existential – worry about their land and future communitarian life.

It is clear by now that the basic needs of the Mapuche-Pehuenche communities of Alto Bio Bío were scarcely covered by the subsistence economy itself and according to life guided by the tribe's own ideas, without a state presence in sight (Moraga 2001; Encuentro Indígena 2005). This would change, however, when the state presence prior to the start of construction of the dam finally became visible, not to provide its service, but to expressly refuse it. The state presence diversified as a variety of state presences, contradictory and in tension among themselves, show the disarticulation of interests and structural – avoidable – faults for the sufficient attention of the needs of the entire population (Rubinstein 2014). To understand this violence it is essential, then, to talk about CONADI and its role in the case.

The *National Indigenous Development Corporation*, CONADI (*Corporación Nacional de Desarrollo Indígena* in Spanish) is an institution created in 1993 by Law 19,253 *(Indigenous Law)*[19] and dependent on the Ministry of Social Development, whose objective is to "promote, coordinate and execute, where appropriate, the action of the state in favor of the integral development of indigenous people and communities, especially in the economic, social and cultural fields and to promote their participation in national life".[20] That is to say, although CONADI is an organ of the state, in its performance "it becomes a sort of intermediary between the state and the indigenous people" (Socialist Deputy Alejandro Navarro, in documentary film *Apaga y Vámonos* 2005:, 30'30"). The highest body of CONADI is its national council, made up of eight representatives from the different indigenous peoples of Chile. The interest of indigenous communities, therefore, is CONADI's focus of action. At the end of April 1998, CONADI became aware of the first roads built by Endesa in the territory protected by the Indigenous Law. The institution initiated inspections and organized meetings for the proper treatment of the issue – meetings in which the Attorney of the *Ministry of Planning* (MIDEPLAN from the Spanish *Ministerio de Planificación*) was also involved. According to CONADI, contracts signed as road easement (authorized by law for up to five years) were, in fact, lease contracts and also damaged the rights and uses of indigenous families, and implied that the roads and works carried out by Endesa were illegal. On June 13, 1998, the delegation went to the affected area

(Alto Bío Bío, Ralco Lepoy) and along with other indigenous people, interviewed the elderly Francisca Curriao:

> With simple words she explained that because she had been very sick, people from Endesa had gone to look for her and taken her to Santa Bárbara with the promise of being attended by medical personnel, and that they had asked her to sign a document that she scarcely understood. Then they made her sign with her thumbprint because she cannot read or write. With her, a relative signed as well. In this way the lease deed was "constituted" through which a road easement was authorized.
>
> (Namuncura 1999: 9, similar testimonies in documentary film *Apaga y Vámonos* 2005: 1', 24', 28', 1:12')

The Technical Mission continued its journey and also interviewed Juan Quipaiñán, who had a copy of the contract signed with Endesa, which expressly stated that a construction permit had also been requested by Endesa from the *Superintendency of Electrical Services* (SEC in Spanish, for *Superintendencia de Servicios Eléctricos*) (Namuncura 1999: 16). The confrontation between this office and CONADI would henceforth continue throughout the Ralco conflict, given that the permit granted by the SEC was in open contradiction with Indigenous Law which, although it allows the lease of indigenous land (under certain conditions), requires the prior authorization of CONADI in cases where such a lease will entail the constitution of any type of lien on indigenous land, such as the construction of a road (*Law 19.253*, art. 13), which implies a purpose beyond the specific purposes of the field itself because of the irreversible impact of the works. Because Endesa had not required this authorization, its works had been initiated in violation of Indigenous Law. The conflict between offices (indigenous interest vs. state interest in investment in the energy field) resulted in the resignation of the first director of CONADI, Mauricio Huenchulaf, who opposed the project.[21] The second director of CONADI, Domingo Namuncura, approached the population to determine, according to the requirements of Indigenous Law, whether the families gave their consent for the exchange of land. After his investigation, which involved 64 interviews, Namuncura came to the conclusion that there was no real willingness to swap on the part of indigenous families (Namuncura 1999: 16). For this reason, because he refused to authorize the works himself on behalf of CONADI, on August 5, 1998, his resignation was demanded. After five months of a leaderless CONADI, a third director was appointed, Rodrigo González (not of indigenous origin), and in a short time and without a single vote from any councilor of CONADI, the project was approved for the first swaps (documentary film *Apaga y Vámonos* 2005: 30').

The establishment of the area as a semi-state, in which a private foreign company could exercise its sovereignty, turned this territorial space into a space, in truth, without a state, and therefore, without the presence of the state to provide services, realize rights and serve the population. "No Chilean authority is present in that reality, only ENDESA" (documentary film *Apaga y Vámonos* 2005: 28'). And, if that were not enough, as it was seen, Endesa is closely related to nondemocratic forms of government leadership. In this context, although the Office for the Development of the Indigenous Population was involved and accepted the economic activity, it was foreseen that the people's unsatisfied needs would remain unsatisfied and that the local people would not see any improvement in their living conditions. Structural marginalization, cultural discrimination and – as will be shown – physical violence would be the state's response.

This is evident when one observes that various public offices were again and again left out of play, given that the economic interest, ruler of that semi-state, weighed more heavily. The task that Professor René Abeliuk was charged with, in order to guide the report that he had to present to the authorities of the MIDEPLAN, was fundamentally to find out whether Endesa had started works without proper permission from CONADI as required by Indigenous Law.[22] His response was positive, that is, Endesa had initiated its work without authorization and in violation of the rights of the indigenous population: "The finding of this irregularity placed CONADI in charge of filing legal charges against the powerful electricity company, which meant initiating a lawsuit in which extremely important political and, above all, financial interests would be brought into play" (Namuncura 1999: 26). The interests of the state were opposed to the interest of the Mapuche. This is reflected in statements from Roberto Celedon: "The State opted for its own interests to the detriment of the indigenous people" (documentary film *Apaga y Vámonos* 2005: 20'); and from the Institute of Indigenous Studies, which complained about the little value that laws have for state offices when these laws are set against the value of money: "Before the authorities, papers continue to be less valuable than the interests of entrepreneurs" (Namuncura 1999: 145).

v. Business, people and the economic situation in the area "during" and "after"

Ultimately, the land in question was polluted to such an extent that the collective coexistence of the Mapuche-Pehuenche, their ancestral land and cultural identity symbols remain endangered (e.g. by the flooding of their cemeteries by water intended for the dam and by the deforestation of the ancestral land that took place in order to facilitate transportation of construction materials) (Saleh & Opazo 2010). The territory has remained de facto under the control of Endesa. There has been neither any account of any annulment of the contracts (even though article 13 of the Indigenous Law provides for annulment in case of contravention) nor criminal prosecution for fraud. Compensatory agreements were made later with protesting families only because they refused to sign the contacts offered by the company; and the amicable settlement signed with the mediation of the Inter-American Court of Human Rights is still pending.[23]

Notwithstanding the economic and energy benefits obtained from the activity of the dam, which amount to millions of dollars, it has not resulted in an improvement to the living conditions of the local population, which is a point of discussion concerning the territorial inequality of the benefits of these generating megaprojects (Namuncura 1999; Rubinstein 2014; Castro 2014).

vi. Structural violence in the region "during" and "after"

The juridical-institutional framework is an unavoidable factor when analyzing the structural conditions that may or may not enable the satisfaction of basic needs, and this is especially so in the case of indigenous peoples. In this regard, it is important to note that at the beginning of the Ralco conflict, Chile had not yet signed ILO Convention 169 on indigenous and tribal peoples in independent countries. This happened in 2008 and implied (or should have implied) a new protection framework. Although the institutional progress regarding the recognition of indigenous people as groups entitled to special protection and, therefore, of dedicated offices for the protection of their rights must be recognized, it is striking that precisely during the time of great state aggression (executive power) with the Mapuche-Pehuenche people in Ralco, and in a time of a significant lack of protection, the offices, commissions and policies touting respect will proliferate, almost as a symbolic recognition of rights that, in practice, will be violated with the same intensity with which they are protected on paper. In the prologue to the document recognized in Chile, it was stated: "As part of this process of recognition, ILO Convention 169 was presented to Parliament for its ratification fifteen years ago. After a lengthy process, it resumes its urgency in December 2006 at the suggestion of President Michelle Bachelet".[24] After 15 years, its treatment was relaunched in December 2006 in the framework of severe conflicts between the Mapuche population and the Chilean government. However, the symbolism of this act did not prevent the lack of genuine crystallization of the commitment which, far from being put into practice, fell back into institutional oblivion, thus betraying – again – the expectations of indigenous peoples. A central basic need, such as cultural identity and its protections, remains, therefore, denied.

In this area, and in the areas where the families were relocated, there is still a situation of deficiencies and unfulfilled promises (labor, economics, housing, health). In this sense, in terms of Galtung, it is noticeable that as a consequence of the project and the lack of state control (protector of the population), diverse basic needs have been seen and continue to be seen as unsatisfied. "At best, some people may consider that [the] dam construction was not a negative process [. . .] But it is hard for people to find positive elements", explained Jeanne Wirtner Simon, a professor of legal and social sciences at the University of Concepción (Radwin 2016)"

Though Endesa promised to compensate those affected with new land and homes, as well as a variety of agricultural and social support programmes,

many Pehuenche said they were still waiting for those promises to be fulfilled more than 10 years later. On top of this, they said the relocation has
created far more cultural and farming difficulties than they had anticipated.

(Radwin 2016)

The affected population itself has translated these needs into legal terms in the
petition before the Inter-American Human Rights System. Thus, various rights
recognized in the American Convention on Human Rights (ACHR), whose
protection comes under the jurisdiction of the inter-American system, could be
compromised in the Endesa-Ralco case. As it was petitioned before the Inter-
American Commission on Human Rights, articles 4 (Right to Life), 5 (Right
to Personal Integrity), 8 (Judicial Guarantees), 12 (Freedom of Conscience and
Religion), 17 (Protection of the Family), 21 (Right to Private Property) and 25
(Judicial Protection) of the ACHR may have been infringed by the Chilean
state in favor of the Endesa company and to the detriment of the Mapuche
people.[25] Although this list does not reflect the extent of the deficiencies that
remain unsatisfied – because rights and basic needs are not exactly equal (see
Chapter 2), the list of deficiencies and violations can be assimilated. For, without
a doubt, they were all avoidable. On its part, Endesa continues to exercise practices of political influence as to the case of being investigated in Spain because of
international corruption in new hydroelectric projects in Chile (Matus 2016).
Furthermore, the pressure on local indigenous population continues as well
(Chile Sustentable 2016; Seguel 2016).

vii. Physical violence in the region "after"

Protests were categorized as terrorist acts. Repression in the region appeared in
the form of the violent presence of the Chilean army and the enforcement of
the International Anti-Terrorism Act (Ley 18.314) against the Mapuche people,
allowing detention without protection for the rights of allegedly subversive
individuals. Physical violence, therefore, was visibly present in the aftermath of
the legal conflict.

Although protest occurred prior to the construction of the dam, it was
not until after the dam's approval that situations of protest and social violence
arose and were repressed by the state. From the moment that the CONAMA
announced the favorable resolution of the "Environmental Qualification of
the Ralco Hydroelectric Project of Endesa", in June of 1997, the country was
submerged in a climate of extreme tension with environmental groups and
urban indigenous people protesting in the cities of Chile (Namuncura 1999).
Several Mapuche leaders were convicted for these protests, and a hardened code
was applied in their cases. For some, even the Anti-Terrorism Law was applied.
This law was sanctioned during Augusto Pinochet's military dictatorship and
was still in force, exclusively in application against the Mapuche people. Thus,
for example, Víctor Alcalá was sentenced to ten years and a day for setting fire
to a truck belonging to an Endesa contractor; Mireya Figueroa was detained

for a year and two months for terrorist associations and, along with eleven others, for terrorist arson. She and 18 others were tried for terrorist associations. For a time, Figueroa was forced into hiding. The trials took place with faceless witnesses ("testigos sin rostro"); that is, the witnesses had their faces covered and testified through voice distortion, all of which is in violation of the most fundamental rules of due process proper to the State of Law legally constituted in Chile and valid for the general population. However, no Mapuche leaders were ever arrested with firearms. The trial focuses on "acts of terrorism with slings and sticks, by lighting grassland fires"; indeed, it was not always clear who the perpetrators had been (documentary film *Apaga y Vámonos* 2005: 52'). The application of this law against the Mapuche people has led to a condemnation of the Inter-American Human Rights System against Chile, for violation of various fundamental rights, due process of law and equality before the law, among other irregularities.[26]

In this context of criminalization of the protest and hardening of the punitive response, there were also investigations of Mapuche leaders who had not been involved in protests or physical violence. Journalists and lawyers who had been involved in telephone conversations found themselves subject to investigation or even detention by plainclothes police for activities carried out in the course of their work, accused of acting as informants, representatives or defenders in the situation of the "Mapuche conflict", as it has been called. In these cases as well, trials took place without impartiality (documentary film *Apaga y Vámonos* 2005: 30', 43').

> When I was going to take the bus to Santiago, a group of plainclothes police intercepted me near the terminal and they arrested me. They did not inform me of the reason for my arrest, they only told me that there was an arrest warrant and they immediately directed me to the city of Lican Rayen (. . .) Once there, at dawn on Friday, they began to question me about my activity related to the production of this film, who were those people, what were they doing in Chile. I have no doubt that the phones of the production had been interfered with, as mine had been, because much of the information they gave me could not have been obtained in any other way than by interfering with my phone.
>
> (Pedro Cayuqueo, in documentary film
> *Apaga y Vámonos* 2005: 43' 20")

The punitive system, thus, has reinforced the structural violence initiated at the political, economic and judicial levels.

viii. Cultural violence in the region "after"

The distance between the indigenous population, on the one hand, and "white" society, the media power and national cultural spaces, on the other, continues to be – if it is not actually increasing – extreme in Chile.

The aforementioned distance is clearly emphasized by the work of the media, when the conservative media (which outnumber the "progressives", as Namuncura points out) use their nationalist and anti-indigenous discourse to provide the basis for explaining corporate and state action, invisibilizing its harmful impact on the indigenous population, or even justifying it.

> There are many economic groups handling the press in Chile. The Mapuche are the sector that is most affected due to the conflict with the State. Chilean society is uninformed about what happens in society. The case of the dam is paradigmatic because people believe that the company Endesa is Chilean, which brings progress and has come to solve an energy problem. Very few know that it is really a transnational company whose real objective is to become the main producer of energy in Latin America. This is unknown because the press works for this economic sector.
>
> (Pedro Cayuqueo, in documentary film
> *Apaga y Vámonos* 2005: 26' 45")

Whereas the press and other media offer their own perspective in favor of economic expansion and development for the Chilean nation, and block the possibility of more understanding and integral improvement for all inhabitants with respect to their living conditions, the environmental impact of the dam goes beyond the physical issue related to soil, plants, animal life and water. Its impact reaches deep into the ancestral culture and identity of the local population. This has led to talk of Pehuenche genocide due to the loss of territorial spaces and symbols of belief that make up a cultural identity. As a kind of honor to them and their people, allow me to recall that due to the effect of the dam, 14 ancient cemeteries are now under water, although it had been assured that no cemetery would be affected – this was a main issue for the Mapuche-Pehuenche in Ralco. Even Endesa later apologized for this (DiarioUChile 2013). Once, when the UN rapporteur approached the place, people showed him bones that had been found floating in the water and somebody said:

> *"They were our authorities. Now there is a lake over our relatives".*
> (Pedro Cayuqueo, in documentary film
> *Apaga y Vámonos* 2005: 1:04' 28")

The whole cultural and physical environment was affected. There is probably a significant symbolic fact of the violence exerted, which should be mentioned here. On December 23, 2013, the body of the most visible Mapuche figure in the struggle against the hydroelectric dam, the body of the elder Nicolasa Quintremán, was found floating in the pool where the water of the dam stocked. She was 74, almost blind, and must have died by an accidental fall into the Endesa's waters (Cuentas Ramírez 2014).

The *MOCASE* case in Argentina

i. The case

This case deals with the formation of the peasant movement known as *Movimiento Campesino de Santiago del Estero* (MOCASE), which, although it has its antecedents in long- and medium-term historical processes dating back to the late nineteenth century, had its moment of institutional consolidation in 1990.[27] In fact, there is a link between the peasant situation and the English investors who had occupied the province at the end of the nineteenth century with the timber company *La Forestal* (see film *Quebracho* 1974).

> Although this problem came to light in the 1990s, with the peasant protest of La Simona, its origin dates back to 1943 when Jungla S.A. was formed – a society linked to English capitals and railways. Its economic objectives revolved around logging, and its interests were guarded by Guillermo Massoni, legal representative in the region. But the nationalization of the railroads and other public policies that harmed the interests of the corporation led to its retirement, leaving the workers adrift.
>
> (Bertolino & Cañada 2004: 3)

This "adrift" situation led to the settlement and beginning of the land work of those families in the areas where they had worked for the company.

> By 1966, the red quebracho (*quebracho colorado*) had practically disappeared and the similar properties of the mimosa, originally from Africa, had been discovered. La Forestal decided to close its facilities down, after the sharp drop in international timber tariffs. "Entire villages, railways, ports and houses (. . .) were abandoned and dynamited [by the company] to prevent the local population from staying in the facilities" (Dargoltz 2003: 9–10).
>
> (Rosso & Toledo López 2010: 12/13)

However, decades later, with the increase in demand for land arising from the increase in international and national interest in the agricultural exploitation, the lands that were already in the possession of these families began to be coveted and claimed by the most diverse means. The situation worsened toward the end of the 1980s. On the one hand, the peasantry in the province of Santiago del Estero was abandoned by the state and its public policies – at that time undergoing an open process of deregulation and unemployment (Guzmán Concha 2002: 16). On the other hand, the state was very much present for the reality of the economic actors interested in the expansion of their cultivation areas. This "commodified" conception of land (Svampa 2017; Gudynas 2015; Gorenstein 2016), understood merely as a "productive resource, with marketable characteristics within the framework of a market economy, which must be exploited in search of the greatest profit in the shortest time possible", contrasts with the sense that land acquires for the peasantry, in which lies a conception marked by their "own identity and culture". This ideological confrontation materializes as a territorial conflict, and the peasantry is in the most disadvantaged situation, therefore, it is the peasants who must overcome the implications of the conflict, leading to a "process of precarization of their conditions of existence, and of rural life in general" (Rosso & Toledo López 2010: 15).

In this framework of dispossession, the MOCASE becomes a symbol of resistance to the model of "development" imposed at the national and international levels, and protest against it is increasingly repressed. It is, therefore, a link between state economic policy, liberalization of cultivation spaces for export and violence exercised and suffered in the territory.

This link, on the other hand, has been strengthened in recent years by the advance of the agrarian frontier (soybeans, crops for biofuel, monocultures in general) that is presented along with the regulatory imposition regarding the use of chemical products, approved seeds or specific technology, all of which prevent the free performance of agricultural activity by peasant communities and small producers. As has been explained, "Agribusiness, as an expression of neoliberal globalization, is installing a new agrarian structure in Argentina [. . .]. The dominant system that always excluded the indigenous peasants now seeks to displace, eliminate and even kill". This is why "since the mid-nineties, but mainly after the crisis [of 2001], new peasant movements emerged in Argentina" (Aznarez Carini 2016: 8). Violent confrontations over the possession and titling of lands, the displacement of the population and their harassment by state institutions are daily occurrences and have become a way of life for MOCASE.

The very birth of the movement is told well by Ángel Strapazzon, one of its founders, today a respected leader of MOCASE and its initiatives – such as the *peasant university*[28]-:

> I came here in 1976. (. . .)I came because it was a group like you, students of philosophy and anthropology; we had chosen to do a thesis on popular culture by finding some old men and old women from the mountains (. . .). [I came, I met some] who already anticipated that, as in the time of La Forestal, companies would come and want to evict the peasants, the producers from Santiago . . . with a model of agriculture for export instead of for food production. That was how the years went by. Actually, the first organizational processes started in Juríes, because in Juríes they had bought a multinational, they had acquired land for a penny and then here [in Quimilí] as well. As we began to see that there were land problems, we did awareness-raising work, of awareness with these grandparents, with these old people and people began to reflect a little, to try to organize. This like 10, 12 years before.
>
> (Desalvo 2014: 282)

ii. Relevance of the specific business area or activity

As Aznarez Carini explains, there was a reconfiguration of the productive model in Argentina, which began in the 1970s with the political and economic transformation that inaugurated the neoliberal state and signified a new turn toward an export-oriented agricultural model. This modification, which deepened in the following decades, marked a productive orientation highly dependent on international demand and prices. During the 1990s, there was even a marked state deregulation of production, which came hand in hand with high prices in international markets and growing financial investment in the nonagricultural capital sector. This implied

> the incorporation to the current market of lands of the interior of the country, hitherto devoted to diversified systems of regional production, or excluded from the export market (when in the middle of the 20th century the foresters extracted from them all their resources).
>
> (Aznarez Carini 2016: 3/4)

More than 80,000 farms, most with fewer than 200 hectares, disappeared and the size of the area exploited during the 1991–2002 period increased, which reflects a process of concentration of activity. For this reason, the author takes up the notion of "green desert", supported by other authors, which emphasizes the scarce presence of workers and producers who participate in large productive units of significant extent, devoted to monoculture for export (Aznarez Carini 2016: 4/5). "The task of appropriation [and expropriation] of the territory beyond the borders of 'civilization' will then begin", so that millions of previously "unproductive" hectares will be guided by the imperative of agribusiness, "and not of the food and development of the 'interior'" (quote by Rubén de Dios, in Aznarez Carini 2016: 5/6).

This marked preference for production destined for export, carried out on the part of big, exploiting companies of immense areas with the most advanced technology, explains the structural disadvantage of the small producers, who do not find policies of support or growth to enhance their own production. This was concluded by MOCASE in its First Congress of November 25 and 26, 1999:

> We see the signs of this reality on a daily basis: the scarcity of soft loans accessible to small producers; the low prices of agricultural products; free competition from products from other countries; the inability to access technology that improves production; excessively expensive inputs; concentration of production, financing, stockpiling, marketing and manufacturing in a few private hands; lack of infrastructure hinders settlement and peasant production, administrative and tax barriers to market and produce.

State activity has promoted the growth of the large companies in the past few decades. Thus, Decree 2284/91 issued by Carlos Menem – known as "Economic deregulation" – at the behest of the International Monetary Fund and other international credit agencies in accordance with the Washington Consensus, deepened the complexity of relations in Argentinian agriculture. Through the aforementioned decree, public offices that had regulation, coordination and control functions, such as the National Grain Board, were eliminated,[29] as were the National Meat Board, the National Institute of Viticulture, the National Sugar Directorate and the Yerba Mate Regulatory Commission, among other deregulatory measures that directly affected the agricultural sector. The decree was based on the laws of State Reform No. 23,694, of the State Police Power (economic emergency) No. 23,697 and Monetary Convertibility No. 23,928. These instruments are what enabled economic and financial groups to enter the productive process, tending to expand private interests in agriculture – in addition to other economic spheres such as hydrocarbons (Barrera 2013; Gorenstein 2016):

> The State was displaced from the place of mediator, which it had assumed in the organization of the links between the actors within the agro-industrial complexes. Today it is large transnational corporations, agrarian capitals and extra-agrarian holders, concentrated and highly mobile, who assume a leading role in the national agri-food and agro-industrial systems.
>
> (Domínguez & de Estrada; 2013: 499/500)

In the agro-economic area and its realization on the territorial map, a reconfiguration is presented, then, given by different factors:

> This is generally highlighted by carrying out the "over-economization" of nature and social relations (Leff 2006), from the presence of social actors associated with land markets or export production (soy, citrus, native wood, beans, rice, cattle raising for later fattening in corral, etc.), the intense rhythm of technological innovation (consolidation of the use of technological packages controlled by a handful of companies), the exclusive deployment of the maximizing rationality of profit in the appropriation of the environment (companies that enter the sector governed by the highest possible profitability in the cycle of rotation of capital or very dynamic sectors of producers capitalized family members who have professionalized or turned to the provision of agricultural services), within a general framework of institutional arrangements that favor the privatization of natural commons (from recognitions of seed breeders' rights, to the role of the agencies of agricultural development or the policies of territorial ordering and agri-food planning).
>
> (Domínguez & de Estrada 2013: 512/513)

All this can be seen as effects of the economic deregulation of the 1990s, which led to the liberalization and privatization of trade (Pierri 2013) and of certain companies and institutions, and even, precisely, to the privatization of the land that leads to a process of land foreignization (Gorenstein 2016: 8)[30] and thus, of the conflicts and their possible resolutions, which were left in private hands.

Foreign investment in the area (transnational and trans-Latin), encouraged and invited by the processes of deregulation, generated in Argentina – as in other Latin American countries caught up in the wave of neoliberal deregulation – extreme conditions and difficulties for the peasant world of the agrarian sector. As Gorenstein explains, "the incidence of transnational capital intensifies long-established trends" and in the agri-food space, for example, transnational companies play a key role in the reconfiguration of dynamics between territory, production and global consumption:

> Through their investments and organizational modalities, they make up complex structures (networks, meshes) and by acting in multiple locations, they exercise the government of different links of the agri-food chains under regulatory and competitive frameworks in which complex national, regional and global instances are combined.
>
> (Gorenstein 2016: 1)[31]

As a provider of agricultural products, the region currently plays an important role in global markets,

> and given its comparative advantage in terms of water and land resources, it could play an even greater role. It exports more than what is imported and, overall, the subcontinent represents 13% of world trade in agricultural products, with an annual growth rate of 8% in the last 20 years.

Besides, Gorenstein explains further,

> in regional agriculture, in addition to soy, other so-called "flexible crops" or wild cards – corn, sugarcane and palm – are disseminated and expanded for purposes of food, but also usable as animal feed or biofuel. This situation marks one of the new trends, of a global nature, associated with the direct influence exerted by energy policies on the price of agricultural products and their consequences on food security.

Added to this, therefore, foreign investment has acquired an impressive "momentum" on land and agriculture in almost every country (Gorenstein 2016: 4). This momentum and this foreign investment, as Brüntrup explains, causes problems for agribusiness in developing countries:

> The consequences of expropriations are, of course, potentially violent social conflicts. And that risk is compounded by the fact that investors are more likely than small farmers to cause environmental damage through the

negligent use of machinery or the application of harmful chemicals, for example. Large areas have been deforested by investors who promised to dedicate themselves to agriculture, when what they really wanted was to have access to the wood and take it away.

(Michael Brüntrup, Instituto Alemán para el desarrollo, in: Romero-Castillo 2012)

iii. Cultural violence in the region

The peasant is a socioeconomic cell, a domestic unit which is at the same time part of a larger social fabric whose center of gravity is the agrarian community. In this sense, then, peasants' forms of communication, of existence and symbols, diverge notoriously from those of people who live in the city and are not linked to the cycles of the earth. In the case of Latin America, on the other hand, the peasantry is in that fusion between white civilization and indigenous customs: "The rites and festivities, indigenous or mestizo, as the traditional forms of government, if any, refer to a specific sociability" (Bertolino & Cañada 2004: 3).

Both traditions and economic logic make the peasantry a population alien to the city dweller, who in general either idealizes it according to outdated and even erroneous gaucho images, or despises it, in the conviction that the field can no longer be the artisanal field, the common subsistence and self-consumption that it once was. Agroindustry is the current model. The idea of development and the technology that dazzles cities does not understand peasant productivity or peasants' genuine solidarity. There are almost always more or less intense forms of community economy such as agreed rotation of plots, common areas of grazing and gathering, nonmonetary exchanges of work, and collective work of common benefit (Bertolino & Cañada 2004: 3).

In this sense, there is a cultural distance which reaches a certain limit. There is a lack of knowledge and, at the same time, a lack of empathy, which makes the peasant, in the eyes of the city dweller, a strange being, and in general, not worthy of state attention, because rural life is often seen as a denial of urban progress which is linked to the progress of the nation and its society.

Like any frontier, agricultural progress in any of its economic fronts, refers to the limit, is inscribed in the production of alterities, makes explicit a type of social relationship in the record of us/others. The new discourse and border practice reinstates a link of alterity with populations made invisible by the narrative of urban-industrial progress and development of capitalism in agriculture, considered non-existent, actively produced as absent from within the homeland, inconsiderate in their forms of knowledge and legality to organize the uses of land and the appropriation of nature, or considered part of but on the margins of the citizenship and the agro-food and agro-industrial system.

(Domínguez & de Estrada 2013: 515)

The peasant, in many senses, is wary of that society. And society makes him pay for it. Cultural violence expresses itself in social indifference, state de-recognition and even physical repression, as will be seen.

iv. Structural violence in the region

By the time MOCASE was born at the beginning of the 1990s and the start of the era of deregulatory policies, the aforementioned modification of the agrarian structure had occurred, and unemployment had led to migrations to urban centers, all of which implies a direct effect on settlers and peasants. The economic units disjoined, as did their dynamics and patterns of integration and reproduction (Bertolino & Cañada 2004: 2). The structural situation, therefore, is serious, and does not promise to change, as it was revealed in 1999 by MOCASE itself in the concluding considerations of that First Congress. On that occasion, a number of unmet basic needs were exposed: the insufficient and poor housing situation of the peasant villagers; the annual family income of the sector, which for most lies below the poverty line, which makes it impossible to improve the conditions of family housing; the high rate of illiteracy and school dropout linked to too few schools, schools without basic resources, too few teachers in relation to the number of children and the great distances children must travel in order to attend school; the deficient nutrition due to the absence of a balanced diet; water unsuitable, in many cases, for human consumption; zonal hospitals without economic resources and deficient care as well as the absence of much-needed, vital medications.

For a specific example of a village that integrated MOCASE, there is La Simona, which had to defend itself against a siege of tractors and security forces, and is in the same situation described in detail: "The fatality of poverty is present in La Simona where, approximately, some 73 peasant families live in the process of de-peasantization and pauperization, of which 35 present problems of land possession".[32] Land, as will be seen, is a central issue. But it is not the only one:

> The struggle for land, although it was a key element to motivate and sustain the organization, was the only one. We also made attempts to improve "the quality of peasant life", through a "greater valorization of work, the mode of production and peasant culture". In this sense, we especially value the contribution of the NGOs, INTA and the various social programs of the state, which offered the possibility of formulating and executing microprojects that included subsidized credit lines as an alternative to the traditional financing of the "bolichero", possibilities of subsidy of the necessary technical assistance to improve or diversify agricultural production, training plans for the organization, promotion of garden and farm activities for self-supply, construction of water systems, construction of rural housing.
> (Concluding considerations of the First Congress of MOCASE
> November 25–26, 1999, Santiago del Estero)

All efforts are needed in order to overcome insufficiencies, because the context is one of a multiplicity of insufficiencies. And land has been the main claim, the foundation of all possibilities of life development for peasant communities. Thus, the context is one of a lack of land titling, and the presence of land in the hands of foreign businessmen in areas where people have lived for decades. Notwithstanding this quality of a 20-year possessor – that legally would lead to entitlement – this situation is often not recognized by the state nor by the private actors, or even worse, peasants sign documents in the false belief that they are "lending" their land while in reality, they are ceding property rights to others (Bertolino & Cañada 2004: 3–4). This led to talk of "silent exclusion" and "silent evictions" (Aznarez Carini 2016: 6, 8 ss., with more references), when they still occurred at times when displacements simply happened, without resistance on the part of the peasants, or visibility of this reality among the rest of the population. This invisibility is constant, as are the "precariousness of their possessions, the informality of the titles of dominion, the scarcity of resources for production and self-consumption and the deterioration of public infrastructure" (Aznarez Carini 2016: 7).

The land that is left to groups- when there is any at all – is not enough to satisfy their needs and exercise their rights peacefully. These shortcomings are what leads to the formation of more or less organized groups, that in the face of state indifference, that is to say, before the repetition of structural violence, opt for the exercise of measures that in some cases result in physical violence, visible to the state, such as the taking of public space or settlements in fiscal territories.

More than ten years after that First Congress of MOCASE, a new organization, the National Peasant-Indigenous Movement, had its First Congress as well. Now joined, peasants and indigenous people expected to improve their situation, to come nearer to the rest of society and become more visible to the state, not only as an "issue", but as part of the population, with their own cultural worldviews, but enjoying the same attention. At that Congress in September 2010, the diagnosis of the situation was no better than it had been decades before, but the analysis – after years of growth in the peasant organization and also all members empowered by the experience – was deeper and more accurate. As they explained:

> The neoliberal model applied its own recipe where the exploitation of natural goods determines the profit of agribusiness and open-pit mega-mining. Agribusiness dominated by large transnational corporations and local groups, controlling the technologies, achieved the expansion of monocultures and transgenics over the productive diversity of indigenous peasant crops, which led to the destruction of montes, forests and yungas, which guarantee a supply of varied, sufficient and accessible food for popular consumption in towns and cities. This model of agribusiness does not want farmers in the fields. Mining companies settle in indigenous peasant territories, damaging water, air and soil; in some cases, they deal out threats

and violence against people who are critical of the mining model. The families that resist on our lands suffer the deterioration of living conditions, we suffer the consequences of the model: difficulty in accessing water for consumption or for production, attempts to expel us from the land where we have lived for generations, the limitations on education for our children and health for our families, violence and persecution towards the families that have decided to defend our land and our way of life.

(Communication of the First Congress of the National Peasant-Indigenous Movement – Peasant Way, September 2010, 11–14)

The foreign investments and the international interest in the agribusiness remain the central challenge. The link to the physical actions and responses on the part of the state and private actors are more visible. Violence, in this sense, has increased. Not only invisible forms remain almost the same, but also more and more visibly violent actions are taking place.

v. Physical violence until today

It is clear that structural and physical violence are interrelated. Sometimes, as in this case, there are not only decisions by the Executive or the Legislative establishing structural obstacles for the realization of basic needs. Often, the Judiciary avoids the realization of rights – those rights which the Judiciary is bound to protect. So they can declare illegal an action of land occupation by peasants or decide that the 20-year possession rule does not apply in the specific case in which a peasant family lives on territory claimed by an entrepreneur or corporation. As they can *pay* for the services of judges, the interaction between state agents and economic actors may be extremely violent, in all possible expressions of violence:

Judges of first instance, more permeable to networks of local power, imbricated with the interests of the dominant economic power (local and/or extra-local), operate by delegitimizing the demands of peasant or indigenous organizations that are affected in the exercise of their right to land or territory, respectively.

(Gorenstein & Ortiz 2016: 22)

And physical action often follows these structurally and culturally violent practices, "when the evictions are ordered by the judges and are executed in the presence of vigilante groups hired by entrepreneurs linked to land grabbing" (Gorenstein & Ortiz 2016: 22).

Judiciary practices and state policies in the normative way, then, cause cumulative impacts. The realization of the pretension of peasants' own agrarian production on their own land, in areas where land has historically been used and cultivated by these families, becomes more and more illusory. The use of direct force by the state and also by private actors enabled – legal and illegally – by the state is in each case traceable to a "framework of specific territorial reconfiguration" (Domínguez & de Estrada 2013: 512).

A map of actors would show several figures on stage, where even the invisible "spatial expansion of large-scale capitalist agriculture" would play a leading role, of course (Domínguez & de Estrada 2013; similar Gorenstein & Ortiz 2016: 21, 22). Different sectors converge in what can be called conflict, but is actually violence, and these actions are interconnected. "On the one hand, the actions of the companies involved in the violent takeover of the land by means of bulldozers and, on the other hand, the State through the police force safeguarding the actions of the companies" (Bertolino & Cañada 2004: 4).

> In this sense, the presence of episodes of violence, and specifically those killed and death, call into question another dimension of agricultural expansion. This is the framework of conflicts resulting from pressure on land and natural assets (forests, water courses, etc.) by companies that are mostly engaged in soy, livestock, or forestry production (. . .). The geographical spaces of greatest conflict over the land coincide with those featuring the most intense deployment of agricultural fronts on lands that had remained relatively untouched by the uses of industrial agriculture, the valorisation by the complexes of the agri-food system and primary exporter, and the real estate markets.
>
> (Domínguez & de Estrada 2013: 512/513)

In this context, the end of the first decade of this century showed an important record of physical aggressions. In 2008, for example, there were numerous cases of home invasions, beatings and arrests by the police, guards and security agents who answered to various businessmen in the area. The complaints, unfortunately, were not always recorded. There are many instances of political economic connections of soybeans and loggers, dating back to the time of La Forestal. Two examples follow:

> Friday, September 5: "Sixteen heavily armed police officers, without orders from a judge, threatened to kill, shoot and beat six members of Mocase-VC, two of whom were later detained in the Santiago prison. They tried to blackmail them by offering them their freedom in exchange for the recognition of possessory rights of the person who has denounced them, Carlos Morel Bullez, a soy entrepreneur from Córdoba, acting with the complicity of the criminal judge Tarchini Saavedra".
>
> Monday, September 22, at midnight: "Forty uniformed police and gendarmerie officers violently raided the homes of peasant families in *El Quebrachito*, in the municipality of *Monte Quemado*, stole tools and money, threatened and beat the heads of families in front of the horrified looks of their children, underage boys and girls. They came under the orders of the municipal councilor Mrs. Villagrán de Coria (wife of Julio Coria, owner of a local real estate agency, and opponent of the peasant communities)".[33]

In 2011, there was the sad and well-known case of the murder of Cristián Ferreyra: this death was anticipated by the previous violence he had suffered, which had not been properly considered or investigated. As MOCASE itself immediately published on its website and then confirmed in the criminal proceedings, on November 16 in the San Antonio area, near the city of Monte Quemado, Department Copo, mercenaries who responded to the orders of the landowner Jorge Antonio Ciccioli (from the province Santa Fé) showed up at the Ferreyra family home and fired on those present, causing the death of Cristián Ferreyra, 23 years old, seriously injuring Darío Godoy and beating a third. On the occasion, a community meeting was being organized to present a complaint to the Forest Directorate for the forest clearing that was being carried out by the businessman Ciccioli. The latter had acquired a field from the businessman Emilio Luque (from the province Tucumán), with whom the community had already come into conflict, which became more acute with businessman Ciccioli. The community of San Antonio, a town near the city of Monte Quemado, a member of the Copo-Alberdi Campesino Central (CCCOPAL) and the Lule-Vilela indigenous people had resisted repeated attempts of eviction and criminal charges. Various businessmen who were at that time in the process of appropriating (grabbing) large areas of land had allegedly hired the services of former policemen in order to confront the indigenous peoples and peasant organizations, which led to situations of extreme violence. This context of violence and hostility was known to the local government, and yet, sufficient prevention measures had not been taken in this regard (Aranda 2011).[34]

On the death of Ferreyra, the page of the *Center for Legal and Social Studies (CELS)*, also the complainant in the case, outlines the "territorial conflict" that had been experienced in the area:

> The expansion of the agricultural frontier and the insecurity of land tenure generate a context in which they deepen violations of the human rights of peasant and indigenous communities, especially their rights to the territory, to adequate food and a dignified life.

The report continues with a clear description of the situation that interweaves visible and invisible violence. The interactions explained on the previous pages are explicitly illustrated here with the example of the killing of Cristián Ferreyra, which made it apparent to the rest of society and the whole country, even in urban centers, how marginalized and violent everyday life in rural areas can be because of the unchecked expansion of export-oriented agrobusiness:

> This conflict results in specific forms of violence in which the boundaries between the State and private actors appear dangerously erased. In different conflicts, police forces intimidate and repress peasants and indigenous people whose claims conflict with the interests of agrarian ventures. In other cases, such as that of Cristián Ferreyra and Darío Godoy, violence

is exercised by armed groups, often comprising ex-policemen. These are private armies hired by businessmen to carry out evictions while the provincial political authorities vacillate between omission and connivance.

Throughout an extensive conflict over lands in that region of Santiago, no political, judicial or security authority in the province intervened to stop land clearings or attacks and threats against peasant communities. MOCASE-VC had warned on several occasions about the presence of armed groups that are threatening and attacking organized peasants who defend their right to territory.[35]

Geographer and teacher Marcelo Giraud offered concrete figures when he analyzed agricultural progress in Santiago: "In 1996, in the province there were only 95 thousand hectares with soy. In 2008 it had jumped to 629 thousand hectares and two years later, in 2010, to the record of 1.1 million hectares." (Aranda 2011).

The killing of Cristián Ferreyra was brought to trial, and on December 9, 2014, Javier Juárez, the material perpetrator of the homicide, was sentenced to serve a ten-year prison term and to pay 900,000 pesos (around US $105,000 at the time) as compensation for the damages caused. The businessman Jorge Antonio Ciccioli, however, despite being directly linked to the homicide, was acquitted of any charge. The rest of the members of the extra-institutional vigilante group ("grupo parapolicial") that had threatened and harassed the inhabitants of the San Antonio area were released from all criminal responsibility.[36]

Less than a year later, a second death occurred under similar conditions. Rafael Galván, a peasant and member of MOCASE, had received a beating. Subsequently, at the end of September, the businessman Facundo León Suárez Figueroa of the province of Salta, in charge of LAPAZ S.A., denounced Galván for "usurpation", and on October 10, 2012, while Miguel – brother of Rafael – was feeding his animals, Paulino Riso, Figueroa's sicario, approached him and stabbed him in the jugular vein. Families from the Simbol area were being harassed by hitmen of the LAPAZ S.A. Agricultural Company, because the company intended to wire part of the territory of the Lule Vilela indigenous communities. The community, on September 15, 2012, had finally managed to carry out a first stage of the territorial survey legally ordered for the recognition and subsequent regularization of the property titles of the indigenous communities – this regularization would mean the land and housing security for which they had been struggling for so long.[37] In this case, Riso was sentenced to nine years in prison on November 2, 2015. Complicity or any other charges against the entrepreneur were unsuccessful.[38]

vi. Cultural violence in the region today

Although the structural conditions have not been modified, but have actually worsened, and physical violence has also increased in the peasant space, there is a particularly favorable aspect regarding the speeches and practices of the peasantry with respect to their non-satisfied needs: the notion that these unmet needs exist, that they should not exist and that there is a legal possibility to reconstruct their own social structure in accordance with their peasant dynamics. Access to information and the (in many cases attempted) access to justice, sometimes underestimated within the basic needs that must be duly met, has seen a profound improvement based on the work of organizations such as MOCASE, in coordination with other actors and agencies. At the beginning of the formation of MOCASE, access to information, still nonexistent, began to be established thanks to joint efforts with, for example, the Institute of Popular Culture (INCUPO), which has found there a new role in its work with rural communities "[that] tries to make people aware of their rights, be able to defend them, and be able to put together a defense strategy" (Aznarez Carini 2016: 11). Thus, it has been possible to think about resisting the eviction of families under a modality not only physical and rustic, but also under the form of law. The possibility for the peasantry to take legal language and know about the 20-year prescription implies a resounding change in subjectivity. This transformation of self-perception entails a new subjectivity, which thus recovers its peasant dignity. As for the land, the peasants have gone from being usurpers to being possessors (Aznarez Carini 2016: 12 ss.).

However, this cultural recovery goes much further:

> The recent political emergency of the peasantry and indigenous peoples in Argentina refers to the emergence of an expressive position surrounding the collective rights to the territory, identity and conditions of material production, which in turn engages in litigation with the systems of agro-food and globalized agroindustry.
>
> (Domínguez & de Estrada 2013: 519, with more references)

As the authors explain, these subjects make criticisms and proposals, identify on the one hand an enemy in the "agribusiness" and "mega mining" at the same time that they define a program based on the need to carry out food sovereignty, an integral agrarian reform and the fulfillment of preexisting, constitutionally sanctioned rights to the State.

This cultural revaluation in the speech itself can be assessed as clearly positive, of course. However, this empowerment can be (and is, in fact) seen as challenging for those who continue to see the peasant and the indigenous as social categories of unproductive units, undeveloped and extinct, or extinguishable. This, undoubtedly, implies restarting the cycle of violence from structural measures that reduce the indigenous peasant pretensions on the one hand, and that repress them even more harshly, on the other (Carrillo 2018).

Violent economy and culture

The four cases presented here in depth share common denominators that become increasingly clear throughout the chapter.

In all of them, a situation of deficiencies and state indifference – or explicit state rejection – toward the population that would later be affected was presented from the beginning. This previous situation of marginality was then affected in various ways, depending on the case.

That is to say, basic needs were identified and made visible such as life, health, work, identity realization or a healthy environment, which became even more difficult to realize from a certain point. In some cases, the difficulty was not a deepening of the known needs, but a new threat that did not exist before. From the beginnings of new activities in the area, or of old modalities with new modalities, going hand in hand with undertakings and economic investments extensive in volume and intensive in their dynamics, the deficiencies began to overlap and multiply.

The activity of a mine, the extraction of petroleum, the construction of a dam or the promotion of agro-export activity, all of which are based on international demand and supposed national conveniences, marked tangible modifications in the lives of the different populations and in their relationship with the rest of society, with the state, and even with their self-perceptions.

Given the territorial extent, the volume of infrastructure and the direct link of the state interest – therefore, knowing from the start about the activity, at least in the offices promoting the investments in question, it is impossible to argue the inevitability of the results on the part of not only the company, but also the state.

Either because of the risk inherent in the activity or because less harmful technology is available but not used, preventability is out of the question. No pollution, geological fissures, illnesses or deaths, neither population displacements nor social dislocations, much less confrontations of physical violence, would be intended here as attributable to the actors involved in these ventures if such harms were inevitable.

The mere fact that the investments are set in discussion tables that often define changes in the internal legislation to facilitate the precise arrival of the new economic group or the start of the activity evidences that everything could have been planned in a different way. Judicial decisions, in the same way, make up the structurally impeding framework for the realization of rights when their intervention is invoked. And the security agents, in principle only the armed and visible arm of the law are in charge of doing the dirty work of the law. As Walter Benjamin said, they come to obey invisible, violent orders not only from the state, but also – and sometimes fundamentally – from the economic actors who pay for their protection, thus making invisible violence visible.

The investments and the income they generate are figures of so many zeros that they are difficult to write or say, and the political weight of those who define these money flows is in direct proportion to those zeros. The support they receive from national and international actors of perhaps even greater economic power turns every claim of impossibility into a confirmation of their lack of will.

No rural population, no child, no brave peasant or self-confident indigenous woman, alone, can counteract the weight of this violence. This is why violence is fed back permanently and directly and physical violence increases. Once this physical violence has been observed closely in the next chapter, it will be seen as less impossible to encourage ourselves to think that this reluctance can be counteracted.

Notes

1 Similar had happened because of the exploitation of the Real de Ángeles mine, also in Zacatecas, which generated the transfer of the community Real de Ángeles, from the eighteenth century, to a spot located 30 km away of the silver vein exploited by open-pit. The exploitation, begun in 1982, left in the area a crater the size of a huge football stadium and soil and air contaminated with lead and arsenic among other toxic substances. See Valadez Rodríguez 2005.
2 Cfr. Environmental Justice Atlas. https://ejatlas.org/conflict/penasquito
3 Cfr. on the vacancy laws *Ley de Tierras desocupadas y colonización*, R.O., Nro. 342, 22.09.1964; *Ley de Colonización de la Región del Amazonas Ecuatoriano*, R.O. Nro 2092, 12.01.1978 and *Ley de la Reforma Agraria*, Ro.O. Nro 877, 18.07.1979; and see also Kimerling (1994: 201). The victims' position is clearly shown in the documentary film *Crude* (2009).
4 Both belonged to the large companies that would have de facto formed a "cartel" of oil, dividing among a few companies the exploitation of the oil existing in the whole land (see on this perspective, Galeano 1984: 257 ss.).
5 At the time (by President Arosemena Gómez), the concession for the exploitation of gas in the Gulf of Guayaquil was signed in similar tenor, to unknown people, who soon passed their rights to a foreign ADA company, which was reason for a great scandal and even later convictions and acquittals by different governments (cfr. Lara 2009: 531 s.). On the unclear interweaving of the concessions to oil companies, by way of illustration, see Jaime Galarza Zavala's famous research literature work, *El festín del petróleo* (1972).
6 On the record of the first oil outbreak (March 29, 1967) and the concession of the exploitation to the Texaco and the Gulf cfr. the *Informe a la Nación* document, written by Galo Pico Mantilla, Minister of Industries and Commerce (Pico Mantilla 1968).
7 Judgment. 2011, February 14. *Corte Provincial de Justicia de Sucumbíos* (Sala única), Exp. 002–2003, 1ra. Instancia, p. 33.
8 Judgment. 2011, February 14. *Corte Provincial de Justicia de Sucumbíos* (Sala única), Exp. 002–2003, 1ra. Instancia, p. 127.
9 Judgment. 2011, February 14. *Corte Provincial de Justicia de Sucumbíos* (Sala única), Exp. 002–2003, 1ra. Instancia, p. 127.
10 The political change as well as details about the *Chevron case* can be followed in the documentary film *Crude* (2009).
11 Judgment. 2011, February 14. *Corte Provincial de Justicia de Sucumbíos* (Sala única), Exp. 002–2003, 1ra. Instancia, p. 80.
12 On the different cases from the Chevron perspective, see the website *Juicio Crudo*: www.juiciocrudo.com/; from the point of view of the plaintiff, the summary can be seen on the website Chevron Tóxico: http://chevrontoxico.com/.
13 Judgment. 2011, February 14. *Corte Provincial de Justicia de Sucumbíos* (Sala única), Exp. 002–2003, 1ra. Instancia, p. 173.
14 Report included in Judgment. 2011, February 14. *Corte Provincial de Justicia de Sucumbíos* (Sala única), Exp. 002–2003, 1ra. Instancia.
15 The documentary film *Crude* (2009) shows real individuals left in the middle of illness and lackness. Even though the film is not sufficiently objective with respect to

governmental positions, the face and voice given to the damaged population make it clear that development in this area is an absolutely nonexisting reality.

16 Judgment. 2011, February 14. *Corte Provincial de Justicia de Sucumbíos* (Sala única), Exp. 002–2003, 1ra. Instancia.

17 See the testimony taken by the own Court, reproduced in Judgment 2011, February 14. *Corte Provincial de Justicia de Sucumbíos* (Sala única), Exp. 002–2003, 1ra. Instancia.

18 See on the link between the Villa family, dictatorial regimes and energy industry sectors: Calvo et al. (2014).

19 *Law 19.253*, 1993, October 5. It establishes norms on protection, promotion and development of indigenous peoples, and creates the CONADI.

20 *Law 19.253*, Art. 39, par. 1.

21 After receiving negative reports in 1996 and dismissing the project as "illegal" in 1997, Huenchulaf finally left office on April 22, 1997.

22 "Did ENDESA commit an irregularity by signing lease contracts with Pehuenche families and through this mechanism achieve the certain fact of advancing the execution of large-scale works, without resorting to the authorization due on the part of CONADI, in the case of works on indigenous lands?" (Namuncura 1999: 26).

23 See the amicable settlement at the Inter-American Commission of Human Rights. *Informe N° 30/04, Petición 4617/02. Solución Amistosa Entre Mercedes Julia Huenteao Beroiza Y Otras, Y Chile.* 2004, March 11. Cfr. TPP 2010; Namuncura (1999). Conversations initiated between Endesa (today, Enel Generación) and the affected communities on the inundation of the cemetery and the claimed compensation are ongoing. www.24horas.cl/regiones/biobio/ralco-a-diez-anos-del-compromiso-parte-reforestacion-pendiente-de-endesa-1910011 [24.02.2016].

24 *Convenio 169 de la OIT sobre pueblos indígenas y tribales en países independientes* (official document by ILO in Chile), 2006: 9. <www.oitchile.cl/pdf/Convenio%20169.pdf>

25 See the amicable settlement at the Inter-American Commission of Human Rights. *Informe N° 30/04, Petición 4617/02. Solución Amistosa Entre Mercedes Julia Huenteao Beroiza Y Otras, Y Chile.* 2004, March 11.

26 ICHR, Judgment, *Norín Catrimán and others vs. Chile*, May 29, 2014.

27 In general, about peasant movements and the history of MOCASE, see Desalvo (2014). For the history of territorial conflicts in Santiago del Estero with a descriptive analysis of its course, see Rosso & Toledo López (2010). Very illustrative from the historic perspective is the film *Quebracho* 1974. On the current situation, see the documentary *Solo se escucha el viento* (2004) and the documentary *Toda esta sangre en el monte* (2012). It was recently also presented with the same name the Film, *Toda esta sangre en el monte* (2018), with a longer and deeper description of the agro-industry in Santiago del Estero and its violence.

28 See the *Universidad Campesina*'s homepage www.mocase.org.ar/secciones/universidad-campesina.

29 The abolition of the National Grain Board facilitated, for example, the cartelization of agribusiness firms concessionaires of port terminals, such as Cargill, Bunge, Nidera, Noble Argentina and Toepfer (Gorenstein 2016: 10).

30 See the figures about land surface ownered by foreign capital in Argentina in Gorenstein and Ortiz (2016: 16–18).

31 On the big four agroalimentary corporations (Archer Daniels Midland [ADM], Bunge, Cargill and Louis Dreyfus, the so called ABCD) and their negative impact and pressure on small producers and local economies, see Murphy et al. (2012).

32 *Nuevo Diario*. November 27, 1998, p. 9.

33 Chronicles in *ColectivoEPPRosario*. 2008, October 6. http://colectivoepprosario.blogspot.com.ar/2008/10/mocase-septiembre-negro-en-santiago-del.html

34 See also "El juicio por Cristian Ferreyra, la violencia rural y los 25 años del MOCASE" *Notas periodismo popular*. 2014, November 10. https://notasperiodismopopular.com.ar/2014/11/10/juicio-cristian-ferreyra-violencia-rural-mocase/

35 CELS homepage: www.cels.org.ar/web/2014/11/juicio-por-el-asesinato-de-cristian-ferreyra/
36 Resumen Latinoamericano. "La maldita impunidad: Absolvieron al empresario sojero por el crimen del campesino Cristian Ferreyra" *Resumen Latinoamericano*. 2015, December 9. www.resumenlatinoamericano.org/2014/12/09/la-maldita-impunidad-absolvieron-al-empresario-sojero-por-el-crimen-del-campesino-cristian-ferreyra/
37 See the MOCASE site on the case: www.mocase.org.ar/noticias/sobre-el-asesinato-de-miguel-galvan
38 See on the judgment: www.mocase.org.ar/noticias/caso-miguel-galvan-sentencia-de-la-justicia-saltena

References

Agencia Reforma. 2013. "Tienen minas ricas y pueblos pobres". *NTR Zacatecas*. February 12. http://ntrzacatecas.com/2013/02/12/tienen-minas-ricas-y-pueblos-pobres/.

Aranda, Darío. 2011. "Otra víctima por defender su territorio". *Página 12*. November 18. www.pagina12.com.ar/diario/sociedad/3-181517-2011-11-18.html.

Aznarez Carini, Gala. 2016. "Un campo en disputa en la Argentina contemporánea: la irrupción de una voz campesino indígena". Paper presented at the *XIII Jornadas Nacionales y V Internacionales de Investigación y Debate*, July, 27–29, Argentina: Universidad Nacional de Quilmes.

Barrera, Mariano A. 2013. "Desregulación y ganancias extraordinarias en el sector hidrocarburífero argentino". *Política y Cultura* (40). January.

Belmontes, Claudia. 2016. "Lo que queda en Salaverna". *NTR Zacatecas*. May 2. http://ntrzacatecas.com/2016/05/02/lo-que-queda-en-salaverna/

Berger, Thomas R./Katz, Claude. 1997. "Los Mapuche-Pehuenche y el proyecto hidroeléctrico de Ralco: un pueblo amenazado. Informe sobre la misión de investigación de la Federación Internacional de los Derechos Humanos (FIDH) sobre la construcción de la central hidroeléctrica de Ralco y la protección de los derechos económicos, sociales y culturales del pueblo indígenas Mapuche-Pehuence". www.derechos.org/nizkor/espana/doc/endesa/fidh.html

Bertolino, Malvina/Cañada, Liliana. 2004. "La resistencia de la sociedad campesina en los tiempos del pensamiento neoliberal de los noventa: Un acercamiento a las luchas de La Simona". Paper presented at the *VI Encuentro Corredor de las ideas 'Sociedad Civil, Democracia e Integración'*. March 11–13, Montevideo.

Calvo, Iván/Velasco, José Luis/Echenique, Pablo. 2014. "La Transición de Martín Villa y las eléctricas". *eldiario.es*. November 6. www.eldiario.es/zonacritica/Transicion-Martin-Villa-justicia-Argentina-franquismo_6_321677853.html

Carrillo, Santiago. 2018. "El conflicto indígena en Santiago del Estero: una familia denuncia mafias en Añatuya". *Perfil*. January 4. http://noticias.perfil.com/2018/01/04/el-conflicto-indigena-en-santiago-del-estero-una-familia-denuncia-mafias-en-anatuya/

Castro, Nazaret. 2014. "Indígenas contra Endesa: 'No queremos más represas en la zona'". *Eldiario.es*. March 13. www.eldiario.es/desalambre/represas-Endesa-conflictos-America-Latina_0_237626997.html

Catalán Leman, Martín. 2011. "Minería, una paradoja en el desarrollo de Zacatecas". *OCMAL*. December 6. www.ocmal.org/mineria-una-paradoja-en-el-desarrollo-de-zacatecas/

Celi, Carla/Molina, Camilo/Weber, Gabriela. 2009. *Cooperación al desarrollo de la frontera norte. Una mirada desde Sucumbíos. 2000–2007*, Quito: Centro de Investigaciones CIUDAD/ Observatorio de la Cooperación al Desarrollo en Ecuador.

Chile Sustentable. 2016. "La renovada arremetida de Endesa con las comunidades de Ralco". November 2. www.chilesustentable.net/la-renovada-arremetida-de-endesa-con-las-comunidades-de-ralco/

Cuentas Ramírez, Sara. 2014. "Nicolasa Quintremán y el territorio sagrado del Bío Bío". *El País*. February 20. https://elpais.com/elpais/2014/02/20/planeta_futuro/1392913018_924314.html

Dargoltz, Raúl. 2003. "Las economías regionales argentinas y la globalización. El caso de Santiago del Estero y la explotación del quebracho colorado". *Revista Trabajo y Sociedad: Indagaciones sobre el empleo, la cultura y las prácticas políticas en sociedades segmentadas*. 6(V), Jun–Sep. http://www.geocities.com/trabajoysociedad/Dargoltz.htm

De la Torre, Héctor Miranda. 2015. *Identidad en los pueblos mineros de méxico. Minería a cielo abierto en Mazapil*, Zacatecas 2013, Thesis, Universidad Nacional Autónoma de México.

Desalvo, María Agustina. 2014. "El MOCASE: Orígenes, consolidación y fractura del movimiento campesino de Santiago del Estero". *Astrolabio Nueva Época* (12), 271–300.

DiarioUChile. 2013. "Endesa pide disculpas públicas por inundación de cementerio pehuenche con central Ralco". February 1. http://radio.uchile.cl/2013/02/01/endesa-pide-ineditas-disculpas-publicas-por-inundar-cementerio-pehuenche-con-central-ralco/

Domínguez, Diego Ignacio/De Estrada, María. 2013. "Asesinatos y muertes de campesinos en la actualidad Argentina: la violencia como dispositivo (des)territorializador". *Astrolabio Nueva Época* (10), 489–529.

Donziger, Steve/Garr, Laura/Page, Aaron M. 2010. "The Clash of Human Rights and BIT Investor Claims: Chevron's Abusive Litigation in Ecuador's Amazon". *Human Rights Brief* 17 (2), 8–15.

Encuentro Indígena. 2005. "Alto Bio Bio, pasado, presente y futuro. El conflicto de la represa Ralco y la historia de los pewenche". www.archivo-chile.com

Fontaine, Guillaume. 2007 reimpr. *El precio del petróleo – Conflictos socio-ambientales y gobernabilidad en la región amazónica*, Quito: FLACSO/IFEA.

Galarza Zavala, Jaime. 1972. *El festín del petróleo*. Quito: Solitierra.

Galeano, Eduardo. 1984 (39th ed.). *Las venas abiertas de América Latina*, Madrid: Siglo XXI Editores.

Garibay, Claudio/Boni, Andrés/Panico, Francisco/Urquijo, Pedro. 2014. "Corporación minera, colusión gubernamental y desposesión campesina. El caso de Goldcorp Inc. en Mazapil, Zacatecas". *Desacatos* 44 México, January–April.

Godoy, Dante. 2017. "Dejan mineras huellas de contaminación". *NTR Zacatecas*. August 30. http://ntrzacatecas.com/2017/08/30/dejan-mineras-huella-de-contaminacion/comment-page-1/

Gorenstein, Silvia. 2016. *Empresas transnacionales en la agricultura y la producción de alimentos en América Latina y el Caribe*, Buenos Aires: Nueva Sociedad/Friedrich Ebert Stiftung.

Gorenstein, Silvia/Ortiz, Ricardo. 2016. "La tierra en disputa. Agricultura, Acumulación y territorio en la Argentina reciente". *RELAER* 1 (2), 1–26.

Gudynas, Eduardo. 2015. *Derechos de la Naturaleza, Ética biocéntrica y políticas ambientales*, Buenos Aires: Tinta Limón.

Guzmán Concha, César. 2002. *Los trabajadores en tiempos del neoliberalismo. Los casos de Argentina y Chile*, Buenos Aires: CLACSO.

Guzmán López, Federico. 2016. "Impactos ambientales causados por megaproyectos de minería a cielo abierto en el estado de Zacatecas, México". *Revista de Geografía Agrícola* (57), 109–128.

Haller, Tobias/Blöchlinger, Annja/John, Markus/Marthaler, Esther/Ziegler, Sabine (eds.). 2007. *Fossil Fuels, Oil Companies, and Indigenous Peoples: Strategies of Multinational Oil*

Companies, States, and Ethnic Minorities: Impact on Environment, Livelihoods, and Cultural Change, Zürich/Berlin: LIT.

Halperin Dongui, Tulio. 2010 (7th ed.). *Historia contemporánea de América Latina*, Buenos Aires: Alianza Editorial.

Kimerling, Judith. 1991. *Amazon crude*. New York: Natural Resources Defense Council.

Kimerling, Judith. 1994. "The Environmental Audit of Texaco's Amazon Oil Fields: Environmental Justice or Business as Usual?" *Harvard Human Rights Journal* 7, 199–224.

Kol, Héctor. 2003. "Corrupción en la Empresa Privada: El Caso Endesa". *Nodo 50*. February. www.nodo50.org/pretextos/endesa.htm

Lara, Jorge Salvador. 2009 (3rd ed.). *Breve historia contemporánea del Ecuador*, Bogotá: Fondo de Cultura Económica.

Leff, Enrique. 2006. "La ecología política en América Latina. Un campo en Construcción". In: Alimonda, Héctor (ed.) *Los tormentos de la materia. Aportes para una ecología política latinoamericana*. Buenos Aires: CLACSO.

Martínez, Esperanza. 2004. "Mujeres víctimas del petróleo y protagonistas de la resistencia". *WRM*. February. http://wrm.org.uy/oldsite/boletin/79/petroleo.html

Martínez Novo, Carmen. 2017. "La minería amenaza a los indígenas shuar en Ecuador". *The New York Times*. March 27. www.nytimes.com/es/2017/03/27/la-mineria-amenaza-a-los-indigenas-shuar-en-ecuador/

Matus, Javier. 2016. "Fiscalía de España investiga a Endesa en Chile por presunto cohecho internacional". *La Tercera*. September 16. http://www2.latercera.com/noticia/fiscalia-de-espana-investiga-a-endesa-en-chile-por-presunto-cohecho-internacional/

Mejía, Irma. 2015. "Mazapil: Pobreza en medio de la riqueza". *El Universal*. August 11. www.eluniversal.com.mx/articulo/estados/2015/08/11/mazapil-pobreza-en-medio-de-la-riqueza

Mocha, Carlos. 2012. *Información estadística de salud actualizada*, publicación del autor.

Moraga R., Jorge. 2001. *Aguas Turbias. La Central Hidroeléctrica Ralco en el Bio Bio*, Santiago de Chile: OLCA.

Murphy, Sophia/Burch, David/Clapp, Jennifer. 2012. "El lado oscuro del comercio mundial de cereales". *Oxfam*. August. www.oxfam.org/sites/www.oxfam.org/files/file_attachments/rr-cereal-secrets-grain-traders-agriculture-30082012-es_3.pdf

Namuncura, Domingo. 1999. *Ralco: represa o pobreza?*, Santiago de Chile: Lom.

Nieto, Bet-biraí. 2017. 'Salaverna: Crónica de un desalojo'. *Ejecentral*. March 5. www.ejecentral.com.mx/salaverna-cronica-de-un-desalojo/

Ollaquindia, Raquel. 2014. "El nuevo impuesto minero no fomenta el desarrollo regional: Darcy Tetreault". *La jornada Zacatecas*. April 12. http://ljz.mx/2014/04/12/el-nuevo-impuesto-minero-fomenta-el-desarrollo-regional-darcy-tetreault/

Ortiz, Gonzalo. 2011. "Los árboles tiemblan en la selva de Texaco". *Taringa*. March 31. http://ipsnoticias.net/nota.asp?idnews=97862.

Pico Mantilla, Galo. 1968. *Informe a la Nación*. Quito: Ministerio de Industria y Comercio.

Pierri, José. 2013. *Efectos de la desregulación económica de la década del '90 sobre el comercio externo de granos en Argentina*. Report submitted at the Conference: *Comercio Agrícola y América Latina: Cuestiones, controversias y perspectivas*, September 19–20, Buenos Aires.

Radwin, Max. 2016. "Chile's Mapuche-Pehuenche: 10 Years After Relocation". *Al Jazeera*. January 31. www.aljazeera.com/indepth/features/2016/01/chile-mapuche-pehuenche-10-years-relocation-160127111719637.html

Raskovsky, Rodrigo. 2017. "Técnicas de neutralización y Arbitraje Internacional de Inversiones". Paper submitted at the *Seminar on Corporations and Humans Rights* at the University of Göttingen, July 20–21.

Romero–Castillo, Evan. 2012. "Inversión agraria extranjera: ¿oportunidad o abuso?" *Deutsche Welle*. May 24. www.dw.com/es/inversión-agraria-extranjera-oportunidad-o-abuso/a-15972448

Rosso, Inés/Toledo López, Virginia. 2010. "Proceso de (des-re)territorialización en Santiago del Estero". *Memoria Académica, Special Issue – VI Jornadas de Sociología de la UNLP*, 1–20.

Rourke, Daniel. 2010. *Estimación de la cantidad excesiva de mortalidad por cáncer y de sus costos por el hecho de vivir en las áreas de producción de petróleo de las provincias de Sucumbíos y Orellana de Ecuador*, publicación del autor – informe requerido oficialmente.

Rubinstein, David. 2014. "La central Ralco y su perversa historia contra los pehuenche". *El Ciudadano*. January 7. www.elciudadano.cl/medio-ambiente/la-central-ralco-y-su-perversa-historia-contra-los-pehuenche/01/07/

Salas Luévano, María de Lourdes. 2013. *Migración y feminización de la población rural, 2000–2005 El caso de Atitanac y La Encarnación, Villanueva, Zacatecas*, Málaga: Fundación Universitaria Andaluza Inca Garcilaso.

Saleh, Felipe/Opazo, Julia. 2010. "El cementerio indígena que incomoda a Endesa". *elmostrador*. December 6. www.elmostrador.cl/noticias/pais/2010/12/06/el-cementerio-indigena-que-incomoda-a-endesa/

Seguel, Alfredo. 2016. "No cesan los atropellos hidroeléctricos en Alto Bio Bio". *Mapuexpress*. www.mapuexpress.org/?p=7155

Svampa, Maristella. 2017. *Del cambio de época al fin de ciclo. Gobiernos progresistas, extractivismo y movimientos sociales en América Latina*, Buenos Aires: Edhasa.

Tetreault, Darcy. 2013. "Los mecanismos del imperialismo canadiense en el sector minero de América Latina". *Estudios Críticos del Desarrollo* 2 (4), 191–215.

TPP (Tribunal Permanente de los Pueblos). 2010. *Report submitted by Permanent People Tribunal to the 4th Session: La Unión Europea y las empresas transnacionales en América Latina*. May 14–15. Madrid.

Urquieta Ch., Claudia. 2013. "La deuda del Estado y Endesa con los pehuenches de Ralco". *elmostrador*. December 30. www.elmostrador.cl/noticias/pais/2013/12/30/la-deuda-del-estado-y-endesa-con-los-pehuenches-de-ralco/

Valadez Rodríguez, Alfredo. 2005. "Minera Real de Ángeles: de orgullo de Zacatecas a paraje contaminado". *La Jornada*. August 23.

Weber, Gabriela (ed.). 2008. *Sobre la Deuda Ilegítima*, Quito: Centro de Investigaciones CIUDAD.

Zanatta, Loris. 2012. *Historia de América Latina – De la Colonia al siglo XXI*, Buenos Aires: Siglo XXI Editores.

Filmography

Apaga y vámonos. 2005. Documentary film. Dir. Manel Mayol. Spain.

Crude: El estigma del petróleo. 2009. Documentary film. Dir. Joe Berlinger. EEUU.

Quebracho. 1974. Film. Dir. Ricardo Wullicher. Argentina.

Reportaje Minera Peñasquito. 2014. Documentary. *La jornada Zacatecas*. www.youtube.com/watch?v=HNGjifVvlF0

Salaverna: El pueblo que hundió Carlos Slim. 2017. Documentary as part of the Report: "La historia de cómo Carlos Slim hundió un pueblo". *Vanguardia*. www.vanguardia.com.mx/articulo/la-historia-de-como-carlos-slim-hundio-un-pueblo

Solo se escucha el viento. 2004. Documentary. Dir. Alejandro Fernández Mouján. Argentina.

Toda esta sangre en el monte. 2012. Documentary. Dir. Martín Céspedes. Argentina.

Toda esta sangre en el monte. 2018. Documentary film. Dir. Martín Céspedes. Argentina.

Chapter 4

Linking economy and visible violence – case studies from Guatemala, Brazil, Peru and Honduras

This chapter is about the visible forms of violence which are directly involved in large-scale economic processes and activities. This sounds similar to the idea of Chapter 3, but it is not. Chapter 3 presented a systematic description of cases and their analysis by following the conceptual lines of violence as it is understood by Johan Galtung (see Chapter 2), and by stressing the chrono-logical development of facts, contextual circumstances and their relationship as well as the shift from one form of violence to the other – especially between invisible forms of violence. The aim was to make clear the often-unperceived general connections, pressures and determinations among large-scale economic politics and the conflicts they promote. The systematic distinction of informa-tion about the situation before, during and after the economic activity allows a disaggregated analysis of facts which otherwise would remain disconnected or invisible.

In this fourth chapter, the method of exposure is another. It is not about elucidating the invisible framework that exists among policies, companies, pro-cesses and negative effects that, as a whole, impede the fulfillment of basic needs. Here, rather, it is about setting the accent on the forms of visible physical vio-lence triggered by economic activity from the beginning. The exercise of the previous chapter made it possible to sharpen the analysis of entire areas, estab-lish links between international economic interests and indigenous protests, for example. After that, the proposal is here to take other more "gross" cases, if the expression is allowed, in which the physical and direct violence was concrete and indubitable.

The task consists in showing the link between this violence and economic activity. Although this link seems to be limited exclusively to the internal logic of each specific case as an isolated case, it is not. We have already seen – in the analysis of Chapter 3 – that the context of each case performs in the time *before*, *during* and *after* the concrete situations of violence exercised and suffered. This violence, located specifically in time and space, is not divorced from the large movements and economic processes which are initiated with political deci-sions and lead to endless small concatenated events that result in deaths, both in the present and in the future. While the previous chapter presented the cases starting from the case with the least perceived violence to the case with most clear violence, this chapter will take the opposite direction. The cases will be presented more briefly and will exclusively emphasize the information that allows the view of physical violence as linked to economic activity.

It will begin with the case of more limited and even intimate physical violence, which attacks a few bodies in a terrible way – even if such violence has not been linked to transnational economic activity – and the level of publicity and "scattering" of physical violence will increase with each new case. The emphasis will remain on violence in its physical form, although it may be less and less perceptible in individualized persons. The previous chapter offered an analysis of contexts and large cases in their violence, even if they were basically invisible. This chapter focuses on smaller areas in time and space, in shorter and more compact processes, almost instantaneous in their physical form, but increasingly longer in the timeline as these forms of violence become increasingly invisible.

The cases and how they will be presented

The four cases deal with transnational corporations and international economic interests that were supposed to promote "development" in the Latin American region. In all cases, it is shown how the promise of development has not been kept and, even more, how there are direct links between those promises and economic activities, and the visible direct violence used against the local population on the part of the state, on the part of the corporate actors, or even on the part of the affected population resisting and attacking in their conflicts with private and state security forces.

The study of these four cases and the order of their presentation aim to emphasize the severity of specific types of harm related to a deregulated economic order.

In short, they are:

1   *Indigenous Women of Lote 8* case, on the rape and death of women in contexts of mining industries and land conflicts in Guatemala;
2   "*El Baguazo*" case, on the explosion of an extremely violent social conflict resulting in several deaths arising from a free trade agreement with the United States, its impact on the situation of the local indigenous population, its territory and its work in the area of extractive industries in Peru;
3   *Matopiba* case, on violent territorial conflicts with physical confrontation and an increasing rate of homicide against local peasants in the context of the expansion of the agrarian frontier promoted by foreign capital and by the state design of a strategic geo-economic area in Brazil;
4   *Valle de Siria* case, on diseases and lethal effects affecting workers and the local child and adult population caused by the contamination of desert soil with heavy metals during gold extraction in Honduras.

Methodologically, there is no unique or repeated structure for the presentation of the cases. In opposition to Chapter 3, the goal here is to show the extremely particular features of each case and context, particularly stressing the level of physical violence. As the cases are read, it is clear that the frontiers between legal and illegal, visible and invisible, public and private actors become increasingly diffuse. Even more, the last case, the *Valle de Siria* case, could be presented exclusively as a case of structural violence. The announced death of a child due to a genetic malformation caused by toxic substances used in gold extraction, however, is a physical death caused by physical causes. In this sense, the description and analysis show the necessary reflection on new categories. In the same vein, the last case in Chapter 3 – the *MOCASE* case on the peasant movement and its resistance and death of some members of the group – is basically a case of a high-level of structural and cultural violence (both invisible), but the step to expressions of physical violence is so short that the boundaries, again, remain fuzzy.

This chapter, like this entire study, aims to contribute to our understanding of these uneasy frontiers and to our understanding of the contextual and complex questions that surround each unsatisfied need in Latin America. The fact that this non-satisfaction is often avoidable explains the need of deep-running analysis on the base of concrete cases and, at the same time, the need of criminological categories that may allow, accordingly, paths of imputation when the unsatisfied needs can be linked to liable actors. This proposal starts with a conceptual ambition, but it later extends to an even more ambitious goal: the analysis and design of norms, institutions and practice. Structural and cultural peace (i.e. nonviolence), in this sense, is the main goal.

The *Indigenous Women of Lote 8* case in Guatemala

The case

In 2006 and 2007, the Compañía Guatemalteca de Níquel (CGN), subsidiary of Hudbay Minerals (Canada) promoted forced evictions of Q'eqchi' communities in the municipality of Panzós, Alta Verapaz and El Estor, Izabal, in the Polochic Valley in order to carry out mining extraction activities. In this context, on January 17, 2007, eleven women reported that they had been gang-raped by several men (security guards of the company, police and army soldiers) who were executing the eviction. All these facts were left in impunity in Guatemala, and they are being investigated in civil proceedings in the process carried out in Canada (see ahead). The case of the *Indigenous Women of Lote 8*, in this sense, is paradigmatic to show the degree of physical violence that can be exercised in the hands of entrepreneurs, employees of companies, hired thugs and members of the various security forces, in activity or retired, when the objective is to ensure territory and economic production at all costs and without presence or state control in genuine protection of its population.[1]

Indigenous women and their especial situation in the face of the mining industry

The predominantly male nature of extractive activity (mining, hydrocarbons, etc.), both in those who work directly for companies and in the management and administration of foreign and local companies, as well as in the male predominance in security forces protecting the facilities, generates a reconfiguration of family, community and social relations in the areas where these activities and their facilities set up. For this reason, mining is one of the most violent industries with respect to the situation of women (Svampa 2017).

The impact is direct in the lives of women (often displaced from their traditional roles and also excluded from the possibility of working with the company, WRM 2003), as it is in their health or in the possibility of their democratic participation in the life of the community. In fact, their situation of inferiority due to the double marginalization implied by their status as women and as indigenous places them, from the beginning, in a situation of disadvantage in terms of the possibility of equal interaction with the company. Note, for example, that their situation regarding education is highly vulnerable, and how this situation leads to further marginalization – as the Inter-American Commission of Human Rights described:

> The literacy rate among the indigenous population in Guatemala is much lower than in the rest of the population, especially among women. In some rural communities, illiteracy in indigenous adult women reaches 90%, a situation that poses an important commitment in the educational formation of indigenous women. In the workplace, they also suffer different forms of discrimination and, in general, have access to less qualified and poorly paid jobs. Many indigenous women work in the domestic area without receiving a living wage, in addition to being subjected to various forms of violence and discrimination. There are also cases of prostitution, exploitation and trafficking of indigenous women in clandestine bars and canteens of the urban area in several municipalities of the country.[2]

Given these limitations for their interrelationships with the modern state and its foreign actors, women often remain within the exclusive framework of the relationship of their primary community ties. As wives and mothers of workers or displaced men of the community, women have to suffer changes in community life, frustration in the men, alcohol problems and unemployment – also in cases in which agricultural or fishing activities are interrupted by the mining activities.

> Alcohol abuse, drug dependence, prostitution, gambling, incest and infidelity are increasing in many mining communities. All this has worsened the cases of family violence against women, active and often brutal discrimination in the workplace, which is frequently sanctioned or ignored by judicial

and political institutions. Even workers' organizations run by men do not denounce human rights violations committed against women. The discussion between these organizations and the mining companies is oriented towards economic issues such as salary increases, subsidies, etc.

(WRM 2003)

The role of women in the family and communities, therefore, is transformed in many ways: they have to nourish, educate and keep children under acceptable hygienic conditions, but the mining impact in the area – as seen in the cases presented in Chapter 3 – does not allow them to do this in the right way. Besides, usually women do not accept external rules, and have to remain constantly available and strong for men and children. It is no secret that women are usually the support of their families, in the practical and emotional sense. This is no exception among indigenous people. For this reason, even though men can be affected by bad working conditions or by physical diseases related to the arrival of new forms of industrial production, women are often affected much more.

Physical violence against women who defend human rights

Given that the institutional response to the violence used by corporations against indigenous communities often remains unheard, protest becomes the only way to demand respect for rights. As mentioned earlier, the violence is present, but not investigated. There is

> Existence of a clear disparity between the institutional response to complaints against members of indigenous communities and the impunity of many of the reported acts of abuse, harassment and physical violence, including sexual violence, against community members, in a context marked by the lack of effective access of indigenous peoples to state organs of administration of justice.[3]

This situation has motivated women present to the UN a formal claim against the violence related to extractive projects. Indigenous and nonindigenous women are together in this petition, especially after the killing of the Honduran activist Berta Cáceres perpetrated as a response to her work in protection of indigenous land and communities. Cases of violence against women who defend human rights extend, actually, through all of Latin America (RLMDDSA 2017).[4]

The cultural discourses and practices, however, are continuously working for the silence and invisibility of these situations, as Carlsen said, talking about the case of Juventina Villa, a human rights defender in Mexico:

> Powerful economic and political forces have a great interest in silencing them. The public often retreats with the versions given by the media – "she

died because she crossed the line", which implies, if you do not cross the line, you are safe.

(Carlsen 2012)

Some women are actively involved in these movements and explain the need of peace; they ask for the common organization of all women to say *"yes"* to life. This was the case of the leader Aura Lolita Chávez Ixcaquic, from Guatemala, specialized in the representation of cases of violence against *Maya* and *Kiche* indigenous women in Guatemala. She explains:

> We are very aware that we face strong opposition – the state is not a friend . . . it's connected, along with the oligarchies, transnational corporations, world powers, and militarism. And all of these have seen us as their enemy.
> This backlash is even stronger against women because we make decisions, and we are clear about our decisions, and we have a lot of energy from nature. And when we say "no", it means "no" and this has generated a lot of repression against us – sisters have been jailed, murdered, threatened.

(JASS 2012)

Even "harmless" aggression against women defending their territory and communities becomes extremely menacing when related to the contextual situation promoted by the state, as in the case of the threat against Isabela Gaspar, a pacifist protester against a hydroelectric project of the company Hidro Santa Cruz, while she was walking with her child and his father: "The aggressor told her 'you should no longer demonstrate because it is development', in reference to the hydroelectric plant" (OMCT et al. 2015).

Development can be a motive for killing. Laura Vásquez, another defender and activist, in this case against a mining plant in San Rafael, Guatemala, was killed in January 2017. Before that, she had spent seven months in prison and suffered defamation. All forms of violence (structural, cultural and physical) working together can be clearly seen in her case (IM-Defensoras 2017). Actually, they appear in all these cases:

> The indigenous and peasant women, especially, became targets of attacks by companies and governments, given their resistance to privatization and looting projects disguised as development. (. . .) Women who work to stop miners, megaprojects, dams and other invasions of their land and rights are in conflict with powerful and brutal adversaries. Private security companies hired by economic interests, government security forces and paramilitary bodies frequently persecute people defending their lands and communities, and women are often at the forefront of battle lines.

(Carlsen 2014)

Besides, if women decide to resist and even to rise up against the exaggerated presence of extractive corporations and their negative impact in Latin America, they expose their families and communities, and not only themselves, to violent responses through sexual assault, grave injury and even death (RLMDDSA 2017).[5] In this context, their bodies and their condition of being women are, in this sense, a vulnerable booty of war. The invisible violence of cultural indifference and discrimination on the part of the rest of society and the state, along with the fragile structural conditions of life in rural or forest areas – favorite areas for mining industries – are together a high-risk combination which leads, in many cases, to the infliction of physical violence against these women on the part of the corporations and their actors. Added to this, the violence exerted on women often remains mute and invisible, given that it comes to an aggression against their physical identity – it is not only the physical fact of the violence, but also the cultural fact of this aggression. In cases where the aggression becomes known, it often leads to revictimization in the form of rejection suffered by women in their own communities:

> They are also abandoned, or worse, attacked – by the government and sometimes by their own communities and families. No matter what they do or what they have done to them, they are presented as if they had provoked their own murders, rapes or attacks.
>
> (Carlsen 2012)

Thus, the *Indigenous Women of Lote 8* case describes the most silent and intimate form of physical violence linked to unchecked economic activity.

Sexual violence in Lote 8

The case of the *indigenous women of Lote 8* is often reported in relation to the case of Sepur Zarco, in which there was also collective sexual rape of women of the Q'eqchi people by soldiers along with the forced disappearances and homicide of their husbands in an operation of land appropriation that occurred during the internal armed conflict in Guatemala.[6] In both cases, the violation of women was a war technique with the aim of instilling fear, displacing population and obtaining economically productive land. In the case of Lote 8, the moment of extreme physical violence occurred on January 17, 2007. It involved the sexual violation of an unknown number of women in the community during the violent eviction of land perpetrated by agents of the company's private security force. The company involved was Compañía Guatemalteca del Níquel (CGN, at that time a subsidiary of the transnational mining company Hudbay Minerals, whose headquarters are in Canada), along with agents of the National Civil Police and the army. It was described that when the agents of the private and state security arrived at the community Lote 8, the men were doing agricultural work in the field. The agents, according to the women's testimonies, trapped the women in their homes or in the surrounding area when they tried to flee, and raped them in front of their children. Many of them were raped multiple times by different men. Later, the CGN guards and state agents burned the houses and the crops, so the women were forced to take refuge in the mountains to escape further repression. Among the physical consequences, women suffered miscarriages, forced pregnancies, inability to conceive again, and pain that lasted for many years, among other ailments. The psychosocial consequences include the impact of silence and stigmatization. The women of Lote 8 kept silent about the rape for several years before encouraging themselves to denounce it (Méndez Gutiérrez 2013).

It is worth mentioning that the women's denunciation took place only after the murder of an indigenous teacher who was a community leader;[7] the retired military officer, and head of the security company in charge of the group that had carried out the aggression and perpetrated the homicide was tried in Guatemala and acquitted. This was, again, an expression of impunity toward acts of violence reported against security agents in the custody of private economic interests and in detriment of the communities (Rivera 2017).

In total, three complaints were admitted by the Superior Court of Ontario (Canada) against the company Hudbay Minerals for crimes of homicide, injuries and sexual violence allegedly committed by security personnel in El Estor (Izabal), where the community Lote 8 is located. The case, still open (as of March 2018), should it result in the company's conviction, would set a precedent in Canada for which a company is judicially linked with situations of physical violence of a sexual nature in the context of its economic activity abroad.[8] Facts such as those reported here are not within the framework of the topics that are usually discussed at tables of commercial, economic or development dialogue, although they belong to a microphysics of power that is decisive for the construction of cultural and social identities.

As Luz Méndez Gutiérrez explains when presenting the case:

> Sexual rape is the only crime for which social shame and guilt rests on the shoulders of the victims themselves and not on the perpetrators. There is the main root of forced silence and social stigmatization. (. . .) Rape is not interpreted as a violation of human rights, as a social and political problem, but as something that corresponds to the realm of the private sphere.
>
> (Méndez Gutiérrez 2013)

It can be seen that the different types of violence, also in this case, are directly interrelated, in barely visible ways. Although the physical violence exerted in principle seems private and even intimate, it is in reality one of the mechanisms of obstruction of human fulfillment at various levels (material, physical, emotional, social), which have a direct impact on the greater or lesser possibilities for personal and social development.

The *Matopiba* case in Brazil

The case

Matopiba is the acronym for Maranhão, Tocantins, Piaui and Bahia, the four states considered together as a region in the process of extending the agricultural frontier in the Brazilian cerrado in order to promote local and regional development (Mathias 2017). This is the institutionalization (and deinstitutionalization after the arrival of Temer in the presidency, in which it was considered that the state had no funds for the project – Mathias 2017) of an area that is presented as geo-economic to the extent of 73 million hectares because it presents a surface as well as optimum soil and climate characteristics for an exportable crop. Therefore, it is expected to increase production, which requires the design and implementation of land distribution reform, infrastructure preparation and technology development. For example, the informant member of the project commission, Irajá Abreu (PSD-TO), presented his favorable opinion on the draft text. Defended the parliamentarian:

> Considering the great challenges to ensure the continuity of the development of the region, it is essential to create a nonprofit organization, of a technical and scientific nature, aimed at promoting the agricultural development of Matopiba and consequently improving the living conditions of the local population.[9]

The project, originally launched at the federal level in response to the interest of the international market, and therefore established in order to attract foreign investment, brought with it a radicalization of violent land conflicts between possible new "owners" and the traditional inhabitants and owners of those lands, whose price is steadily increasing. This has even led to the liberalization of actions by public and private security forces in the struggle to obtain land in the area. The area, historically, has experienced the attention of large landowners and violence going as far back as the 1970s with the green revolution, and later with the rise of agribusiness, which goes hand in hand with agrochemicals as well as fertilizers and pesticides, as well as transgenic crops, all of which have increased in the Matopiba project. In all cases, those projects and political actions have been carried out with the promise of "zero hunger" and development. To this day, despite having been an area with a rise in its agrarian exports in the past few decades, the population continues to live in conditions of marginality and suffer the highest rates of violence in Brazil.

The interest of the Matopiba project for economic development

The agrarian exploitation proposed by Matopiba would lead to greater industrialization and higher technology in machinery, and therefore, to less labor, along with the use of chemicals that affect the health of workers, peasants and neighboring populations, who would thus lose their own crops. If we add that it is generally managed in terms of monoculture, this also brings the problem of the loss of food sovereignty because both the seeds (through the imposition of large firms and their patenting thanks to reforms in intellectual property regimes – Gorenstein 2016: 9) as well as the loss of land – or its contamination – leave small and medium farmers at a disadvantage. If these farmers yield to pressure, they become workers in the best case, or become unemployed or must live as internal migrants in the cities (*favelization* is a key word here, related to the processes of increasing urbanization and the marginalization processes in the suburban areas – Documentary *Tierra en transformación* 2013: 4'). If they do not fold, they end up in judicial conflicts that revolve around the problem of untitled possession, the *grilagem*[10] and the lack of legislation in line with democratic agrarian reform as provided for in the 1998 Federal Constitution, or in conflicts of physical violence because of their resistance to the evictions.

In this case, the interest of the transnationals is clear, as is their merger with local capital:

> The companies use market structures as a joint venture – an association of two or more companies to start an economic activity – and create international funds in partnership with national companies that can circumvent the law that limits the purchase of land by foreigners. Thus, it seems that the land was acquired by only one company, hiding the participation of foreign pension funds, whose holdings are majority through its subsidiaries, such as TIAA-CREF Global Agriculture HoldCo.
>
> (Prof. Fabio Pitta, University of São Paulo in
> Campelo 2017, see also REDE 2015)[11]

As he has explained elsewhere as well:

> With a capital of approximately 866 billion dollars, the TIAA-CREF (Teachers Insurance and Annuity Association) invests in everything that promises good returns. But it does not do this directly and, rather, it creates companies (holdings) for the purpose of managing different types of financial applications through the participation in other companies. In the case in point, TIAA-CREF established a holding company; the holding company created a Brazilian company with foreign capital; this company joined in 2008 a large Brazilian sugar and ethanol company (Cosan) to create Radar S/A, whose business is to speculate on the price of land.
>
> (Mathias 2017, also FIAN 2017)

Not only the agrarian business and speculation with land prices find foreign interests attractive in Matopiba. This interest and the consequent opening and facilitation of investments by the Brazilian state also arises from other factors, such as the fact that the territory presents large tracts of land "still at a low price"; water, "even with all the threat to the sources of the Cerrado"; and the possibility of connecting with infrastructure projects to flow production such as the Tocantins-Araguaia waterway and railroads such as Ferrogrão and Carajás (Campelo 2017).

The statements of the then-Minister of Agriculture, Livestock and Supply (MAPA), during the creation of the Development Agency of MATOPIBA, on March 7, 2016, are convincing: "The master plan will be instrumental in attracting investors and entrepreneurs worldwide. Everywhere in the world where I've been, everyone just wants to know about this new Brazilian agricultural frontier" (Campelo 2017).

Despite the interest and impulse of the former minister, since the inauguration of the new president, this situation was changed by a presidential decree of October 18, 2016, in which the Matopiba Regulation Office was closed. Given that the state withdrew from the regulation and direction of the project, it continues, but is now governed by the private hands of the market, in a true process of deregulation of a sector placed first on the table based on private interest and then later motivated by the state;[12] the population of the place, finally, is currently exposed to foreign entrepreneurs and corporations which are clearly excited about the economic landscape advertised (Mathias 2017).[13] Even the World Bank, in a 2007 report, claimed that the country combined a high degree of availability of land and water (Ceratti 2016). International interests and the national attitude thus led to the idea that "expropriation becomes regularized" (Mathias 2017).[14]

For the market, even without the state support of a specific office, the conditions are optimal – and perhaps more. The context promotes not only the obtaining of land, but also the infrastructure projects that the new agrarian area entails: "There are ports, large storage terminals, railroads, highways, waterways, hydroelectric plants and power stations that guarantee the conditions for large-scale production to be sent outside the country. Almost always to the other side of the world, to China" (Mathias 2017). And this makes the proposal especially attractive for international capitals interested participating in such infrastructure works dedicated to facilitating the export of resources from the South to the Global North. This agroexporting and economistic vision of reality is celebrated even in other countries through their media, which share and endorse this vision, thus promoting different spaces of cultural violence. It is not surprising that the Argentine newspaper *Clarín*, directly linked to the interests of the Argentine agricultural groups, presents with admiration the growth of the Brazilian countryside without taking into account the aggressive consequences of this growth (Castro 2017). The consequences are serious and are linked to a synergy between the international economy and the national state that exacerbates the fragile living conditions of the local population.[15]

New markets for foreign investors, new land for speculation (Campelo 2017), land grabbing in few hands and deforestation[16] with state permission: these conditions do not sound compatible with the promised development for the population. Besides, two specific aspects need special attention because they lead the issue to an even more violent step – *visible*, this time.

The structural and physical negative impact – water and agro-toxics

Because of mechanized agriculture, the soils are compacted, hinder the penetration of water into the substrate during the rain catchment, leading to a gradual decrease in the volume of water in the aquifers (underground natural spaces of fresh water) with a consequent decrease of water in the rivers and streams that flow from them. This lack of water, in an area that has been called "berço das aguas" ("cradle of the waters") (Mathias 2017: 14), is another effect of the expansion of the agrarian frontier to areas with a biosphere not accustomed to intensive industrialization, and brings drought and lack of water to local communities – and the country in general (Gonçalves de Souza 2017: 12–13; Mathias 2017).

The other side of this situation is that when lands with groundwater are left in the hands of foreign capital, that water is also available to these foreign interests. Researcher Isolete Wichinieski explains:

> By 2030 the planet will have 10 billion inhabitants. And we will have 40% less water available than today. Brazil owns 12% of all the fresh water in the world, so we are starting to realize why international capital is very interested in the *cerrado*. Water will be the gold of the next centuries.
>
> (Mathias 2017: 15)

In a conflict over the qualification of underground water collection carried out by the company Sudotex, the suspension and then granting of the permit generated tension between the executive and judicial authorities, and finally the extraction was authorized by the Court of Justice. Its arguments were the same as those given opportunely by the Institute of Environment and Water Resources (Inema), and these arguments are economic: "Without water, the company could have to suspend its operation". The inhabitants, meanwhile, see their life becoming increasingly dry, which has led to the organization of protests and the adoption of measures of force, such as the retention of machinery in order to force dialogue (WRM 2015).

To conflicts over land and lack of water, pollution and the negative impact on health caused by the increase in the use of chemical products are added. By 2000, International Labor Organization (ILO) estimated that, among workers in developing countries, pesticides and chronic poisonings are responsible for deaths as well as for acute and chronic nonfatal diseases – each year, there are around 170,000 agricultural worker deaths because of accidents and/or poisoning (ILO 2000).

In sum, the testimony of an observer from the Investigative Delegation of Matopiba, which collects data and testimonies on the living conditions of the population and organizes public hearings in order to listen and provide information to the population, has summarized the picture eloquently:

> In all the different communities that the delegation has visited, it has denounced a lamentable absence of the state. The inhabitants, as a rule, do not have public services such as schools, electricity, infrastructure or health centers and are discriminated against by the police, which fail in their duty to protect them. As stressed by delegation member Altamiran Ribeiro (CPT-Piauí), state intervention is essential for the survival of these communities: "Either we help these communities or they are sentenced to death".
>
> (FIAN 2017)

Physical violence

In many cases, this death sentence is, with increasing clarity, also linked to is physical exposure to direct, individual violence in the struggle for land.

The processes of concentration of land and the conflicts they bring contribute high figures to the statistics of physical violence (Gilvander Moreira 2017):

> The CPT's [Pastoral Land Commission] 2016 Violence Report revealed an average of five murders per month with 61 deaths among quilombolas (descendants of black slaves settled in rural areas), indigenous people and activists of the landless movements, an increase of 22% compared to 2015. The same report states that death threats had also increased by 86% and assassination attempts by 68%. Since 1985, agrarian conflicts have ended the lives of 1,834 Brazilians, and most of the killings have gone unpunished: only 31 people have been arrested for ordering any of those deaths.
>
> (Martín 2017)

The aforementioned *grilagem*, the fraud carried out to obtain property titles, goes hand in hand with the physical violence that is exerted to expel resident peasants and indigenous communities from the acquired areas. This is usually done with a direct violent intervention that begins with threats and can even end in massacres of entire families at the hands of hired gunmen, employees of companies or big farms, or even members of the security forces, both active and retired (De Olho 2017). As the Spanish daily *El País* informed readers:

> The massacres of peasants have returned (. . .) The rural landowners, protected by the government, have a license to kill and the State's policy is one of open repression against the agrarian movements. Collective assassinations of indigenous populations have returned. It is a very propitious context for death. Private militias, sometimes led by retired or active military,

act with hoods on, firing bullets, shooting and burning everything, seeking to instill fear.

(Martín 2017)

On situations of extreme violence against peasants and indigenous communities, the newspaper describes:

On April 30 [2017] in Maranhão, in northeastern Brazil, a community of Gamela Indians was massacred for having occupied a farm in the territory of their ancestors, now in the possession of ranchers. The landowners summoned people living outside the area to a big party, and then expelled and tortured the Gamela people by cutting their wrists and shooting them in the head.

(Martín 2017)

Maranhão is one of the states where the Matopiba project is situated. If the report is read on its own, it seems to be just an extremely violent form of adjustment of accounts. In the context that is being described here, the dimension is quite different. It is not possible to dissociate these kinds of collective massacres from the economic sphere. In another state, outside Matopiba but near to it and with similar land and agrarian conflicts, there was another case at that time: "In Pau D'Arco, in the north of the country, ten 'landless', who occupied a hacienda located on public lands and awaited their recognition, were killed by the police and another 14 were injured" (Martín 2017). The situation for the relatives is not easy, because they remain in the area. Migration is not a better option. Concerning this case, a Brazilian report informed the public in 2017 that around 200 families remain there, living in precarious conditions. The conflict was initiated because of a land dispute four years before; first investigations in the case had proved that it was an "execution scenario with indication of commissioned crime" (G1 2017).

The names of the actors who could have commissioned the crime, of course, were not disclosed.

According to the Pastoral Land Commission (CPT), there are three main factors for the increase of conflicts in 2015.[17] These are the impunity related to conflicts in the countryside, the dismantling of public bodies and the absence of a state policy aimed at the democratization of the land, because when governments do not act, "the [peasant] movements are those that directly conflict with the large estate" and, finally, the expansion of agribusiness, "the advance of large economic corporations in the countryside and of large infrastructure works", which want the territory of traditional communities for the wealth that it contains (Seigner Ameni 2017).

Impunity, linked to invisible violence through the fibers that are most intrinsic to their tissues, is a clear legitimation that perpetuates violence. This is clear and seems irremovable beyond any complaint. Take the fact that only two days after the astonishing report of the CPT cited previously was released, nine peasants were brutally murdered (Vida Nueva 2017).

The *Baguazo* case in Peru

The case

In 2009, with the aim of facilitating the operation and optimizing the obtaining of economic benefits by foreign and national companies operating hydrocarbon and minerals the national government promoted the normative deregulation of activities through legislative decrees that consolidated the commitments assumed by the signing of a free trade agreement with the United States. The decrees, as denounced by the Awajún and Wampis peoples, went against their right to prior consultation, recognized by Peru in 1995 with the signing of ILO Convention 169. The decision of the executive power generated a conflict in the province of Bagua, which was already in a state of alert because of the reduction of the Reserve land of Cordillera del Cóndor. Most of this area was delivered to Mining Afrodita and implied in this way that the extension of the land as an Awajún–Wampi Biosphere Reserve of 1,642,567 hectares would be reduced to 88,477 hectares.[18] This nonrecognition of the area's reserve status, along with the signing of the decree laws, led to the taking of a Petroecuador Station by the Amazonian Awajún people in May and the consequent roadblocks that remained in place until June 5, 2009. The state was asked to repeal the decrees which, among other measures, reduced requirements for the disposition of community and forest lands. That day, the conflict reached its peak of tension and evolved into the facts known as "Baguazo" or "massacre of Bagua", which resulted in the deaths of 34 people and more than 200 injured. A superior police officer remains disappeared ever since.

The free trade agreement with the USA

In the course of 2008, a package of legislative decrees (DL) was issued that, among other matters, modified the regulations on the right to own forest lands (DL 1090), the disposition of indigenous lands (DL 1015) and cultural identity (DL 1064). A free trade agreement formerly signed with the United States was the framework of economic commitment that motivated the issuance of the decrees in order to adapt the domestic regulatory order to said treaty and enable and facilitate the investments of that country according to the set terms. For this reason, given the requirement of the Awajún people that these decrees should be left without effect, the government's response was intransigent and the Minister of Foreign Trade, Mercedes Aráoz, explained that the requirement could not be met because the repeal of these decrees could entail international responsibility for noncompliance with a bilateral agreement, thus exposing Peru to being brought before an arbitration panel (Documentary *La espera* 2014: 12').

However, in that package of decrees – which generated much controversy in the country – the government exceeded the issues strictly related to the FTA in order to impose its development model (Romero Cano 2014). In that tension, once the conflict arose, the executive branch and the legislative branch passed responsibility to each other and left the definition of the problem in the hands of the other state area, while the indigenous peoples continued to wait for a response.

These decrees corresponded to the idea of government and economic orientation espoused by the president of Peru at the time, Alan García, who had presented in various writings published in the newspaper *El Comercio*, between 2007 and 2008, his "theory" of "the gardener's dog syndrome" ("*el syndrome del perro del hortelano*").[19] According to this theory, there were actors – such as indigenous peoples and representatives of civil society identified with the struggle for indigenous rights and a respectful vision of the environment – who neither used the resources offered in abundance on Peruvian soil, nor allowed them to be exploited by third parties – national or foreign investors. That is, they were analogous to "the gardener's dog", who neither eats what is in the garden nor allows other animals to eat it. In accordance with these ideas, the government then set in motion regulatory modifications that made it easier for land and areas that were considered idle (in the Amazon, in the sea, in the mountains) to be offered for private exploitation. In the words of the former president, the reference to the unsatisfied basic needs of a large part of the population, especially of the rural indigenous population, is explicit in relation to the conditions of nutrition, health, education, housing and democratic participation. In this sense, the idea of economic development that his doctrine promulgated was clear about the needs that had to be met, especially with respect to the indigenous population. Consider that the population first affected in the Bagua case is the indigenous population of the Peruvian Amazon, historically marginalized from state attention. In brief words, the lawyers Mejía and Quispe indicate:

> The Amazonian ethnic groups have been traditionally forgotten, excluded and discriminated against by the Peruvian State and society. And in contemporary Peru, this reality of state exclusion and lack of protection is reflected in the high rates of poverty, illiteracy and malnutrition.
>
> (Mejía & Quispe 2017)

However, the mechanisms put into operation would not allow, in the short or long term, any change to their situation.

The lack of democratic representation and institutional attention to internationally accepted commitments for the protection of the rights of the people belonging to indigenous groups implies the obstruction of the satisfaction of basic needs: the collective manifestation of the affected indigenous peoples was prevented through legislative decrees, as was their participation concerning matters of direct impact on their private and working lives. The obstacle, in this case, is presented as avoidable, given that the political decision was unilaterally adopted without consultation or dialogue with the affected population, and another decision would have been possible without presenting any obstacle to the development of hydrocarbon economic activity. Another decision – the consideration of the concerns of the affected indigenous peoples – was possible. The eventual reduction of facilities or economic benefits for business actors was not an explanation of inevitability. The political decision, in short, was not a force-majeure decision. It can, therefore, be analyzed as violence in its manifestation of structural violence. In a similar sense, an anthropologist, analyzing the case, said that "the violence came from the moment when there were rules contrary to indigenous rights"; that is, that sanctioning of laws contrary to indigenous rights, is violence in itself: "That is a way of exercising violence, not just shooting or bullets, acting against the recognized rights of the people is to exercise violence, and this violence generated more violence" (Paucar Albino 2017).

Unchecked physical violence

On June 5, 2009, about 2,000 indigenous people were occupying a Petroperú station; 35 police officers and 13 civilians had been taken hostage. Faced with the government's refusal to respond to the demand for respect of their rights, the protesters decided to leave the place the next day, and this was made public. However, from Lima, the eviction was ordered. The reason for this measure, unnecessary – given the protesters' decision to leave – had, again, a purely economic motive. As explained by the President of the Congressional Investigative Committee on the *Baguazo*, Guido Lombardi:

> It is because of the taking of the Number 6 fire station of Petroperú that the denouement occurred, and the government's desperation somewhat as well, because they are the oil companies that had stored the oil they produced for those forty days. After forty-two days they had reached their storage capacity and, therefore, they needed to close the wells. It was because of this, according to all indications, although there are no records of the Council of Ministers meeting, that President Garcia says a phrase like "So, Minister, it's about time".
>
> (Documentary *La espera* 2014: 28')

The reference was to the Minister of the Interior, Mercedes Cabanillas, who gave the order for the eviction without sufficient preparation or respect for the complexity of the situation on the ground. A certain level of conversation between protesters and the officer in charge had been reached. However, under the command of another officer who came to the site exclusively to move forward with the eviction, the minister's order culminated in tragedy for police and indigenous people, and yet it did not entail any kind of political responsibility for Cabanillas or any other political authority or legislative official – in

Congress, despite awareness of the tensions that were being experienced, the urgent treatment that should be given to the law that would define the repeal of the legislative decrees under question was delayed.

There were protest demonstrations that led to the death of 34 people. This violence is directly linked to the economic activity whose deregulation was under discussion, because it was unleashed by the protesters in rejection of the presence of the police, sent by the government from Lima with the pressure to end the protest – which the demonstrators had already decided to end and had subsequently informed the police – who were in clear numerical disadvantage regarding the indigenous protesters on the route: "What happened is the last act in a chain of events" (Documentary *La espera* 2014: 01'50").

Thus, a violent physical confrontation took place between indigenous people who had taken the station, cut off both the road and the police stationed there because of economic decisions and orders coming from the executive power – far from the direct and personal stress scenario – so that the Baguazo "was the product of police action ordered by the Government [. . .] The Government ignored the protesters and sent troops and what happened happened. The violence was unleashed by the arbitrary, abusive and arrogant Government" (Paucar Albino 2017).

It is not only the members of the Awajún people, but also the police sent to carry out the eviction, who have been considered victims of the political attitude and the primacy of the economic interest over the protection of the general population. The father of a deceased policeman, like other parents of the police officers who intervened in the conflict, and like other citizens who were injured by police activity in towns near the roadblock, feel directly injured and abandoned by the state.[20] As Renán Delgado, frustrated and contrite, remembers his son:

> He participated, as did his colleagues of the DINOES [Dirección de Operaciones Especiales, a special police force in Peru] . . . in protecting the mining companies, protecting private and public entities . . . (. . .) Really . . . the feelings have always been contradictory. On the one hand . . . of impotence, of not being able to do anything to arrive at the truth, of not being able to make the guilty ones pay. Impotence because in the entity, in the institution to which my son belonged, they are left in the background by the authorities in charge. Impotence because the press does not allow us to give our version of what happened, and yet Ms. Cabanillas goes from television program to television program giving her version. And we see that in our country we are not finding justice. And depending on how the facts are given, we see that this will continue like this. That's why every time I see the picture, I see the information, it makes me so angry . . . [*he cannot continue, tears interrupt him*].
> (Documentary *La espera* 2014: 1:05'15")

Two days after the confrontation, in his speech for Flag Day, President Alan García blamed the indigenous population for the tragedy and assured that he would not let the country's enemies impede its economic advance:

It is only a long, ongoing struggle that we live, defending the homeland from its adversaries. What is happening with our country, which does not defend the fundamental importance of its progress, which is a progress envied by other peoples? We have suffered an aggression that is the product of a conspiracy, which is that of those who do not want Peru to progress. They do not want progress because they have external interests, or because of their elementary ignorance. I know that the vast majority of Peruvians want development, want employment, and want modernity. That is the majority and modern country that must oppose formulas of savagery and barbarism that reappear.

(Speech by former President Alan García, June 7, 2009)

In the aftermath

As for the conflict itself, the situation has not changed, as protests and confrontations often recur due to the regulatory conditions governing the extraction of hydrocarbons and minerals and their direct impact on the living conditions of the local population. It can be said that "the causes of what is known as 'Baguazo' are maintained and the rights of indigenous peoples continue to be violated" (Paucar Albino 2017).

In the procedural field, in September 2016, the 52 indigenous people who had been incarcerated and accused of being responsible for the deaths of 12 policemen in Baguazo were acquitted by Peruvian justice. No other person was condemned. The attribution of responsibility, therefore, remains pending.

The Afrodita mine is still present and is even trying to reinitiate its mining activity in the area (Chamiquit et al. 2016).

The modality of the activity, and the living conditions of the inhabitants of the area, have led over the years to the exacerbation of the confrontation and the deficiencies since the incidence of diseases related to the toxic activity of oil companies (regular activity and spills) have increased in the area while living conditions have worsened. There are daily spills which, in the face of insufficient preventive intervention and repair by the State and the company, directly involve the Awajún population, not only as affected by pollution, but also directly addressed in cleanup work. Companies offer a pittance for adults and children, without protective clothing or equipment, to take buckets and collaborate in the cleanup of the spills by entering the areas and collecting the oil directly, as happened in February 2016 in Chiriaco due to losses of the Norperuano Pipeline, in the province of Bagua (Correo 2016; Hurtado 2017). This daily life increases their exposure to toxic substances and diseases, which occur from an early age. On that occasion,

> Several children of the community came to a sector of the shore, where the dark and toxic substance was concentrated. Carrying small buckets, some holding bottles and kitchen utensils, they worked between two hours and

one day. They had no protection over their bodies. Their presence there was explained in the offer that an engineer from Petroperú had made – some versions indicate that there were two engineers – of 150 soles for each large bucket of recovered oil.

(Hurtado 2017)[21]

Many deaths and many injuries in *Baguazo*, further, remain "invisible" to the state (Prado 2017).

Regarding the state attention provided to the basic needs of the population, anthropologist Alberto Chirif said, "The arbitrariness of the authorities who believe that they can do anything to bypass the rights of the people remained, although these were well-defined in the prior consultation; the prepotent action of the authorities remained" (Paucar Albino 2017).

This review of subsequent events in the political sphere provide a good example. Five years after the *Baguazo*, 70 civilians were investigated and no political authority was found responsible for the order. Minister Aráoz denied having suggested that the FTA with the United States could fail if the legislative decrees in favor of the indigenous request were repealed (Documentary *La espera* 2014: 1:08'40"). The decreed laws were annulled, and the FTA continued in force. Minister Aráoz, with a seat in Mexico, advises the Inter-American Development Bank. Minister Cabanillas was condecorated. June 5 – the anniversary of the Baguazo – was declared the National Day of Peruvian Rum by Alan García the following year. In speeches that the former president addresses to entrepreneurs, the tenor of his words continues to endorse economic intervention without regard for the consequences that it entails: *"The oil capital of the world is looking for where to invest. By God . . . how can we waste that?"* (Documentary *La espera* 2014: 1:10'27").

The *Valle de Siria* case in Honduras

The case

In 1995, in an exclusively agricultural area (Valle de Siria, Francisco Morazán, Honduras), a valley known both for its scarcity of surface water and for the extreme poverty in which its inhabitants live, the new gold rush of the international markets intensified interest in new regions. The Honduran government authorized and started exploration works of gold deposits by the company Mar West Resources, then Goldcorp (Canada) through its Honduran subsidiary Entre Mares. The exploitation was extended until 2008, when the activity ceased without information being provided to the general public or the community regarding the process of deactivation of the mine. Exploitation was carried out using the open-pit method, and this generated various forms of environmental damage both during the exploitation and after the closing of the mine (superficial and deep contamination of the land, cyanide-based contamination of water and air). As a consequence, this led to injuries to the physical integrity, health and lives of the inhabitants as well as severe negative effects at the socioeconomic level (Trucchi 2014; Torres Funes 2016; Cálix 2017). As summarized by the testimony of Carlos Amador, teacher and member of the Environmental Committee of Valle de Siria:

> Entre Mares S.A. came to the Valle de Siria with the theory of giving employment and development to thousands of people. What was actually generated were about 330 jobs and more poverty for thousands of peasant families who were left without income. Everything was a big lie, and we went from being the first producer of basic grains in the Francisco Morazán department to one of the most affected and poisoned areas in the country.
> (Trucchi 2014)

The environmental damage, therefore, came hand in hand with social disarticulation, the displacement of the population and the illness or death of its inhabitants.

The promise: regulatory simplification to achieve development

According to the Institute of Environmental Law of Honduras (IDAMHO) the Environmental Impact Study submitted to obtain the exploitation concession recognizes that during 1995 and 1996 "Minerales Entre Mares S.A. carried out geological, geochemical and geological mapping surveys throughout the concession". In 1996, five drilling operations were carried out, and between that year and 1999, two separate deposits were defined, called Rosa and Palo Alto, which later became the epicenter of the entire San Martín mining operation. The projections resulting from the exploration indicated that the Rosa Tajo would be active for extraction over the first five or six years of the project. Its surface area would cover around 43 hectares, and it would have a depth of 120 meters. On the other hand, the Tajo Palo Alto would operate between four and five years from year five of the project. Its surface area would cover about 25 hectares, and would have a depth of 200 meters. During this stage, the population was not consulted about the exploration activities or about the potential impact of a mining operation.[22] The communities and residents were also not properly informed about the scope and real risks of an extractive activity of this magnitude and its potential positive and negative impacts with respect to health, the environment, society and community or the economy. Minerals Entre Mares developed its exploration activities on the basis of agreements with the central government and on the basis of the provision of Article 12 of the Constitution of the Republic, which establishes the state's right of ownership (exercise of sovereignty) with respect to the subsoil of all the national territory. However, the provisions of article 1, paragraph 3 of the Covenant of Economic, Social and Cultural Rights, which has constitutional status and prevails in cases of conflict with the same constitution and other national laws (article 18 of the current Constitution) were not complied with. In this way, the right of communities to exercise self-determination over their economic, social and cultural rights was violated (IDAMHO 2012: 42/43).

A rural teacher warned that life would not improve under those conditions:

> They have defined what development is and told us that this is because a company will come to extract the materials. That is not development. That's looting sand, water, which is what happened here. And the looting of minerals. (. . .) Nowhere in the world is going to develop by extracting the materials.
>
> (Hada Zúñiga, Director of the Instituto Polivalente Holanda,
> El Pedernal, El Porvenir, in Francisco Morazán)
> (Documentary *La Mina San Martín* 2013: 12'36")

Juan Almendares of the Mother Earth Ecologist Movement summarizes the situation in a few words, saying that it is a

> disaster how the issue of mining has been handled. A total disaster, and by that I do not mean this government, but I mean practically everyone. SERNA [Office for Natural Resources and Environment] has caused a disaster, as has the Environmental Procurator Office.

And adds, shortly after,

> When it was said that the state is supporting what a community decides . . . a community may be right or not, but . . . where is a state policy? The policy of the State must be to defend life. And mining companies violate life in our country.
>
> (Documentary *La Mina San Martín* 2013: 2')

This violence happens not only in a structural and gradual way, but also even in a "violent" way, when the local population meets and forms an Environmental Committee for the claim for the situation, and its members are later criminalized, as in the case of Carlos Amador, who was detained with other comrades on July 5, 2011, for alleged obstruction of forest management – deforestation of 1,800 hectares of forest on the hill La Torrecita – and then declared innocent 18 months later (Trucchi 2014).

Death in slow motion

Clara Vega, Director of IDAMHO, also referred to the authorizations given by the state without considering the results, and explained that granting an environmental license to develop a mining project does not imply a previous environmental impact study (Documentary *La Mina San Martín* 2013: 7'50"). This lack of attention is reflected in the consequences, because more than 50 million tons of land were removed to extract gold, affecting agricultural production, which fell by 70%. In addition, 19 of the 21 existing water sources have dried up; those that remain are contaminated with heavy metals, which "generated an unprecedented water emergency", explained Pedro Landa, a mining specialist and member of the Coalition of Environmental Networks (Trucchi 2014).

Moreover, pollution is extremely serious: "We are poisoning these people" (Documentary *La Mina San Martín* 2013: 1'35"). It is not only pollution of surface water, but also the deep pollution of the earth. The acidic drainage generated there will remain for more than 100 years, contributing sulfuric acid to the permanent release of heavy metals (Documentary *La Mina San Martín* 2013: 8'58").

This grave contamination and release of heavy metals in open-pit mining led to the emergence of various diseases both immediately and in the medium and long term. During the operation of the mine, many workers and residents suffered hair loss and sores on their bodies. As time went by, even after the mining activities had ceased, skin damage was seen, as were new health problems such as malformations, miscarriages, premature births, and cancer. Due to the reports and studies that were carried out, it was finally decided to take samples from residents in order to assess the level of contamination contained in their blood. In the 62 cases surveyed after long studies lasting between three and four years, dramatic results were officially recorded: in all cases, the studies confirmed the presence in the blood of heavy metals such as lead and mercury in levels that are plainly lethal. Since 2007, when these results were announced, these people and other residents of the Valle de Siria have not received medical treatment (Torres Funes 2016).

Two concrete references on the case provide a better idea of the seriousness of the situation:

> The research study "Water pollution in the area of mining exploitation of the San Martín project and repercussions on human health", carried out by Flaviano Bianchini in 2006, reveals that in one of the communities affected by mining exploitation, infant mortality reaches the value of 300‰ (per thousand), that is 12 times higher than the national average. These values increase markedly for the children of mine workers. In this case the mortality rate reaches 833‰ or 33 times the national average.
>
> (Trucchi 2014)

Children are dying, but nobody sees it because they are not being shot or beaten by a physical individual in a concrete action. Physical violence is instantaneous and visible, and for this reason, individuals resorting to this violence can be held responsible for it. Physical diseases and death from poisoning, on the contrary, are neither instantaneous, nor visible, and can be attributed even less to individualized persons. It happens inadvertently. Slowly. This is what can be called death in slow motion ("*muerte en cámara lenta*").[23]

A specific case can explain this and show that a sufficiently detailed report can make that death visible even before it happens. In this case, health was affected by environmental conditions even before birth and generated a direct effect on health and life from the very conception of a baby girl. This was caused by her own and her parents' exposure to heavy metals such as those produced in the leaching processes that took place during the mining exploitation in the valley.

> In the case of the girl – 10 – of New Palo Ralo, there is no indicator of Werdnig-Hoffmann syndrome in the parental history. The girl has blood values of 173 ug/dl of lead and 263 ug/dl of arsenic. Both metals, and others that could be present in their blood, are teratogens, that is to say they cause genetic mutations, and are transmissible between mother and daughter via the placenta. Then the most likely cause of the disease is that the pollutants to which the parents and the girl herself have been subjected for years have caused the genetic mutation on chromosome 5 in the girl, causing Werdnig-Hoffmann syndrome.
>
> It can be affirmed from now on, this girl's days are numbered. Soon her lungs will no longer be able to move alone and her stomach will not be able to fulfill the movements necessary for digestion. If it is possible, the girl could be fed by a tube leading directly into her stomach, and helped with an artificial lung for some time, but it will not be possible in the long term and the girl will die very young.
>
> (IDAMHO 2012: 68)

Traceable economic violence

In the four cases presented in this chapter, physical violence in diverse forms was presented as the climax to each situation.

The cases were different and were made public differently as well. In some cases, it was media information that prevailed, whereas in others, it was testimonials, and in some it was scientific sources. In all, however, regardless of the method of disclosure and where the principal attention was focused, the last part of the story was a description of the "traditionally" violent, that is, a situation of physical direct visible violence.

All four cases could have been seen out of context and described as particular cases of unscrupulous policemen, mafia businessmen, soldiers accustomed to authoritarian violence or company employees who violated the mandate and aggressively abused the situation when seeing women alone. Any of these explanations, however, though they may describe "the picture" with some veracity, would simply repeat the bias with which these episodes have been studied, and attention would be reduced to the observation of physical violence.

Even if the alleged perpetrators of acts of direct violence were prosecuted, as was the case in some of the situations, for crimes of homicide, assault or rape, for example, the approach would remain partial. This is what happened in the case of the murders of Cristián Ferreyra and Rafael Galván of MOCASE, the last case reviewed in the previous chapter, where there were criminal convictions to those directly responsible for homicides ordered by businessmen, but none of businessmen were convicted. The *film* remained unknown, or it was so desired that it remain unknown as context of that *photo* of the material responsible, so that only this picture of someone with a gun firing at a minor or driving a knife into someone's throat was condemned, a picture that was captured in an instant, and in only one of the many negatives that made up the tape.

This is what was revealed here: the moment of physical violence can be very brief and entail only a few hours of shots and machetes in a conflict spanning months, a few minutes of carnal access, and blows in an invasion of territory can last a couple of hours but be motivated by a territorial conflict going back years, a child can stop breathing in less than a second because of heavy metals carried in her blood, or her parents' blood, since before she was conceived. Each of these brief moments, almost ephemeral, is part of a network of relationships, systems and structures, as Galtung would say, that intrinsically shape the moment of shooting, stabbing, aggressive carnal access or the cessation of breathing.

These relationships, systems and structures were necessary conditions for the moment of direct violence to take place. Although it seems that the presence of violence cannot be perceived, it is very much present. It is invisible, of course, but it can be made visible.

It is not a matter of bringing every politician or legislator to criminal trial, nor every businessman who decides to invest and thus seeks the means to extend productive lands or to maximize his yields. It is a first step – a big step – not to deny that those decisions are the ones that could engender physical violence. And the physical violence that always appears in connection with violence that remains invisible must be addressed.

If political and economic measures, and in particular the deregulation that by transnational impulse has been increasing over the past few decades, can lead to an improvement to the state economy and to national development in general, this must be measurable, not only later, when the plans do not work, but also before.

The study of the interrelations among structural, cultural and physical violence has the objective of facilitating the possibility of tracking links, untangling the skein and working patiently on the detection of knots and threads.

Only in this way can it be thought that noncompliance with the promises of development, directly linked to the perpetuation of violence, can be considered differently.

How interrelationships occur over time will be studied in more depth in the next chapter through an analysis of the cases presented in this chapter and the previous one. The rotation of the triangle of violence, which explains the vicious circle between international and transnational interests in the economy, as well as the deficiencies and violence in local areas, must be able to reveal the differences between the film and the photo, between the visible and the invisible and, especially, between the traceable and the untraceable in the responsibilities. This will form the substance of the next chapter.

Notes

1 I would like to mention and thank Silvina A. Alonso, a member of the Research Group on Corporations and Humans Rights that I lead, and a PhD student and a lecturer at the Law School of the University of Buenos Aires, because she first spoke to me about this case, and I could see that it was a story, as Galtung says, worth telling. See different cases analyzed by the Inter-American Commission on Human Rights about the links among economic actors, security forces and physical and sexual aggression in its 2016 report on Guatemala, par. 137–138, 213 (ICHR 2016, *Situación de los Derechos Humanos en Guatemala*, OEA/Ser.L/V/II. December 31, 2015).

2 ICHR 2016, *Situación de los Derechos Humanos en Guatemala*, OEA/Ser.L/V/II. December 31, 2015, par. 80.

3 UN, A/HRC/16/xx. 2011. *Observaciones sobre la situación de los derechos de los pueblos indígenas de Guatemala en relación con los proyectos extractivos, y otro tipo de proyectos, en sus territorios tradicionales*, Informe del Relator Especial de Naciones Unidas sobre los derechos de los pueblos indígenas, March 4, p. 17.

4 As another example, about Mexico, see Carlsen (2012).

5 For data about concrete cases of violence against women related to mining projects in various countries, see Solano Ortiz (2015).

6 In both cases, the analysis by Luz Méndez Gutiérrez offers detailed information and several critical thoughts needed for an integral understanding of the complexity and context of Guatemala today. See interview by Garay Zarraga and Gago Menor (2013).

7 "On September 27 of the same year (2006), employees of CGN/HudBay Minerals tried to violently and extrajudicially evict the inhabitants of Las Nubes, claiming that the inhabitants had occupied land reserved for the project. That day, a strong contingent of National Civil Police, members of the Army and private police, under the orders of retired Lieutenant Colonel Mynor Ronaldo Padilla González, using company cars and accompanied by the departmental governor Luz Maribel Ramos Peña, tried in vain to evict to the inhabitants. When the governor had left, the villagers went to the road, where employees of the mine were waiting for them. They wounded at least 8 people and killed the teacher Adolfo Ich Chaman, who, according to his son, was shot and then cut with a machete by private guards and Mynor Ronaldo Padilla González himself" (CMI 2014).

8 See information on the Hudbay lawsuits (sexual violation against women, and homicide of a community leader and teacher) and the current stand under: www.eldiario.es/the-guardian/Indigenas-Guatemala-enfrentan-multinacionales-canadienses_0_718129021. html; https://business-humanrights.org/en/hudbay-minerals-lawsuits-re-guatemala-0#c134836 and www.chocversushudbay.com/la-demanda?lang=es.

9 See the official announcement on the website *Cámara Notícias – Câmara dos Deputados*. 2017, August 17.
    http://www2.camara.leg.br/camaranoticias/noticias/agropecuaria/539298-agricul tura-aprova-criacao-da-agencia-de-desenvolvimento-do-matopiba.html

10 About the *grilagem* as a process of documentary fraud and physical appropriation of public lands, and the violence that this entails, see Mathias (2017).

11 Representatives of the rural sector are currently trying to make this restrictive law more flexible (Draft 4059/12).

12 See Temer's campaign video in relation to the agrobusiness: www.youtube.com/watch?v=rs2B2dhJtQQ

13 Specifically, as explained by Karina Kato, researcher at the Observatory of Public Policies for Agriculture, "What happened was a deinstitutionalization: you no longer have in the Ministry of Agriculture a structure that controls or tries to articulate these national and international private investments. Which can even speed up the process, because you leave the whole dynamics in the hands of private initiative" (Mathias 2017: 17).

14 This refers to the fact that in the State of Piauí, for example, the new Fund Regularization Law (6,709/15) does not recognize the right of possession and proposes individual titling for small producers, or in the State of Bahia, State Law 12,910 of 2013 states that if communities are not recognized by 2018, they will lose the right to regularize their territory.

15 In general, to understand the history and expansion of agribusiness in Brazil in particular, and in Latin America in general, see the documentary *Tierra en transformación* (2013).

16 "Deforestation grew by 61% between 2000 and 2014 in Matopiba, and the area of soybean cultivation increased by 253% between 2000 and 2014 (from 1 million to 3.4 million hectares), expanding this monoculture mainly to areas of native vegetation of Maranhão e Piauí" (Mathias 2017: 14).

17 On this increase, see also Maina (2017).

18 See general information on the case in the documentary *La espera* (2014).

19 Cf. Articles *El síndrome del perro del hortelano* (October 28, 2007), focused on indigenous communities and defenders of the environment and community lands; *Receta para acabar con el perro del hortelano* (November 25, 2007), where emphasis is placed on actions and the need to reduce state control, acceleration of licensing procedures for enterprises and investments and redistribution of state assets in private hands is raised; and *El perro del hortelano contra el pobre* (March 2, 2008), an aggressive article against defenders of rights and those who demand the need for structural social services and assistance from the state, in which data are presented that would confirm the government's attention "to the poor", and that would legitimize its action before those "communists" who do not want the poor to do well, and therefore hinder or minimize the achievements made by the state in this regard. The articles are no longer available on the *El Comercio* newspaper page, but they are accessible online: www.google.com.ar/url?sa=t&rct=j&q=&esrc=s&source=web&cd=6&ved=0ahUKEwiqx624vODaAhWEIZAKHX-UC3IQFghEMAU&url=http%3A%2F%2Fperuesmas.com%2Fbiblioteca-jorge%2FAlan-Garcia-Perez-y-el-perro-del-hortelano.pdf&usg=AOvVaw1PPk44Z56JPa4TXWVl4aaa

20 On the injured civilians who have not received any answer or reparation from the state, see Prado (2017).

21 Note: 150 soles corresponded to around US$45 at that time.

22 The "silent" way for companies to arrive is repeated again and again when the gold rush requires more and more. As an illustration, see the documentary film *Gold Fever* (2013).

23 My recognition to Marco Abudara Bini, an engaged future colleague, who in his first research exercise on this topic in the seminar on Corporations and Human Rights (School of Law, University of Buenos Aires) was able to see invisible violences and to explain them in a touching way. He suggested the expression *death in slow motion (muerte en cámara lenta)*.

References

Cálix, Martín. 2017. "El Valle de la Esperanza". *Contracorriente*. October 4. https://contracorriente.red/2017/10/05/el-valle-de-la-esperanza/

Campelo, Lilian. 2017. "Terras na região do Cerrado viram alvo de especuladores". *Racismo Ambiental*. February 6. https://racismoambiental.net.br/2017/02/06/terras-na-regiao-do-cerrado-viram-alvo-de-especuladores/

Carlsen, Laura. 2012. "Matar a la mensajera: Crece la violencia contra las defensoras de derechos humanos". *Pensamiento Crítico*. December 10. www.pensamientocritico.org/laucar0113.htm

Carlsen, Laura. 2014. "¿Por qué una mayor seguridad trae mayor violencia contra las mujeres en América Latina?" *DesInformémonos*. March 23. https://desinformemonos.org/por-que-una-mayor-seguridad-trae-mayor-violencia-contra-las-mujeres-en-america-latina/

Castro, Jorge. 2017. "El boom de la producción agrícola en Brasil". *Clarín*. January 20. www.clarin.com/rural/boom-producci-agr-cola-brasil_0_H1t0e-nIg.html

Ceratti, Mariana. 2016. "Brasil: dueño de 20% del agua del mundo, pero con mucha sed". *Banco Mundial*. August 1. www.bancomundial.org/es/news/feature/2016/07/27/how-brazil-managing-water-resources-new-report-scd

Chamiquit, Clelia Jima/Mayan, Augustina/Perez, Wrays. 2016. "Minera Afrodita tiene permiso de explotación en Cordillera del Cóndor". *SERVINDI*. August 24. www.servindi.org/actualidad-noticias/23/08/2016/minera-afrodita-tiene-permiso-de-explotacion-de-oro-en-cordillera-del

CMI. 2014. "Níquel: Minería, Militares y Muerte en Guatemala". *Red CMI Guatemala*. April 8. https://cmiguate.org/niquel-mineria-militares-y-muerte-en-guatemala/#rf11-3971

Correo. 2016. "Bagua: Alarma por contaminación de petróleo en río Marañón y Chiriaco". *Dirio Correo*. February 12. https://diariocorreo.pe/regional/bagua-alarma-por-contaminacion-de-petroleo-en-rio-maranon-y-chiriaco-video-653301/

De Olho. 2017. "Violência no sul do Piauí lembra a do Pará, aponta Fiocruz". *De Olho nos ruralistas*. January 5. https://deolhonosruralistas.com.br/2017/01/05/violencia-no-sul-do-piaui-lembra-do-para-aponta-fiocruz/

FIAN. 2017. "La Caravana Matopiba insta a las autoridades brasileñas a tomar acción, alerta a los inversores". *FIAN International*. September 19. www.fian.org/es/noticias/articulo/caravana_matopiba_urges_brazilian_authorities_to_take_action_warns_foreign_investors/

G1. 2017. "Perícia e recontituição em Pau DArco confirmam cenáro de execução com indício de crime encomendado". *O Globo*. September 3. https://g1.globo.com/pa/para/noticia/pericia-e-reconstituicao-em-pau-darco-confirmam-cenario-de-execucao-com-indicio-de-crime-encomendado.ghtml

Garay Zarraga, Ane/Gago Menor, Andrea. 2013. "Luz Méndez, investigadora y activista guatemalteca: 'Las mujeres en Guatemala se organizan y piden justicia'". *Revista Pueblos*. July 26. www.revistapueblos.org/blog/2013/07/26/luz-mendez-investigadora-y-activista-guatemalteca-las-mujeres-estan-luchando-en-guatemala-se-organizan-y-piden-justicia/

Gilvander Moreira, Frei. 2017. "Concentrar terra para crescer o capital e a violência". *MST*. November 23. www.mst.org.br/2017/11/23/concentrar-terra-para-crescer-o-capital-e-a-violencia.html

Gonçalves de Souza, Ivonete. 2017. "Eucalipto y el veneno silencioso: expansión del monocultivo en el extremo sur de Bahía, Brasil". *Boletín del Movimiento Mundial por los Bosques Tropicales (WRM)* 233, 8–13.

Gorenstein, Silvia. 2016. *Empresas transnacionales en la agricultura y la producción de alimentos en América Latina y el Caribe*, Buenos Aires: Nueva Sociedad/Friedrich Ebert Stiftung.

Hurtado, Jonathan. 2017. "El destino de los niños afectados por petróleo en el Perú: A un año del derrame en el Chiriaco". February 11. www.caaap.org.pe/website/2017/02/11/el-destino-de-los-ninos-afectados-por-petroleo-en-el-peru-a-un-ano-del-derrame-en-el-chiriaco/

IDAMHO (Instituto de Derecho Ambiental de Honduras). 2012. *La mina San Martín en el Valle de Siria. Exploración, explotación y cierre: impactos y consecuencas*, San Ignacio: FM/IDAHO/OXFAM.

ILO. 2000. *Safety and Health in Agriculture*. International Labour Office.

IM-Defensoras. 2017. "Guatemala. Asesinan a Laura Leonor Vásquez de Pineda, defensora del territorio". *Iniciativa Mesoamericana de Mujeres Defensoras de Derechos Humanos.* January 18. im-defensoras.org/2017/01/alertadefensoras-guatemala-asesinan-a-laura-leonor-vasquez-pineda-defensora-del-territorio/

JASS. 2012. "Maya K'Iche' Leader Says No to Violence Against Women". *JustAssociates.* https://justassociates.org/en/womens-stories/maya-kiche-leader-says-no-violence-against-women

Maina, Lucía. 2017. "MST de Brasil: 'La violencia en el campo aumentó drásticamente'. Interview with Maura Silva". *La Tinta.* August 17. https://latinta.com.ar/2017/08/mst-brasil-violencia-campo-aumento/

Martín, María. 2017. "Una nueva matanza revela la barbarie por los conflictos agrarios en Brasil". *El País.* May 27. https://elpais.com/internacional/2017/05/25/actualidad/1495737149_649329.html

Mathias, Maíra. 2017. "Matopiba: na fronteira entre a vida e o capital". *EPSJV/Fiocruz.* September 19. www.epsjv.fiocruz.br/noticias/reportagem/matopiba-na-fronteira-entre-a-vida-e-o-capital

Mejía, Rocío/Quispe, Juan. 2017. "El Baguazo ocho años después". *Lamula.pe.* June 4. https://redaccion.lamula.pe/2017/06/04/el-baguazo-ocho-anos-despues/redaccionmulera/

Méndez Gutiérrez, Luz. 2013. "Guatemala: Abriendo brecha en la búsqueda de la justicia – las valientes mujeres q'eqchís". *visionews.net.* October. www.visionews.net/es/guatemala-abriendo-brecha-en-la-busqueda-de-justicia-las-mujeres-valientes-q%C2%B4eqchis/

OMCT/FIDH/UDEFEGUA. 2015. *Guatemala. 'Smaller than David': The struggle of Human Rights Defenders.* International Fact-Finding Mission Report. February 23. www.fidh.org/es/temas/defensores-de-derechos-humanos/17044-mas-pequenos-que-david-la-lucha-de-los-defensores-y-defensoras-de-derechos

Paucar Albino, Jorge. 2017. "Experto en temas amazónicos advierte que las causas del Baguazo se mantienen". Interview with Prof. Alberto Chirif *Lamula.pe.* June 5. https://redaccion.lamula.pe/2017/06/05/baguazo-2009-bagua-conflicto-peru-alan-garcia-causas-aniversario-pueblos-indigenas/jorgepaucar/

Prado, Manuel Angelo. 2017. "Las víctimas invisibles (y colaterales) del Baguazo". *lamula.pe.* June 4. https://redaccion.lamula.pe/2017/06/04/las-victimas-invisibles/manuelangeloprado/

REDE. 2015. "A empresa Radar S/A e a especulação com terras no Brasil". *Rede Social de Justiça e Direitos Humanos.* www.social.org.br/files/pdf/RevistaREDE2015paranet%202.pdf

Rivera, Nelton. 2017. "Izabal: La Justicia es solo para las empresas mineras". *km 169 – Prensa comunitaria.* April 18. www.prensacomunitaria.org/izabal-la-justicia-es-solo-para-las-empresas-mineras/

RLMDDSA (Red Latinoamericana de Mujeres Defensoras de los Derechos Sociales y Ambientales). 2017. *Letter Asking for the Stopping of Violent Extractive Activities in Latin America.* www.salvalaselva.org/peticion/1044/mujeres-denuncian-que-proyectos-extractivos-generan-violencia

Romero Cano, Ana. 2014. "Bagua a 5 años del TLC con EE.UU". *Diario Uno.* June 6. http://diariouno.pe/columna/bagua-a-5-anos-del-tlc-con-ee-uu/

Seigner Ameni, Cauê. 2017. "Democracia já tem quase 2 mil assassinatos políticos no campo". *MST.* March 20. www.mst.org.br/2017/03/20/democracia-ja-tem-quase-2-mil-assassinatos-politicos-no-campo.html

Solano Ortiz, Lina. 2015. "Mujer, violencia e industria minera". *Otros mundos.* August 31. www.otrosmundoschiapas.org/index.php/temas-analisis/32-32-mineria/2070-mujer-violencia-e-industria-minera

Svampa, Maristella. 2017. *Del cambio de época al fin de ciclo. Gobiernos progresistas, extractivismo y movimientos sociales en América Latina*, Buenos Aires: Edhasa.

Torres Funes, Ariel. 2016. "Valle de Siria: Oro, pobreza y resistencia". *El Pulso HN*. September 27. http://elpulso.hn/valle-de-siria-oro-pobreza-y-resistencia/

Trucchi, Giorgio. 2014. "Actividad minera en región de Honduras deja rastro de enfermedades, destrucción ambiental y desempleo". *Nicaragua y más*. September 7. https://nicaraguaymasespanol.blogspot.com.ar/2014/09/actividad-minera-en-region-de-honduras.html

Vida Nueva. 2017. "La impunidad perpetúa la violencia rural en Brasil". *Vida Nueva Cono Sur*. May 2. www.vidanuevadigital.com/2017/05/02/la-impunidad-perpetua-la-violencia-rural-brasil/

WRM. 2003. "Los impactos de la minería sobre las mujeres". *Boletín WRM*. June. http://wrm.org.uy/oldsite/boletin/71/mujeres.html

WRM. 2015. "Brasil: Paren con el monocultivo de eucalipto!" *Boletim WRM*. October 14. http://wrm.org.uy/es/articulos-del-boletin-wrm/seccion2/brasil-paren-con-el-monocultivo-de-eucalipto/

Filmography

Gold Fever. 2013. Documentary film. Dir. J.T. Haines, T. Haines and A. Sherburne. USA/Canadá/Guatemala.

Tierra en transformación: Agronegocio o agroecología. 2013. Documentary. Dir. Nils Bucher, Michaela Danielsson, Lisa Persson. Brasil/Sweden. www.dailymotion.com/video/xt2vm3

La espera. 2014. Documentary. Dir. Fernando Vílchez Rodríguez. Perú. www.youtube.com/watch?v=pVkONDVbe-w

La Mina San Martín en el Valle de Siria. Un ejemplo de los impactos de la minería en Honduras. 2013. Documentary. Realized by IDAMHO. Honduras. www.youtube.com/watch?v=LeoBg41Ow-c

Tierra en transformación: Agronegocio o agroecología. 2013. Documentary. Dir. Nils Bucher, Michaela Danielsson, Lisa Persson. Brasil/Sweden. www.dailymotion.com/video/xt2vm3

Part III

Chapter 5

The vicious circle of deregulated international businesses and violence

The case studies from Mexico, Ecuador, Chile, Argentina, Guatemala, Peru, Brazil and Honduras in the previous chapters have shown relations between domestic and international economy, and their relations with violence in each respective country. Concrete data and stories were presented and located in specific times and places and, at the same time, a panoramic view should have been reached. This previous work may now allow an integral analytical-conceptual approach in terms of social, economic and institutional dynamics over time.

This chapter, therefore, is marked by the idea of process. The vicious circle of the relationship between deregulated economic activities and violence in Latin America should be understood as a process, begun more than five centuries ago, formed in turn by the synchronic and diachronic framework of minor processes. These processes – many of them illustrated in the aforementioned chapters – can be thought of in terms of progressive mutation following the logics of circularity, as if it were a spiral in that each loop would seem to return to the same point, but in reality, it does so with a slight displacement.

It is probably apparent that the richness of some contexts, which are increasingly rich, is nourished by the poverty in other contexts, which are increasingly poor. Or, in other words, that development in some contexts is based on maldevelopment in others. As it was said by a Mapuche leader, Alihuen Antileo:

> The economic decisions that affect the large sectors in this country are taken in Spain, they are taken in the United States, in Japan, in New Zealand, or at the different stock exchanges of New York, Tokyo, or anywhere else. What we have in Chile are servile political classes subordinated to those great economies, and that economic model is the one that is depredating our natural resources, wants to continue advancing into the ancestral Mapuche territory and condemns us to slow genocide. So to speak, the opulence of the economic system that can develop in Europe is financed by the misery of my people and by the misery of many peoples in both

America and Africa and the rest of the world, who have been called Third World peoples.

(Documentary film *Apaga y vámonos* 2005)

If opulence is financed by misery, misery will never stop, because opulence does not know any limit. This view seems realistic, and it has been in some way confirmed by the cases presented in Chapters 3 and 4. However, this vicious circle – this is exactly what it is, a vicious circle – cannot be accepted as a natural, unavoidable reality. To accept it would be to become an accomplice of cultural violence; it would mean accepting conditions as given and would be, therefore, a silent justification of the status quo. Some are not capable of considering another way. To them, this acceptance of the vicious circle of violent economic models and all kinds of violence can be explained as unavoidable. To politicians, economists, entrepreneurs and scholars, this naturalization of the status quo is inexcusable because this way of thinking is avoidable. As Galtung explained: although it is true that the natural quality of a country is given, precisely, by nature, it is not the same thing to recognize this fact of reality as it is to state in economic terms that there is no law that can modify a country's production profile. We must agree with Galtung that this affirmation only crystallizes as real a political and conceptual economic decision that, in many cases, leads precisely to unsatisfied needs. That is to say, it is about the exercise of cultural violence by a theoretical and political proposal that justifies in a certain context that the potentiality of realization of certain needs and their satisfaction is not achieved (Galtung 1996: 206).

To stop this way of thinking, thus, it is suggested that we see not only the whole picture (the photo), but the whole film, or at least as much of it as possible. There are moments in the film which should be captured and should not be ignored. Willful blindness is not acceptable when life and death are at stake.

In the first part of the chapter, then, the phases that can be perceived in the vicious circle between deregulating unchecked economic policies and measures and violence will be presented with examples of current processes in the region. It will be seen that some special features are central in these processes: territory and dissociation among the actors linked to this territory. There are extremely empowered actors on the one hand – who are often far from the territory – and then there are individuals who are dejected and neglected in terms of their life needs and human integrity: these people are immediately related to the territory. These two features, evidenced time and again, are symptomatic of what Michel Foucault explained about the sovereign strategy of power seen in Europe over the centuries. Because their conceptual considerations appear as useful explicative tools, the second part of the chapter will present a Foucauldian approach to sovereign power and biopolitics. Last, the third part will focus on an explanation of the utility of this approach for the Latin American situation and its failed development. This explanation is intended as a base for the further description of maldevelopment as a criminological conceptual category in the next and last chapter.

Phases of the vicious circle of violence in the regional long-term perspective

Preexisting invisible violence

In all the cases presented in Chapters 3 and 4, both in those concerning specific extractive enterprises – the cases of *Salaverna* (Frisco) and *El Peñasquisto* (Goldcorp), *Texaco/Chevron*, *Ralco* (Endesa), *Valle de Siria* (Goldcorp) and *Indigenous Women of Lote 8* (CGN/Hudbay), and also in those in which new measures and political economic interests have begun to shape new policies and changes to the territory – the cases of *MOCASE, Baguazo* and *Matopiba*, it is noted that the communities or people directly affected by these interests were those the most underserved by the State and that they were hardly considered as "equal" by the rest of the population.

There is the paradoxical situation that in these cases, those most in need of constructive state attention receive such attention, but in the opposite direction to that required. It is precisely the high level of invisible violence suffered by these parts of the population which ends up justifying the objective of the new measures or new ventures: the "lack of development" seems to justify the state's interest in dealing with the area and its people, and these words are spoken and are acted out locally, nationally and even internationally through political and economic spokespeople – often widespread, thanks the time conceded to them by the media. The arrival of *Texaco* in the province of Sucumbíos, which was at that time not even given consideration in the statistical information of the State, was carried out with "civilization" promises, and Goldcorp also started, in *El Peñasquito* in Mexico and in *Valle de Siria* in Honduras, activities under the promise of more opportunities for the local population. The development claimed by representatives of the Peruvian and Brazilian Executive branches before (and also after) the massacres of the *Baguazo* and of Brazilian peasants because of *Matopiba* respectively, were also touted as development possibilities for the most marginalized population, who would be favored by the new measures. The high rates of unemployment explicitly mentioned by the inhabitants in the *Salaverna, El Peñasquito* and *Valle de Siria* cases, the lack of peaceful access to sufficient means of subsistence in cases of peasants and rural communities (the *MOCASE* and *Matopiba* cases) – among other necessities that the local population knows and suffers permanently, sometimes even because of prior large economic projects which have left them without work or without land, clean water or a natural environment for them to produce their traditional food (all cases!) – seem to feed the hope that "this time" the state's concern is genuine and that the new activity or economic measure can have a positive impact. On the other hand, there is usually not much choice. Again and again, local populations are exposed both to the state and to potential economic actors, who redouble their chorus of promises.

In fact, in cases in which such promises are not so readily accepted, physical violence begins to take place in the form of repression or criminalization much earlier than in cases where the people decide to give the new venture a chance. Another important spectrum of deficiencies must be added to the previous economic, labor and educational situation as it has been observed. In terms of information and access to state offices through which demands for control and protection should be promoted, the lack of service has been egregious in all eight cases. The elderly from the Mapuche population in *Ralco* had to travel a long distance to the responsible office, indigenous people from the province of Bagua (*Baguazo* case) were not even heard and the *Indigenous Women of Lote 8* and people from Sucumbíos (*Texaco/Chevron* case) were in areas where the state was not present at all.

The sum of unmet basic needs is hence the existential platform of the local population. From a victimological point of view, it is not difficult to see this context as a catalyst of multiple victimization processes, as will be shown.

New forms of invisible violence

To see new forms of invisible violence, it is useful to present the areas in which international and foreign economic and political investments and interests, as well as international regulations, have been taking place throughout the twentieth and twenty-first centuries, and to review how such initiatives were presented when they arrived in Latin America and were translated at the national level. It is necessary to note the large number of cases in which these international and foreign interests were mobilized at the national level in Latin America in the context of development programs. Significant examples could be the promise of food in agriculture that leads to more poverty (as it did in the *MOCASE* and *Matopiba* cases), the promise of energy that is then used by the industry (as in the *Ralco* case), the promise of more work in the exploitation of natural resources that not only does not generate a significant amount of local labor, but also reduces production to metals that leave the country in order to be manufactured and gain value abroad for the foreign population, while the local towns and their inhabitants become displaced, impoverished and sick (as in the *Texaco/Chevron*, *Salaverna*, *El Peñasquito*, *Valle de Siria* and *Indigenous Women of Lote 8* cases). In a few cases, these major programs invest in education or technical and vocational training.

The formation of "human capital", in economic terms, does not belong to the field of investments that are interesting in the international sphere, and therefore, they are not encouraged by national governments in their international relationships either. For this reason, the division of labor at the international level (as mentioned in Chapter 2) does not seem to be able to change. New structural needs are added to old structural needs. For this reason, the promised development is never achieved: what is presented as "development" is, in fact, the intensification of mechanisms that stall the economies and policies of the Global South.

The deepening of the self-perception of excluded individuals on the one hand, and the perpetuated conviction that foreign countries can better administrate their economies on the other hand, can be seen as renewed cultural violence reinforcing the non-satisfaction of self-realization in a population's own cultural identity and at the same time a justification in the hands of powerful actors who explain that the conditions cannot be changed at the local level.

This reiteration of dynamics perpetuates the role of the South as a supplier of primary products and of cheap and unqualified manpower to the center or Global North, as already mentioned. It is a division of labor on an international scale that leaves insufficient room for structural changes at the local level. Some figures make this evident as well with respect to the land question:

> A study by the British NGO Oxfam launched in November 2016 concluded that fewer than 1% of Brazilian farms possess 45% of the rural area of the country. Correntina ranks among the most unequal cities, where large estates occupy a significant 75% of the total area of agricultural establishments. The report, which compares several databases, shows that the agribusiness bonanza is in the hands of a few. According to the latest Census of Agriculture made by the IBGE in 2006, the Gross Domestic Product (GDP) of Correntina was R $ 786 thousand, a wealth that if divided by the 31 thousand inhabitants, would give just over R $ 25 thousand per capita. As far back as 2012, data from the Federal Government's Single Register for Social Programs showed that poverty reached 45% of the rural population and 31.8% of the general population. The human development index (HDI) of the municipality was 0.603 in 2010, below the national average (0.813). And the city's land concentration index is 0.927 on a scale where the maximum is 1. Oxfam conducted the same survey in 15 other Latin American countries and found that the development logic based on the intense exploitation of natural resources prevails in the regions which favor the concentration of land and wealth in the hands of a few families, and worsens the economic and social indicators for the rest of the population.
>
> (Mathias 2017)

The same thing has happened in the history of metal mining, hydrocarbons, renewable energy (hydroelectric, wind), infrastructure industries (roads, bridges and facilities for those who produce the aforementioned and for their transport), at the expense of the environment and the living conditions of the population originally living there, which receives with open arms the promise of progress, and is then seated next to its open mountains, its contaminated soils, its deforested forests and its diversity of crops replaced by the extensions of harmful monocultures, designed for the feeding of other populations or for the generation of energy or consumer goods to be consumed in other regions.

The concern for the continued loss of structural conditions is even shared by some political actors from the Global North and has been crystallized in the form of consultation, for example to the European Union, regarding the transnational purchases of land for agriculture in countries in development in which States of the Union operate. In the question, there are data offered and later confirmed by the European Union in its answer – which also expressed its concern and explained that it is working, through regulations and directives, to counteract these practices:

> The report entitled "Transnational Land Deals for Agriculture in the Global South", published in April 2012 by a European consortium of research institutes and centres, affirms that investors or State agencies in rich or emerging countries have purchased more than 83 million hectares of arable land (approximately 1.7 % of global arable land) in the poorest developing countries since 2000.
>
> The study identifies how approximately 45 % of purchases of existing arable land and almost one third of the land acquired may pose risks to biodiversity. Furthermore, according to the report, the aim of more than 40% of these projects is to export food to the countries of origin, which may suggest that food security is one of the main reasons to buy land, even at the expense of the countries where the land is located.
>
> Another report entitled "Our Land, Our Lives", presented by Oxfam International in October 2012, refers to 21 formal complaints brought since 2008 for violation of land ownership rights by communities affected by World Bank projects.[1]

The permanent internationalization of the actors is, therefore, another of the central themes that make up new structures and, at the same time, new impediments to the realization of basic needs. States, economic unions, corporations and international financing institutions are international actors shaping the structural conditions at the local level, which has been described as *crimes of globalization* (Friedrichs & Rothe 2015, see next Chapter).

This internationalization contributes, in turn, to the complexity of conflicts and the possibilities of unraveling them on the part of the local population, as can be seen with the example of land in Brazil related to the *Matopiba* case:

> If the agrarian question in Brazil was already a barrel of gunpowder due to the grilagem,[2] to the extent that landowners cease to be the familiar colonels to become opaque capitals, the situation tends to complicate. The owners of the land have no relation to it: we do not even know who they are. The joint venture has no face; the pension fund has no face. Before it was the Brazilian landowners, now they are also the foreign landowners. And the people who were meant to access the land in Brazil never did. From the point of view of the struggle, getting to the foreign landlords will be impossible. They are untouchable. Conflicts tend to intensify.
>
> (Daniela Egger, in Mathias 2017)

Due to the intensification of the conditions of structural violence, conflicts are increasing. Hence, the recourse to physical violence is becoming more immediate.

New forms of visible violence

Whereas international standards have a direct impact on national economies, economic policies have an immediate influence on social life. Furthermore, when this economic and social life develops in a context of structural violence, it has been seen that physical violence and insecurity in individual, social and political life is often an immediate consequence. This physical violence can be seen in at least four different ways of expression, also present in the cases described in the former chapters.

A first expression is physical violence *on the part of individuals and communities affected* by the economic projects. In this case, physical violence appears as the last resort for rejecting structurally violent conditions and claiming through this visible mean for the respect of their own rights, such as acknowledgment of legislation or due access to justice spheres, which have been disregarded by the state until then. The physical violence unchecked in the *Baguazo* case, in which indigenous people and policemen died, and one officer has even remained disappeared until today, is an example of this expression. Better conditions in the coming new relations with the arrived new actors or policies is also a common claim in these cases. As Galtung explains, this violence is physical violence, but it cannot be labeled as aggression – as many political actors do:

> Homo occidentalis, first as Catholics and then as Protestants, traveled all over the world making "discoveries", using direct violence to build this gigantic world pyramid of structural violence with democracies still on top. More direct violence followed, in self-defense, as revolutionary efforts to change the order and as counter-revolutionary violence to preserve it. To see the non-initiating as non-belligerent is not only bad politics but also bad social science, as it neglects third variables. When somebody is sitting on somebody else, chances are that the latter will move first; to call that "aggression" is somewhat far-fetched.
>
> (Galtung 1996: 52)

A second expression of physical violence arises *on the part of the corporations, businessmen or entrepreneurs* in protection of their facilities and investments, or in order to improve the obtained economic benefit through the expansion of their territorial domain. In the first case, the physical violence can be materially inflicted by agents of the corporation, as was the case of the employees of the mine who beat, threatened and raped *indigenous women of Lote 8* in Guatemala, invading their land and burning houses, for example, in order to achieve the goal of making these families abandon the area wanted by the company. The use of bulldozers to knock down a house, if this is done against the will of the inhabitants, or even to advance on people in a menacing way, as was the case with families in the *Salaverna* and *El Peñasquito* case, is physical violence as well. A different way is present in the rural areas in terms of land grabbing by means of aggression, homicide and even massacres against peasant communities, as in the cases *MOCASE* and *Matopiba*. In all these cases, along with the material perpetrators related to the economic actors, there were state agents present who were related to the inflicted violence – even though there were no judgments against them. Canadian companies, further, which are directly involved in mining projects (think about the cases *El Peñasquito*, and *Indigenous Women of Lote 8* and *Valle de Siria*) are known because of the violence related to their activity. Hence, "since 2010, at least nine opponents of Canadian mining operations in Latin America have been killed, five in Mexico, three in El Salvador and one in Guatemala. Hundreds more have been beaten and arrested during peaceful protest demonstrations" (Tetreault 2013: 208).

A third form of physical violence is used *on the part of the state in defense of the established order* (structurally violent conditions of the established order) and in the protection of the specific economic activity, that is, in support of an economic measure – even if this measure is against the law or against the fundamental rights of the population that will be primarily affected. The occupation and reappropriation of territories usually require the private security forces as well as paramilitary forces, even those protected by the state (Altvater 2011: 52). Further, the criminalization and repression of social protest are common cases, evidenced for example in the investigation, prosecution, detention and even sentencing of activists, human rights defenders and community leaders, as can be seen in relation to severely damaging projects such as the case in *Valle de Siria* or *Texaco/Chevron*, as a consequence of state policy favoring an aggressive extractive impulse in Honduras and Ecuador. The highest rates of prosecutions and repressions against environmental defenders can now be seen. In the *Ralco* case, the use of the Anti-Terrorist Act on the part of the Chilean state against Mapuche people defending their rights and territories was closely related to the military protection of the area in direct support of the Spanish energy investor Endesa, a traditional partner of authoritarian governments in Spain and Chile. The Executive order of eviction of the Awajún people in the *Baguazo* case and the violence triggered in the terrain because of the offensive intervention of the policemen following this order – even after the protesters had decided to leave the road and the facilities of the oil company – can be counted here as well. Both the Anti-Terrorist Law from the Pinochet era, which is still implemented in Chile today, and the immediate order of a minister causing police to advance in an area of high tension, seem to be mere political decisions. In this sense, the violent procedural methods in the first case and the massacre in the second seem at first glance to be the sole responsibility of the low-level agents who enforced them. Low-level state agents are usually the armed wing of the state. The harm they produce, however, is by no means primarily attributable to them. They are acting to protect and maintain the economic status quo of *development* just for some:

> But one has to observe carefully, for those most interested in the mainte-
> nance of the status quo may not come openly to the defence of the struc-
> ture: they may push their mercenaries in front of them. In other words, they
> may mobilize the police, the army, the thugs, the general social underbrush
> against the sources of the disturbance, and remain themselves in more dis-
> crete, remote seclusion from the turmoil of personal violence. And they can
> do this as an extrapolation of the structural violence: the violence commit-
> ted by the police is personal by our definition, yet they are called into action
> by expectations deeply rooted in the structure – there is no need to assume
> an intervening variable of intention. They simply do their job.
>
> (Galtung 1969: 179–180)

A fourth form of physical violence occurs *on the part of individuals working with or in relation with the newly arrived facilities* and the dynamics that are brought in with the new projects. These are individual forms of harm and sometimes are simply social disorder that can be caused in the microphysics of the new rela-tions in the area; they are more identifiable with common, ordinary crime and incivilities, and are, therefore, not registered in the general information about the cases themselves. Drugs and alcohol consumption increases and leads to trafficking networks, and gender violence and prostitution increase as well, as does trafficking in women. Svampa explains the idea of this kind of violence that has always taken place as a side effect of the large extractive and industrial projects in Latin America and can be seen as the result of the "masculinization of territories" that comes with these kinds of industries, which fundamentally employ men as leaders and as workers, and which also leads to an increase in the presence of men working with the state security forces or for private secu-rity services in charge of protecting facilities and investments (Svampa 2017: 119 ss., 121).

These four categories of physical violence related to the presence of newly deregulated economic areas and projects not only are a result of, and therefore implicated with, the deregulated business activities and their conditions, but, of course, also are closely entangled with them. They can be called "chains of violence" (Svampa 2017: 119).

The Inter-American Commission of Human Rights, in its Report on Extrac-tive Industries, has also detailed the cumulative resort to physical violence through criminalization of groups that are asking for state attention, through the enforcement of criminal law against human rights defenders, abuses against demonstrators and their right to gather in public spaces, through the use of spe-cial units for the intimidation of collectives and communities and through the increased use of police and military forces for the protection of economic units and projects in indigenous territories (IACHR 2015: paras. 297 ss.).

The context of violence, visible and invisible, therefore, is usually worse after the opening of new industrial or mining plants in a specific area. However, as it is well known, what comes *after something* is, at the same time, always, something that comes *before something* else.

Reconfiguration and deepened conditions of invisible violence – again

Recall the cases *Salaverna* and *El Peñasquito*, which are set in Zacatecas, Mexico. Both refer to extremely harmful mining units and to populations living in extremely structurally violent conditions until today. And now, read these words from the governor of Zacatecas (Montes de Oca 2018):

> I tell the mining concessionaires, entrepreneurs and potential investors of the mining sector that they count, and they will continue to count, invariably, with the firm support of the State Government. I am their friend and I am their ally.

These words were said on January 29, 2018, at the signing ceremony of the Coordination Agreement between the Mexican government and the government of Zacatecas to establish the foundations and mechanisms for each authority, within their respective faculties, to promote improvements in the products and services for potential investors and mining entrepreneurs. Through this agreement, the Inter-Institutional Committee for the Competitiveness of the Mining Sector was also installed to increase the productivity and competitiveness of the sector. This committee is made up of the Federal Undersecretary of Mining, the State Secretary of Economy, a delegate from the Ministry of Economy and the president of the Association of Mining Engineers, Metallurgists and Geologists of Mexico. From the reading of those words, the emphasis on the idea of productivity and competitiveness contained in the agreement, as well as the officials who are part of the new committee, it can be assumed that social rights and environmental issues remained outside the core of the negotiations and the political strategic interest, oriented in terms of economic "development", but not of development in terms of realization of rights or satisfaction of needs. Once again, this betrays an intensification of economic activities and business benefits at the expense of the living conditions of local people.

The anthropologist Alberto Chirif expressed this circularity in the form of apathy when he took stock of the situation eight years after the massacre that took place during the Baguazo, while explaining that the conditions had not changed, that no one authority had been found "guilty" and that indigenous rights with respect to the working conditions and population consultation of indigenous peoples in relation to hydrocarbon exploitation activities had not changed: "Nothing has changed, there is no learning, there is no will, there is no capacity to recognize errors or to act according to what democracy really means" (Paucar Albino

2017). In fact, everything indicates that the mining company Afrodita will once again receive permission to exploit – notwithstanding the legal obstacles. To the affectations that are to be feared as concomitant with the mining activity is added the immediate threat to the economic income of many indigenous families who today live off the cacao crop with organic certification, which they sell in the context of a project of the European Union (Chamiquit et al. 2016).

In a similar sense, the link between today and the past, from democracies to dictatorships, is another manifestation of reiterations and perpetuations of historically circular political economic relations. Thus, related to the land and agrarian issue seen in the *Matopiba* case, a researcher outside the legal world explained the circularity of violence structures in a clear, explicit way:

> It is also important to highlight how history repeats itself. Since the political-legal-media coup to dismiss President-elect Dilma Roussef, the decline in workers' rights has deepened, while agribusiness stimulates the advance on traditional peasant, indigenous and quilombola lands. In Bahia, about 300 families were evicted from the areas in which the conflict with Vera-cel Celulose developed. You can also see the confrontation to weaken the regulatory and oversight bodies, such as the National Health Surveillance Agency (ANVISA), responsible for the evaluation and revaluation of agro-toxics. While the industry of agrochemicals and eucalyptus for cellulose already benefited from the civil-military coup of 1964, the representatives of the agribusiness, which is intimately linked to the agrotoxic industry, appointed Blairo Maggi to the Ministry of Agriculture of the current government. Maggi is nationally known as the "king of soya" and author of Bill 6299 of 2002, known as the "Poison Law Project", which provides for the commercialization, use, storage and transport of pesticides. There are strong indications that the current coup, such as that of 1964, is based on strengthening companies in this sector. Thus, history repeats itself and, in this case, as a farce devoid of modesty or ethics.
>
> (Gonçalves de Souza 2017: 13)

We share that history repeats itself, or rather, it constantly circulates in similar channels, always remaining by means of these forms of relationships and violent systems, the latent physical violence, which continues and manifests itself again and again in these cycles.

The same Chirif explained it in a few words in a way that is applicable to all cases, to all state processes and attitudes that claim inability to act differently: "It is a terrible way to state things on behalf of the State because it is accumulating violence, and at any moment this can be unleashed" (Paucar Albino 2017). And, if it is actually unleashed, the physically violent expressions will come to the forefront again.

Maybe the more illustrative and, at the same time, paradoxical case of circularity in violence is the case of the promise of development in terms of the satisfaction of one of the most basic needs – food – and the consequent failure to fulfill this promise. The issue deserves a special section in this chapter.

Agrarian production "for export" and unmet needs at home

The industry and agricultural market, according to the FAO, declined in the 2000s and has presented a sustained growth curve since 2009. The latter occurred largely as a result of the global economic crisis that prompted a change of view and the focusing of the market on grains and crops, which is subject to less volatility than financial investments. This increase in interest in the area brought with it an intensification in the supply of technology for the development of the agrarian economy in Latin America (as it had already done in the 1970s), basically through two main areas: that of chemical fertilizers and pesticides, on the one hand, and that of the genetic manipulation of seeds, on the other. This interest, along with the growing scarcity of sufficient raw materials in other contexts (think of China or India, and not only of Western countries) for both food and the production of nonfood consumer goods and energy, has brought consequences of relevance in the territorial, legal and social configuration of many Latin American countries through the promotion of monocultures and through the increasing number of conflicts over land. All this has been mentioned before with respect to specific cases, and here it must be taken as a general context to understand the idea of circularity that this movement implies. Moreover, this is not the first time that it has happened.

Both in the 1970s and in the first decade of the twentieth century, the motivation that was heard both from external actors and in the different national areas was the slogan of "zero hunger". Both the green revolution and the current agribusiness have encouraged national, local and individual commitments under the premise that they would generate better production conditions, and therefore more food, and better market conditions and further greater profits for producers. In neither case has this been confirmed. The result has been quite the opposite.

According to a study carried out by the German Institute for Development, poverty rates in rural areas are not modified by technology or the internationalization of agricultural production (Romero–Castillo 2012). This can be explained in part by the conditions promoted in international spaces and in the multinational and binational agreements that lead to the deregulation (or reregulation) of economic relations (Gorenstein & Ortiz 2016). That is, through the signing of FTAs, the delivery of large tracts of land to foreign or large national landowners (e.g. through liberalization of nonproductive territory) is enabled. This "delivery", on the one hand, can mean the displacement of small and medium farmers, forcing them to migrate and play an active part in the processes of urbanization and urban marginalization or, on the other hand, they become commercial "partners" that are subject to and dependent on the purchase of technological packages. This way of a "partner", on the other hand, implies that the gains from increased production (ensured by the use of agrochemicals) does not really mean healthy nutrition because it generates permanent diseases in the production areas, just as it raises many doubts as regards the future production of damages to health and life to those who could have access to these foods, affectations not yet revealed but already presumed for the foods subject to genetic manipulation and toxic substances during their production. In addition, being a "partner" does not mean an increase in profits either, simply because higher production does not result in a greater return for the small or medium local farmer, but rather for the big players and consortia of the agribusiness and food industry (Documentary *Tierra en transformación* 2013).

This presumed promise of "zero hunger", therefore, not only is not fulfilled by this expansion and intensification of the agrarian industry, but even leads to the greater impoverishment of small producers, the loss of independence and productive quality of the medium producers and a permanent bureaucratic and physical conflict in relation to the lands in which they work. As for "nonproductive" lands in terms of traditional economic development, the promise of rural development and modernization brings with it displacement and violence due to the loss of land from communities not formally recognized as engaged in agrarian production, such as indigenous, peasant, afro-descendant and tribal communities.

As the FAO stated in its report in 2000:

> While optimistic liberalism prevails today, such a perspective is nevertheless considered by many economists to be an unobtainable mirage. Quite apart from the imperfections of the real markets – for example, increased economies of scale, monopolies, monopsonies, asymmetry of information, transaction costs – we cannot fail to ignore the fact that, in just a few decades, the international food markets have been able to absorb vast historical national and regional economic entities, with significant disparities in development and productivity. (. . .)
>
> In addition, over the last 20 years of free movement of goods, services and capital but not of people, the massive outmigration from agriculture has greatly exceeded the capital accumulation and employment-generating capacity of the world economy, notably in the South; and disparities among and within countries have widened, as has the scale of mass poverty. (. . .)
>
> If at the beginning of the twenty-first century, we continue down the path of liberalization of trade in food, other goods and services and capital, without the free movement of people and without providing the material and regulatory means for everyone to enjoy basic economic rights, extreme poverty and chronic undernutrition can be expected to persist in rural areas. The migration of agricultural workers, unemployment and low wages can also be expected to persist in the poorer countries that have no or few resources other than agriculture. This will contribute towards keeping the prices of exported goods and services and private and public incomes at

very low levels in these countries, thus denying them the resources needed to provide the minimum public services required for development and good governance.

(FAO 2000: 195–196)

Liberalization of trade food, in the same terms as we are discussing here of the deregulation of extractive industries, means the deepening of insufficiencies. And the situation brings an everyday issue to those immediately affected by these policies.

Those who do not have the fortune of nucleating in organizational communitarian spaces (they are the overwhelming majority of indigenous people and peasants affected), remain after the programs of "zero hunger", "agrarian revolution" and the like, in much more precarious conditions than before. Before! Often they had their own cultivation spaces for their subsistence, and fundamentally, the dignity of the self-satisfaction of the basic alimentary need, of their own cultural and environmental space, and with insufficient health service but without the iatrogenic intervention of investments that aim to improve the economic and social situation of the population and, instead, worsen it.

The greater economic dependence on loans assumed for the "improvement" of their own production, the created need to acquire seeds and technological packages from the companies that monopolize the agricultural market, the loss of lands, the socio-environmental conflicts, the diseases generated by the manipulation and consumption of pesticides by workers, the surrounding population and the immediate consumers as well as the unbundled displacements that have taken place over the decades: all this generates, in each subsequent cycle, the need for an intensification of promises that will justify (cultural violence!) the increasingly intense economic–institutional intervention of population and territories:

> Another emblematic case of this "development" is the Campos Lindos Agricultural Project, in Tocantins. Created in 1997 by the then governor José Siqueira Campos, the project is characterized in academic circles as agrarian reform in reverse. The politician expropriated for lack of productivity the Santa Catarina farm, allocating its 90,000 hectares to large producers (among them Senator Kátia Abreu) who paid only R $ 10 per hectare. But, of course, those lands were not empty. "The establishment of the grain production center by the former governor ignored the 160 families who lived in this region of the Serra do Centro, some of whose families had been there more than a hundred years. Most were expelled, some resisted. They are there, but surrounded by soy. The creek that existed before no longer exists because it silted up, it cleared everything", says Rafael Oliveira, agent of the Pastoral Land Commission (CPT) of the regional Araguaia-Tocantins, which accompanies the peasants who, moreover, had to face a

long battle in the courts. Today there are seventy families who have recently had to renounce their right to tenure to live in the now legal reserve area of the property. Like Correntina, Campos Lindos is an example of "development": for years it has been the state champion of soybean exports, for years it has figured in IBGE statistics as a record in poverty and inequality.

(Mathias 2017)

Only when the displaced peasants manage to gather in cooperatives or communities, as was the case of the *MOCASE* in Argentina or those formed around the *Rurais Sem Terra Movement* of Brazil (MST) – *Matopiba* case – is there a possibility of resistance that brings with it both the *redignification*, as the generation of spaces of technical training and the individual, social, cultural, economic empowerment, and in short, the fulfillment and satisfaction of basic needs. These, however, are cases that speak of paths of struggle and confrontation against political and economic powers that legally and factually bid to leave them out, and only reluctantly "yield" the portions of land occupied for the formation of these settlements when the social conflict scale takes on extreme dimensions. Dead bodies remain in the claimed territory, abandoned by the State, and mourned by the communities. It is the struggle of the *homo sacer* against the sovereign. Permanently, the *homo sacer* demands to be recognized as *zōé* – in his needs and rights. To understand this idea better, a new theoretical framework is presented in the following section.

Violence again and again: the sovereign power that is never overcome

In a present that seems alien to the territorial struggles and that seemed to have overcome the wars that took place face to face, or that showed a king in command of his men advancing on insurgent plebeians, it is interesting to verify what style of conflicts and confrontation is being discussed here. The high technologies, the era of communication and digitization (see Chapter 1) could not exist without the resources that certain regions, such as Latin America, have in their land. And this land leads us to think of a logic of the exercise of power that can be very well explained in the terms proposed decades ago by Michel Foucault, when he spoke of sovereign power. In Latin America, it is the never-extinguished presence of sovereign powers that use the power of death and the sword when the interest of the sovereign so deserves.

In Chapter 2, it was mentioned that the economy required safekeeping, and that this happened through directives, as Carl Schmitt called them, that had to carry out this task. If those ideas are retaken, after the analysis of the violence carried out up to this point, it is not difficult to notice the existing relationship, on the one hand, between the visible and invisible forms of violence that occur in harmful processes of reiteration in their relation with the national and international economic policies and, on the other hand, the forms of sovereign power just mentioned. For this reason, it seems useful here to explain the links that can be seen in these theoretical proposals, and that allow historical circularity to become clearer and more profound, and even the stagnation of relations in the Latin American context, which in turn leads to the permanent nonsatisfaction of basic needs. What is this sovereign power about? In what sense can this analysis really clarify the functioning of the vicious circle of violence, and the reasons why in the current century, this circularity has still not been interrupted?

Sovereign power, governmentality and biopolitics

The strategy of *sovereign power* is that which Foucault identifies as typical of the forms of domination that appeared in the twelfth century – in its beginnings only in France and England – and that predominated until the end of the sixteenth century and the beginning of the seventeenth. This power was exercised fundamentally on the land, its agricultural products and the wealth and goods of the subjects, and this exercise of power was based fundamentally on the law, which enabled in a rather predatory manner the confiscation of goods for the benefit of the sovereign (Foucault 1995: 77). The territory was important in this context not only because of its productive potential, but also because it determined the physical limits of the power of the sovereign. That is why the defense – and in the best of cases the enlargement – of the territory was one of the fundamental tasks of this form of power that was self-legitimated and self-conserved in the figure of the sovereign. Any threat to the territory or the law, which was the basis and embodiment of that sovereign, was answered by the exercise of power in its most characteristic form: the right to life and death of its subjects or, in fact, the right of death, which was the right to dispose of life and to decide the moment of death of its subjects (Foucault 2002: 163 ss.). This power of death, explained Foucault, was to be modified throughout the centuries, but it would remain present through the exercise of a form of power that would have as its goal the defense and conservation of power in itself; which would extend to its territory, its goods and, in modern societies, to its population – which since its discovery as a collective body had become the foundation and *raison d'être* of that sovereign power.

The inefficient and unproductive form of this strategy of power had laid the very foundations of its weakening, which was accentuated between the sixteenth and seventeenth centuries, when it began to glimpse the gradual development of another strategy of power analyzed by Foucault, which he called *governmentality* (Foucault 1993). Governmentality would have begun to develop alongside the growing recognition of a population as a biological body, as a sum that is more than a simple set of disciplined individuals (Foucault 1977b; Goffman 1968). This emergency was fundamentally highlighted in the nascent cities, where biological issues such as diseases, aging or birth were palpable and affected production not only in the agricultural sphere, but also primarily the manufacturing sphere as well, and were, therefore, registered in early statistical reports on the life of the population.

Dispersed economic and commercial traffic at that time became a source of wealth generation no longer isolated, but general and fundamental for the population. The political economy would develop, therefore, according to Foucault, as a logic of government and not of domination, and this growth would occur shoulder to shoulder with the maturation and expansion of liberalism. The idea of government, against the idea of domination, would imply that riches would not be confiscated by a sovereign, but that their generation would be fostered for the welfare of the population. Therefore, the emphasis was placed on governmentality, on the promotion and guarantee of natural and economic processes, of the circulation of goods and people, all of which had the purpose of keeping the population and the economy healthy and capable of developing uninterruptedly. It was about the promotion and assurance of processes, through their regulation and through the establishment of mechanisms that prevent strong imbalances or interruptions. Since then, governmentality has been this strategy of power that began to develop in the sixteenth century and has had the population as its main target, whose most important form of knowledge is political economy and whose essential technical instruments are security mechanisms (Foucault 2004: 162).

To understand with sufficient clarity the idea of sovereign power that helps explain the vicious circle of violence in Latin America, it is not enough to present governmentality as a strategy of power that developed as its counterpart, but also to understand a central idea in the Foucauldian proposal, which links both strategies: biopolitics. Biopolitics is a technology of government, that is, a way of carrying out government which acts and manifests itself not so much on and through isolated and individual phenomena, but on and in the midst of a population as a living body, with its own biological, economic and ultimately existential developments (Foucault 2004: 70 ss.). Biopolitics is a form of "administration of life", of "care of 'all living'", as Ojakangas says (2005: 6). According to these ideas, the conditions of growth of the population must be encouraged, which at the present time depends fundamentally on the economic promotion of the spheres of freedom, and this not necessarily in a mercantile sense, but of production, exchange and distribution. These development conditions must be protected and defended, which requires the implementation of both assurance techniques – risk control – as well as security strategies – elimination of hazards. "Everything" that is necessary and circulates around population life is the subject of biopolitics. Because "biopolitics must then concern the biological, social, cultural, economic and geographic conditions under which humans live, procreate, become ill, maintain health or become healthy, and die" (Dean 2001: 47). Biopolitics is thus the technology used by the governmental strategy when putting into practice and regulating life (and normalizing it), and is, in turn, the explanation for the existence of sovereign power at present, where the sovereign feels impelled to exercise his characteristic "power of death" regarding what is considered dangerous and in protection of that life – as will be seen later.

In order to make biopolitics and its concerns about life more comprehensible, Foucault (1996) analyzes three different examples of the emergence of social medicine, highlighting the importance of life as a state problem. First, he mentions state medicine (as part of a political science), which originated in Germany at the beginning of the eighteenth century, with the idea of a state's efficient and organized intervention to increase the health level of the population. Based on hospital reports and the independence of medical study programs and the appointment of medical officials responsible for the health of a region, a first medical policy had been developing since 1764. In France, city medicine began to develop at the end of the eighteenth century. According to this model, it is no longer the state but the city structure that cares about improvements in the living conditions of the population. Sanitation measures for urban construction were the first target, so that crowding had to be avoided, and the free and fresh circulation of air and water had to be promoted. Plague and leprosy were regulated in this way, and individuals suffering from plague and leprosy were isolated – for the general health of the population. In this way, public hygienism was born as the political and scientific controlling authority with regard to the vicissitudes of the environment. Finally, in England, as a third example, labor force medicine has existed since the nineteenth century. With the "Poor Laws", the idea came up to carry out controlled, free medical assistance in favor of the poor (Foucault 1996). In this way, the worker possessed the necessary health to work, and wealthy citizens freed themselves from epidemics. In these three examples, the life force of biopolitics is clearly visible.

This explanation in long terms can be understood as an exhibition of a virtuous circle of attention in the sense of turns increasingly dedicated and matured for the care and health care, minimization of conditions and damages, from the structural to the individual, and with positive effects in various orders of life. It is just the opposite of what would happen if all those spaces were abandoned, at different levels. A feedback of negative, cumulative impacts would be given – as in the Latin American cases presented here.

Normality – in one direction or the other, one could say, is promoted and formed by these biopolitical mechanisms – or by their negation.

Norm and law

The *norm* as a measure of decision and judgment is becoming more and more firmly established, whereas the law – the prototype of sovereign forms of rule – if it remains formal or ideal, is actually suffering from a gradual and permanent weakening of its influence. Foucault explained that since the emergence of biopower, we have lived in societies that are no longer legal societies. The legal society was the monarchical one. From the twelfth to the eighteenth century, European societies were largely legal societies in which the problem of law was the fundamental problem and they fought for it and made revolutions because of it. In the societies that since the nineteenth century constituted with their parliaments, legislative procedures, codes and courts, represented as societies of law, in reality a quite different mechanism of power prevailed and it obeyed nonlegal forms. Its basic principle is rather the norm and not the law, and its instruments are no longer the courts, the law and the judiciary, but medicine, social control, psychiatry and psychology (Foucault 2005: 237).

It seems clear then that it is no longer law but norm that guides the practice of power. It is no longer legal forms, but the nature of things that determines the practices of politics, and the norm is increasingly "naturally" determined. However, this does not mean that the law is going to dissolve or that the institutions of justice are disappearing, but that the law is increasingly functioning as a norm, and that the judiciary is becoming more and more integrated into a continuum of regulating institutions (health, administrative, economic) (Foucault 1977a: 157). A fine example of this is a conception of the state law scholar Stahl in 1878 when he said about the state and its functions: "The state is therefore merely an institution for external order and promotion of social life" (Šarčević 1996: 20).

The law as an instrument of the state then had to implement the ideas of order and promotion of social life. Discipline and biopolitics, so to speak, were the technologies, the norms that were regulated by law. The legal theorists did not create the "natural" norms, but interpreted them and translated them into a legal language. The law is probably replaced by nature as a regulatory mechanism, and nature is also partly replaced by economic deregulations and neoliberalism. Not only the "natural" nature, but also the "desired" nature of the processes – through economic conditions necessary for circulation, distribution and for the processes within the population – are promoted and protected. However, it is still the case that the law no longer has the most important voice.

Foucault warns us:

> Let us not be deceived by the introduction of written constitutions around the world since the French Revolution, by the innumerable and ever-changing codes of law, by ceaseless and noisy legislative activity: these are all forms which make an essentially normalizing power acceptable.

Behind the law, there is always the threat of death. Death is, therefore, the "most outstanding" weapon of the law, because the law cannot be unarmed (Foucault 1977a: 157, 156), because it originally belonged to the field of sovereignty, the field of the power of death (Krasmann 2007).

Therefore, "the original relation of the law to life [. . .] is not its application, but its abandonment [l'Abbandono]" (Agamben 2002: 39). Over the centuries, and especially since the period of bourgeois revolutions and the beginning of, let's say, modernity, the law has pretended to be a component of life power – opposite of death power – as legal protection against the sovereign's attacks.

This is why the law no longer acts "openly" as an instrument of death power. The sovereign power can, therefore, because of biopolitical or bioeconomic necessity, appear only as a legal exception.

Power of life and death

If there are recurring threats to the population or "things" connected with it – including the economy – then how does the governmental strategy respond? How does this power of life react? The power of life can protect its object – the population and its "things" – only and insofar by relying on the sovereign power of death. It is as Foucault said, a biological type of relationship explained more or less in this way: The more low genera disappear and the more abnormal individuals are destroyed, the fewer degenerates there are in the genus, therefore, the better I will be – not as an individual, but rather as a species – I will live, be strong, be powerful and thrive (Foucault 1999: 296). As was seen in Chapter 2, the economic policies and the violence exercised by the state against excluded individuals and segments of the population occurred through the excessive recourse to the criminal system. That relation has also been explained in the terms of biopolitics. This is what happens in ordinary politics in Latin America as well. Those who are not accepted as part of the society that must be defended and promoted in their liberties, are in some sense exposed to being treated as low genera and abnormal, or at least, as undesirable and superfluous. In the Latin American context, this happens in urban areas between the different individuals and subcultures living in nearby areas, and this also happens with respect to the disregard for issues happening outside the urban areas: rural, peasant and indigenous, forests and rainforest. People living there seem to be, for central administrations, as useless and superfluous as people excluded from the social and state meshes in the cities.

Biopolitics is the fundamental technology of governmentality, while the art of government itself is not directly related to biological life, but rather to economic processes. Sovereignty therefore confronts itself several times with the governance of the (neoliberal) economy, whereby the illiberal elements of liberalism are evident and make the talk of "demonic societies" possible (Dean 2001; Ojakangas 2005):

> It is no longer so much the right of the sovereign to put to death his enemies but to disqualify the life – the mere existence – of those who are a threat to the life of the population, to disallow those deemed "unworthy of life", those whose bare life is not worth living.
>
> (Dean 2001: 53)

This sovereign power takes on different forms than mere killing. A biopolitical understanding of this question would explain, as Foucault suggested, that there are some who are not needed, and there are others – one's own population – that must be given priority. Priority is understood here as more security forces for their protection in rich urban areas in detriment of the civil rights of undesirable individuals passing by there, or as development through more mining industry, more hydroelectric dams for more energy production or more territory at the disposal of actors with more vision than poor peasants and in detriment of people living in the territories of those rich soils, rivers or lands. All of this is a kind of state work in favor of some, in detriment of many others. Governmentality for some, and the dark side of it, the sovereign power, for many others. This dark side is the expression of the metaphor – not always only a metaphor – of the power of death.

Bare life, exclusion and exception

How exactly does exclusion, which is set by the norm and can lead to the killing or non-protection of life, work? To see this relationship explained on the individual level, the work of Giorgio Agamben is of benefit. For his analysis of a political logic of exclusion by inclusion and the associated idea of the excluded as mere physical life, Agamben draws extensively on two useful entries: first, he takes over the Greek separation of the terms *bíos* and *zōé*. *Zōé* is the naked life, the unpolitical, only physical and biological life. *Bíos*, on the other hand, is the political, social and bourgeois life. Not everyone owns, more precisely, not everyone is adjudged as bíos. While the bare life of *homo sacer* means an absolute absence of civil and political attributes and rights in ancient Greece, *bíos* is the enjoyment of social existence. Life without political life is just biological life that has to be eliminated if it is "sick" or "dangerous". The logic of the state of emergency, according to Agamben, begins with this possibility of explicitly invoking the bare life, which in the normal situation seems connected to the manifold forms of social life, as the ultimate fundament of political power – to separate this bare life from its ways of life and from its possibilities of life, which is "potentiality always and above all" (Agamben 2006: 13, 17). The possibilities of life, in terms of Galtung, are also called potentialities, and in this sense, the link between the two authors is highly interesting. Whereas Agamben analyzes the conceptual possibility of deprivation of social potentialities and even of vital potentialities as the transformation of *zōé* into *bíos*, Galtung explains that the obstruction – when avoidable – of the realization of the potentiality is violence. It is the transformation of individuals with human rights, we could say in other words, into individuals without rights. This distinction progresses in the same vein in the explanation provided by Agamben as well.

Bare life is the condition of the separation between those who are only this bare life and those who are also *bíos* – for whom the life-form has been preserved; it is a separation that is most evident in the distinction between *People* and *people*, as in the Roman distinction between *popolo grasso* (the rich and lords) and *popolo minuto* (the common people) (Agamben 2006: 34 s.). On the one hand, People [Popolo], political existence, inclusion, *bíos*. In contrast, people [popolo] stands for bare life, exclusion, *zōé*. Thus, Agamben describes:

> On the one hand the crowd <People> as an integral political body, on the other hand the subordinate <people> as a fragmentary variety of needy and excluded bodies; here an enclosure that tolerates no rest, there an exclusion that knows no hope.
>
> (Agamben 2002: 187)

The political inclusion in terms of recognition of rights and satisfaction of basic needs sees itself, hence, confronted with exclusion in terms of the negation of rights and multiplicity of unsatisfied needs in important sectors of the Latin American population as well.

The bare life "is excluded", that is, by a power intervention, the mere life is separated from the life-form. In this sense, therefore, the exclusion is made by the inclusion:

> According to Agamben, bare life is excluded from the political realm, from the realm of the normal situation, in the very same sense that the Schmittian sovereign is excluded from the normally valid legal order. Here lies the hidden bond between bare life and sovereignty, between biopower and sovereign power.
>
> (Ojakangas 2005: 8)

Through the law or the normative, rights are modified and social and institutional structures are abolished. The law, Agamben would say, is applied according to the power of death in the hands of the sovereign power. The exclusion of rights from the population is done through their inclusion as receptors of the regulations that exclude them from the realm of *bios* (Agamben 2004: 9, 33, 41), rights and development, it could be said.

Economization and internationalization of biopolitics

This exclusion, however, can be applied not only to individuals, but also to entire populations and even states, as a sort of return to the origin of the bellicose concept of security and killing of enemies. Today, further, it can sometimes arise even from tensions stemming from purely economic reasons.

The German criminologist Fritz Sack has, several times, mentioned the main role of the economy or of neoliberalism as the control of contemporary politics and as the main aspect responsible for the new punitivist streams which lead to the abolition of legal rules and the rise of warlike rules (Sack 1995, 1998, 2003, 2004, 2006):

> It is economic transactions and their carriers and agents that invade and transgress the limits that underlie the processes we call "globalization",

a term that makes States tremble and disintegrate, no matter how highly equipped and totalitarian they may be; a term that makes legal systems surrender and causes the breaking of moral principles.

(Sack 2003: 10)

The economy determines the style of government and creates a place for the emergence of sovereignty, which is achieved even if not always visible, by the exception. The economy leads the government and is at the same time the reason for the declaration of a state of emergency, just as life directs biopolitical governance and is also the reason sovereignty occurs by means of the exception. It is certain that biopolitical life – biocultural life as Connolly calls it (2004) – is based not only on the "bio" but also on all other elements vital to the preservation of the population. Economics is perhaps most important in the current neoliberal era, because only the economy and the rules of corporate society emerge as determinative for the (post-) social (Rose 2000; Lemke 2002; Sack 2003; Krasmann 2003). There is a shift from life in the narrow sense of the term to life in the broadest sense, that is, to life as all things and processes that are not only inherently about life, but that must be promoted and created for this life.

The role of the economy as part of the power of life is then protected by a power of death. Therefore, warlike measures are taken when the economy is in danger or threatened. This economization is one of the two main transformations to be considered in the analysis of governmentality and sovereign power. The other is connected to the economy, but has an independent meaning.

Sovereignty, once considered exclusively state power, is increasingly thought of as interstate power. Globalization, the internationalization of protective mechanisms and the international exchange of resources, individuals and information to an unprecedented degree, makes it possible to imagine governmentality and sovereignty not necessarily within states or "internally", as Foucault has done. It is actually complementary, as Dean explains, because sovereignty – he speaks of sovereign states – and governmentality – arts of governing – need not only intra-states, but extra-states as well.

> The relation of the arts of governing and sovereignty is not the replacement of one by the other but each acting as a condition of the other. On the one hand, the existence of nominally independent sovereign states is a condition of forcing open those geopolitical spaces on which the arts of government can operate. On the other hand, a set of supranational agreements and regulations of populations is a necessary condition of the world inhabited by these sovereign states.
>
> (Dean 2001: 50)

Economization and internationalization of biopolitical technology seem to be the most interesting transformations that should not have escaped Foucauldian analyzes of actuality, and they are directly linked to the processes analyzed in this book.

Back to the (sovereign) violence in the Latin American territory

The population of the Global South, in many senses, today sees itself considered as a bare life in the international capitalist project. It is as if these parts of the world could be eliminated as a side effect, or externality, along the path of progress (Agamben 2006: 36). The international legal exceptions have been created long time ago. For example, for refugees who have no national rights, there do not seem to be any human rights on European territory, or for migrants without formalized permission in the United States, or for indigenous and peasant communities in Latin America. Some thoughts from Hannah Arendt are telling here. Human rights, she claimed, do not seem to apply to all people. Human rights, as they can be recognized, can also be withdrawn. The idea of a constitutional state or of a state of law has turned into a national state which cares only for the members of its own nation, and this, in turn, could not mean anything other than that national interests are superior to any legal order, which means, in her example in that time, that what was right was what benefited the German people (Arendt 1962: 414). Stateless persons and minorities have no human rights, as they have no civil or political rights – and human rights are seen only as part of those others. If their rights are no longer the rights of the citizen, then man is truly sacred [sacro] in the sense that this term had in ancient Roman law: *consecrated* to death (Agamben 2006: 27).

As in the case of Foucault, this does not necessarily mean physical death. Rather, we could speak here of a situation of exposure to structural, cultural and physical violence and it would be equally correct.

The sovereigns and their protected territories

The territory was once the foundation of the power of death. Sovereign struggles took place in and because of territories. The sword has almost always had the objective of protecting power and territory (Altvater 2011: 41, 52). If, hence, in international relations and transnational economic relations there are societies and states where the governmental strategy is exercised upon most of the population – many countries of the Global North – the sovereign power of death that is used against those who are a threat for those societies and states will reach for its sword. In the Latin American region, according to the historical review presented in Chapter 1 and the analysis of failed development as violence, explained in Chapter 2, and after the elucidation of eight cases in Chapters 3 and 4 describing concrete discourses and practices in different particular cases, after all this, without a doubt, it is possible to say that the territorial struggles and the different structural, cultural and physical expressions of violence in the context of transnational economy and economic domestic policies, and the deregulation of protective forms for the domestic population as well as the nonrecognition of their basic needs and interests, are manifestations of a sovereign power that is never overcome. The social division of labor at the international level, which has been mentioned before, can also be explained according to the internationalization and the economization of biopolitical logic. Territory, the game board for the struggles of biopolitical tension, remains therefore in Latin America the central issue: the sovereign needs this territory for the improvement of life and protection of interests in his kingdom, the Global North. For people living in this territory, however, this demand represents a daily threat to its life. They are not recognized as *bíos*, and thus the realization of their potentialities is neglected.

For them, the territory remains the place of the defense of their bare life, at least. There, social relations are perpetuated in relation to this tension and threat. In this sense,

> we refer to territory when we speak of an appropriate space for a particular social relationship that produces it and maintains it from a form of power. Under this analysis it is possible to infer that, by modifying power relations, even if it is an external imposition and not a decision taken by the will of those who built the territory until then, the form of appropriation of the territory is modified and therefore the Society-Nature relationship.
>
> (Rosso & Toledo López 2010: 6)

The modification of the Society-Nature relationship, therefore, is the result of the permanent defense of one's own space, and this explains the new forms of resistance that have taken place in Latin America over the past decades and that have been conceptualized as "the ecoterritorial turn of the resistances" ("giro ecoterritorial de las resistencias", Svampa 2017: 88 ss.) also thought as "socio-territorial conflict" ("conflicto socioterritorial") (Altvater 2011: 41 ss.).

This is then related to the threefold result of the land question in current Latin America: the resistance is against large-scale transactions in terms of capital and territory; the resistance is against national and, principally, transnational actors; and the resistance arises because the territory means specific control forms of this territory (Gorenstein & Ortiz 2016: 7). The abandonment of resistance, in this context, would probably lead to the definitive reduction of the population in these areas, to *zōé*. Actually, this happens all the time.

There is a disinvestment in the social field and a hyperinvestment in the economic sector without sufficient regulation, or with regulation that facilitates precisely the economic action disconnected from its social impact. The economic aspect increases more and more the need for social construction, which does not take place from the institutional side – quite the opposite – and leads only to the increasingly deliberate presence of economic interests that clearly pursue economic returns, and not public service. This happens particularly under governments which adhere to neoliberal deregulatory policies, fundamentally but not exclusively. As we have seen, it also happens in economic orders of social and progressive vision which, however, do not attend to the impact that the excessive economic exploitation of natural resources has on the population living there. The political sovereign and the economic sovereign continue to decide on the territory, regardless of whether the subjects have or lack the possibility of designing, managing and performing with their own abilities the forms they choose for the personal and social realization of their area, or at least, the satisfaction of basic needs that could potentially be made reality.

The sovereign power, then, is the one that exercises the invisible structural and cultural violence as well as the visible, physical violence directly linked to it.

Conclusion

Territorial peace as an objective (Galtung 1996: 196; Suelt Cock 2017) is, therefore, still in need of hard work. And this, also, because today there is not only one sovereign acting in the territory; there are many.

Under these conditions, it is not surprising that development becomes maldevelopment, that the subjugated remains a subjugated (or in reality, *homo sacer*) and that the king has never been decapitated.

Whoever dares attempt this "decapitation of the king" (resistance), is subject to a violent physical criminal policy inspired and sustained by cultural violence and embodied in structural violence. The king, sovereign, or sovereigns, and even their feudal lords, in fact, lie beyond any possibility of judgment in this scheme. Neither the political power for its acts against the interests of its citizens, nor the economic power that is governed only by the rules of the free market, are held liable or judged – although formally there are possibilities, only sporadically are they valid enough to become a reality.

The exception is generated in these areas in which everything is valid for them, everything is regulated or deregulated by them, and therefore, the ultimate decision on which rules apply and which do not, and who deserves to live and who does not, depends on these sovereigns. This puts them in that position so well described by Foucault and Agamben, outside of that order that should promote life, but that does not receive sanctions when it not only does not promote it, but also destroys it. It is the essence of sovereign power. In the case of Latin America, much of the political and economic order seems to be internally and geopolitically very much on the outside of that governmental strategy so well described for the Global North.

In the Global South, there are still kings showing the sword. And this, in some way, is what must be modified, even to the extent of setting the kings, in principle from the analysis and concepts, in the dock of those who must answer for their actions. To remove from them the power of impunity that their investiture confers upon them will mean, at the same time, dethroning the sovereign and strengthening the possibilities and reality of democracy and its possibilities for fulfilling needs and rights.

This requires, among many other things, broader conceptual tools in the criminological field for the visibilization and explanation of these processes, for the outline of possible ways for the determination of liability and, essentially, for the interruption of this vicious circle, its prevention and the repair of the damages that it has produced.

The crime of maldevelopment as a criminological conceptual category is offered in the next chapter as a first step toward a response to this need.

Notes

1 Question formulated by Antolín Sánchez Presedo to the European Union on *Transnational land deals for agriculture in the "Global South"*. 2013, January 22. www.europarl.europa.eu/sides/getDoc.do?pubRef=-//EP//TEXT+WQ+E-2013-000610+0+DOC+XML+V0//EN. Answer from the EU on 2013, March 13, available at www.europarl.europa.eu/sides/getAllAnswers.do?reference=E-2013-000610&language=EN
2 The *grilagem* is a specific fraud technique related to land titles. It is explained in the context of the *Matopiba* case in Chapter 4.

References

Agamben, Giorgio. 2002. *Homo Sacer. Die souveräne Macht und das nackte Leben*, Frankfurt a.M.: Suhrkamp.

Agamben, Giorgio. 2004. *Ausnahmezustand*, Frankfurt a.M.: Suhrkamp.

Agamben, Giorgio. 2006. *Mittel ohne Zweck*, Zürich Berlin: Diaphanes.

Altvater, Elmar. 2011. *Los límites del capitalismo. Acumulación, crecimiento y huella ecológica*, Buenos Aires: Mardulce.

Arendt, Hannah. 1962. *Elemente und Ursprünge totaler Herrschaft*, Frankfurt a.M.: Europäischer Verlagsanstalt.

Chamiquit, Clelia Jima/Mayan, Augostina/Perez, Wrays. 2016. "Minera Afrodita tiene permiso de explotación en Cordillera del Cóndor". *SERVINDI*. August 24. www.servindi.org/actualidad-noticias/23/08/2016/minera-afrodita-tiene-permiso-de-explotacion-de-oro-en-cordillera-del

Connolly, William E. 2004. "The Complexity of Sovereignty". In: Edkins, Jenny/Pin-Fat, Véronique/Shapiro, Michale J. (Hrsg.). *Sovereign Lives: Power in Global Politics*, New York/London: Routledge, 23–41.

Dean, Mitchell. 2001. "Demonic Societies: Liberalism, Biopolitics and Sovereignty". In: Hansen, Thomas B./Stepputat, Finn (Hrsg.). *States of Imagination*, Durham: Duke University Press, 41–64.

FAO (Food and Agriculture Organization). 2000. *The State of Food and Agriculture*. www.fao.org/docrep/x4400e/x4400e00.htm

Foucault, Michel. 1977a (orig. 1976). *Sexualität und Wahrheit. Der Wille zum Wissen*, Frankfurt a.M.: Suhrkamp.

Foucault, Michel. 1977b (orig. 1975). *Überwachen und Strafen*, Frankfurt a.M.: Suhrkamp.

Foucault, Michel. 1993 (orig. 1976). "Las Redes el poder". In: Foucault, Michel (ed.). *Las Redes del Poder*, Buenos Aires: Almagesto.

Foucault, Michel. 1995 (orig. 1978). *La Verdad y las Formas Jurídicas* (Die Wahrheit und die juridischen Formen), Barcelona: Gedisa.

Foucault, Michel. 1996. *Diskurs und Wahrheit: die Problematisierung der Parrhesia*, Berlin: Merve Verlag.

Foucault, Michel. 1999 (orig. 1970). *Die Ordnung des Diskurses*, München: Carl Hanser Verlag.

Foucault, Michel. 2002 (orig. 1976). *La voluntad de saber* (Historia de la sexualidad, Tomo 1), México D.F.: Siglo XXI.

Foucault, Michel. 2004. *Geschichte der Gouvernementalität I. Sicherheit, Territorium, Bevölkerung. (Vorlesung am Collége de France 1977/1978)*, Frankfurt a.M.: Suhrkamp.

Foucault, Michel. 2005 (orig. 1976). "Die Maschen der Macht". In: Foucault, Michel (ed.). *Analytik der Macht*, Frankfurt a.M.: Suhrkamp, 220–239.

Friedrichs, David/Rothe, Dawn L. 2015. *Crimes of Globalization*, London: Routledge.

Galtung, Johan. 1969. "Violence, Peace, and Peace Research". *Journal of Peace Research* 6 (3), 167–191.

Galtung, Johan. 1996. *Peace by Peaceful Means: Peace and Conflict, Development and Civilization*, London: Sage.

Goffman, Erving. 1968. *Stigma: Notes on the Management of Spoiled Identity*, Harmondsworth: Penguin.

Gonçalves de Souza, Ivonete. 2017. "Eucalipto y el veneno silencioso: expansión del monocultivo en el extremo sur de Bahía, Brasil". *Boletín del Movimiento Mundial por los Bosques Tropicales (WRM)* 233, 8–13.

Gorenstein, Silvia/Ortiz, Ricardo. 2016. "La tierra en disputa. Agricultura, Acumulación y territorio en la Argentina reciente". *RELAER* 1 (2), 1–26.

IACHR (Inter-American Court of Human Rights). 2015. Informe de la Comisión Interamericana de Derechos Humanos sobre *Pueblos Indígenas, comunidades afrodescendientes y recursos naturales*. OEA/Ser.I./V/II. Doc. 47/15. December 31.

Krasmann, Susanne. 2003. *Die Kriminalität der Gesellschaft. Zur Gouvernementalität der Gegenwart*, Konstanz: UVK Verlagsgesellschaft mbH.

Krasmann, Susanne. 2007. "Folter im Ausnahmezustand?" In: Krasmann, Susanne/Martschukat, Jürgen (eds.). *Rationalitäten der Gewalt. Staatliche Neuordnungen vom 19. bis zum 21. Jahrhundert*, Bielefeld: Transcript, 75–96.

Lemke, Thomas. 2002 (3rd ed.). *Eine Kritik der politischen Vernunft. Foucaults Analyse der modernen Gouvernementalität*, Hamburg: Argument.

Mathias, Maíra. 2017. "Matopiba: na fronteira entre a vida e o capital". *EPSJV/Fiocruz*. September 19. www.epsjv.fiocruz.br/noticias/reportagem/matopiba-na-fronteira-entre-a-vida-e-o-capital

Montes de Oca, Claudio. 2018. "Promueven competitividad en minería". *NTR periodismo crítico*. January 29. http://ntrzacatecas.com/2018/01/29/promueven-competitividad-en-mineria/

Ojakangas, Mika. 2005. "Impossible Dialogue on Bio-Power: Agamben und Foucault". *Foucault Studies* 2, 5–28.

Paucar Albino, Jorge. 2017. "Experto en temas amazónicos advierte que las causas del Baguazo se mantienen". Interview with Prof. Alberto Chirif *Lamula.pe*, June 5. https://redaccion.lamula.pe/2017/06/05/baguazo-2009-bagua-conflicto-peru-alan-garcia-causas-aniversario-pueblos-indigenas/jorgepaucar/

Romero-Castillo, Evan. 2012. "Inversión agraria extranjera: ¿oportunidad o abuso?" *Deutsche Welle*. May 24. www.dw.com/es/inversión-agraria-extranjera-oportunidad-o-abuso/a-15972448

Rose, Nikolas. 2000. "Tod des Sozialen? Eine Neubestimmung der Grenzen des Regierens". In: Bröckling/Krasmann/Lemke (eds.). *Gouvernementalität der Gegenwart*, Frankfurt: Suhrkamp, 72–109.

Rosso, Inés/Toledo López, Virginia. 2010. "Proceso de (des-re)territorialización en Santiago del Estero". *Memoria Académica, Special Issue – VI Jornadas de Sociología de la UNLP*, 1–20.

Sack, Fritz. 1995. "Prävention – ein alter Gedanke in neuem Gewand. Zur Entwicklung und Kritik der Strukturen ‚postmoderner' Kontrolle". In: Gössner, Rolf (ed.). *Mythos Sicherheit. Der hilflose Schrei nach dem starken Staat*, Baden-Baden: Nomos, 429–456.

Sack, Fritz. 1998. "Conflicts and Convergences in Criminology: Bringing Politics and Economy Back In". In: Ruggiero, Vincenzo/South, Nigel/Taylor, Ian R. (eds.). *The New European Criminology: Crime and Social Order in Europe*, London/New York: Routledge, 37–51.

Sack, Fritz. 2003. "*Von der Nachfrage- zur Angebotspolitik auf dem Feld der Inneren Sicherheit*". In: Dahme/Otto/Trube/Wohlfahrt (eds.). *Soziale Arbeit für den aktivierenden Staat*, Opladen: Leske und Budrich, 249–276.

Sack, Fritz. 2004. "Strukturwandel und Kriminalpolitik". Paper presented at the *Institut für Konfliktforschung*. Verein Deutscher Strafverteidiger: XXXIII. *Symposion 'Neue Lust auf Strafen'*. March 27–28.

Sack, Fritz. 2006. "Die gesellschaftlichen Ursachen der Punitivität. Einige Notizen". Paper presented at the Institut für kriminologische Sozialforschung der Universität Hamburg, *'Im Gespräch. Zur Aktualität der Kriminologie'*. January 13–14.

Šarčević, Edin. 1996. *Der Rechtsstaat: Modernität und Universalitätsanspruch der klassischen Rechtsstaatstheorien; eine Bilanz der Rechtsstaatslehren zwischen aufgeklärtem Liberalismus und Nationalismus*, Leipzig: Leipziger Universitätsverlag.

Suelt Cock, Vanessa. 2017. "Las violaciones de DDHH por parte de empresas del sector extractivo en Colombia. Retos para el Estado del postconflicto". Paper submitted at the *Seminar on Corporations and Humans Rights*, University of Göttingen. July 20–21.

Svampa, Maristella. 2017. *Del cambio de época al fin de ciclo. Gobiernos progresistas, extractivismo y movimientos sociales en América Latina*, Buenos Aires: Edhasa.

Tetreault, Darcy. 2013. "Los mecanismos del imperialismo canadiense en el sector minero de América Latina". *Estudios Críticos del Desarrollo* 2 (4), 191–215.

Filmography

Apaga y vámonos. 2005. Documentary film. Dir. Manel Mayol. Spain.

Tierra en transformación: Agronegocio o agroecología. 2013. Documentary. Dir. Nils Bucher, Michaela Danielsson, Lisa Persson. Brasil/Sweden. www.dailymotion.com/video/xt2vm3

Chapter 6

The crime of maldevelopment as a needed conceptual category of criminology

The possibility of dethroning the sovereign power, to those who are the sovereigns who exercise structural, cultural and physical violence within the dynamic of a vicious circle of economic interests, economic undertakings, state (*dis*)interest and remarginalization, requires first that we recognize the possibility of their responsibility. Thus, the objective here is to conceptualize a crime of maldevelopment as a category of study and analysis which enables the thought that not only individual crimes, but also structures and processes of violence, far from being anonymous or historically impersonal, can be tracked and identified in order to design mechanisms for accountability, including forms of reparation and, of course, prevention.

It is often heard – as a kind of fate – that it is not possible or that it is too naïve to think about "responsible" actors when talking about hunger, corruption and desertification, the influence of the mass media, poverty or toxic industries. To a certain extent, in fact, it is not easy to find visible individuals responsible for these "disasters". In reality, however, the cultural and historic structures of our thinking are what prevent us from analyzing from another perspective. Governments, transnational corporations, the global economy and the social structures are commonly thought of as natural and given, as Harari states (2014: 36).

If these categories are considered "real", they will be real with all their circumstances and consequences. They will be, then, the explanation and justification for the perpetuation of sovereign powers everywhere. And these sovereign powers, as is well known, are protected by the "exception". The sovereign cannot be judged, cannot be reached or touched. Leaving aside the "natural" essence attributed to these categories and putting them in question could be the first step toward explaining that there is a direct link between that ubiquitous exception and the non-liability of the main actors and processes responsible for hunger, corruption, desertification, mass media influence, poverty or toxic industries. The veil can be removed if the invisible mesh of structural and cultural violence is revealed, if the trail of breadcrumbs can be followed.

The exception must be excluded even from the analytical scenario if we are to open the door to responsibility for the most silent and invisible damages caused by economic processes. Agamben, again, can help with the first step, which will be explained in the first part of this chapter. Thereafter, maldevelopment as a violent harm attributable to whom, by action or omission, intervenes in the failed promise of development will be presented. Further, why this violence of maldevelopment should be thought of as a criminological issue will be explained. The third section will make a review of previous criminological works and authors who have already explained aspects of politics, violence, crime and economy as interrelated in some way. This review will be followed by the presentation of some Latin American scholars who, from the perspective of the Global South, have approached these interconnections as well, going even further with a suggestion of making the field of criminological studies broader. In the last part, on the basis of this panoramic review, the specific features of the crime of maldevelopment as a conceptual category of criminology will be explained.

Accountability without exceptions

For Agamben, the problem of sovereignty does not lie in biopolitical interplay (see Chapter 5), but rather in the paradox that the state needs absolute authority to clarify open questions about the law. This paradox, however, is that this authority itself lacks a previous law that regulates the authority of the state, because at the same time, the sovereign stands outside and within the legal order (Agamben 2002: 25). There is, therefore, no law, but biopolitical mechanisms that make decisions in an emergency. It is not the law, but rather its rescindment, not the rule, but the exception that applies in cases where a suspension of the valid order is necessary in order to secure its very existence (Agamben 2004: 41):

> In truth, the state of emergency is neither outside the legal order, nor is it immanent to it, and the problem of its definition concerns precisely a threshold or a zone of indeterminacy, in which inside and outside do not exclude each other, but rather de-determine themselves [s'indeterminato]. The suspension of the norm does not mean their abolition, and the zone of anomie that establishes it is not unrelated to the law (or at least pretends not to be).
>
> Hence the interest in theories such as the one by Schmitt, which translates the topographic contrast into a more complex topological relationship, in which the boundaries of the legal order itself are in question.
>
> (Agamben 2004: 33)

The specificity of the state of emergency is not so much the lack of separation of powers as the separation or dissolution of the force of law from the law:

> The state of emergency defines a state of the law in which the norm is valid, but is not enforced (because it has no "force"), and on the other hand some acts that do not have the range of laws gain "force".
>
> (Agamben 2004: 49)

For the cases analyzed in this work, the statement could lead to the idea of law being valid but not applied (*law without force*).[1]

Since law and violence are so invisibly linked and language also has a defining, invisible bond with nature – a bond that has led to the point of indistinguishability between law and violence – one should try thinking beyond any known law and beyond any known logos. For this reason, Agamben suggests that if there is today a social potency, it should aspire to its own powerlessness in the sense of a renunciation of "making law and preserving law"; in so doing, the social potency would break the interdependence between violence and law as well as that between life and language (Agamben 2006: 98).

This idea of seeking a new logic of life beyond the law leads Agamben even further, to the hope of a certain happy life, which is possible without the intervention of the law. The happy life that should be the basis for political philosophy can be "just a 'satisfying' and absolutely profane life that has attained the perfection of one's own potency and one's own mediateness, and to which the sovereignty and the right no longer have access" (Agamben 2006: 99).

These explanations and suggestions by Agamben are useful for the understanding of law exceptions and possible ways of banishing them in social life. However, before happy (peaceful and nonviolent) life beyond the law is possible, some adjustments of the current order should be attempted in order to achieve a better balance. This would be possible through, on the one side, a prior visibility of the law, its exceptions and the sovereigns who benefit from these exceptions and, on the other side, through the design of mechanisms for the identification of responsible actors, the implementation of responsibility channels and the implementation of repair and construction processes with nonviolence as the horizon, that is, the aim is development in the sense of a construction of economic, cultural and legal peace. All basic needs should be satisfied, and all potentials should actually be realized. There are no exceptions in this sense.

Of course, there is a shortage of resources in the world. In fact, this is the reason why a scientific and political discipline called economics has been developed, whose object of study is the generation and administration of scarce goods (see Chapter 5). However, if there is a shortage of certain basic goods for life, it does not mean that such scarcity entails a complete lack. Much less does it imply that this lack can be used as an excuse for those who manage scarce goods causing, as a consequence, the exponential increase of deficiencies for certain populations in favor of the reduction of deficiencies for others. When the Minister of Defense of Peru was questioned after the violent confrontation provoked by the state in Baguazo (see the *Baguazo* case in Chapter 4), and when the journalist suggested that the indigenous populations were the great "forgotten" ones of the Peruvian state, the Minister justified the situation of deficiencies and detached the state from all responsibility regarding the situation in which many communities live, alluding to the "impossibility" of satisfying all needs. If there is not enough for everyone, he said, it is not forgetting. And he closed with an eloquent, "*No me jodas!*" ("*Don't fuck me!*") (Documentary *La espera* 2014: 17'30"). If there was not enough for everyone, there could be no forgetting, nor could there be violence. But the reality is that there is enough. In the areas most affected by unmet needs, wealth is not scarce. The scarcity occurs only if the observation is made in a global sense. There are shortages in certain areas, and wealth in others. Redistribution, therefore, could generate a balance in the populations of the globe if resources were not always displaced in the same direction, generally from the Global South to the Global North, or from the peripheries to the centers, to use Galtung's language (see Chapter 2). Therefore, the Minister, despite his indignation, is not correct in his justification – which is similar to the explicit and implicit justifications of the institutions throughout Latin America, which through ways of thinking exercise cultural violence which makes structural violence a natural consequence. It is neither acceptable, nor is it accepted that the legislation should allow written and factual exceptions in favor of the sovereigns. The tracking of the responsibility for maldevelopment is a proposal of visibility of the possibilities and potentialities that can be realized; it is also a proposal for explaining that unmet needs are not always inevitable, as political space and more orthodox economic doctrines have proclaimed for centuries through their innumerable channels of cultural violence expansion.

A first exercise to trace lines of responsibility can be made following the proposal of the Inter-American Commission on Human Rights, in its statement of state obligations in the context of indigenous populations, people of African descent and natural resources.[2]

> [T] he Commission considers that the state obligations in these contexts revolve around six central axes, consisting of the duty to:
>
> i   adopt an adequate and effective regulatory framework,
> ii prevent violations of human rights,
> iii supervise and supervise extraction, exploitation and development activities,
> iv guarantee mechanisms for effective participation and access to information,
> v   prevent illegal activities and all forms of violence, and
> vi guarantee access to justice through investigation, punishment and access to adequate reparation for human rights violations committed in these contexts.
>
> (Para. 5)

The Commission demands legal frameworks, monitoring and supervision of activities, effective participation, prevention of violations generated by activities, prevention of violence and access to justice. These formulas are necessary and essential, but not sufficient if they are proposed only by an international organization without the capacity to effectively sanction states, and without direct interference in business activities. The purely legal-institutional demands are explained, obviously, because it is a regional body for the protection of human rights. But the law, even written and institutionalized, as Agamben explained, does not necessarily apply, and many other rules, unwritten, govern with their norms, in Foucault's terms, the daily reality of the forgotten populations that have been thrown under the train of the promised development. This framework, therefore, is necessary as a guide, but not sufficient. On the other hand, it is not only the responsibility and sanction of what should not happen, but the way to get to the cradle of maldevelopment, that is probably a concurrent project with the mechanisms of what should happen in terms of realization of basic needs. Violence is not only what can be negative, but also the result of the absence of construction mechanisms in terms of economic, cultural and legal peace. There must be a deep interrelation between the reduction of the negative and the promotion of the positive, so that the promises (including, if it is the case, that of development) can be realized.

In the cases outlined in Chapters 3 and 4, it was shown that in all of them, the states made promises and explained the objectives of the activities and measures adopted in terms of development. They were sovereigns speaking to the people, promising an improvement in the quality of life, and then acted like sovereigns, arbitrarily preventing all obstacles to such plans, even when the promise offered with great fanfare had clearly not been met, and even when that promise had harmed daily life among the populations that were directly in contact with such ventures. Recall, as an example, that during the parliamentary debate on the *Matopiba* project the rapporteur, deputy Irajá Abreu (PSD-TO), presented a favorable opinion on the text of the project. "Considering the great challenges to ensure the continuity of the development of the region, it is essential to create a nonprofit organization, of a technical and scientific nature, aimed at promoting the agricultural development of Matopiba and consequently improving the living conditions of the local population";[3] and Alan García, defending the signing of the FTA with the United States and the need for the decrees that led to the *Baguazo*: "I know that the vast majority of Peruvians want development, want employment, want modernity".[4]

Whether in terms of civilization, improvement of living conditions or development, employment and modernity, in all cases, the measures taken and business activities are presented as positive and even necessary for the growth of the country, and especially for the sustainable growth of the local population. With these promises, it is logical that every form of opposition be presented as an obstacle, as Alan García did with his theory of the "gardener's dog", when he blamed the local population and its defenders responsible for the capricious obstacle they had set in the path of national development.

The state, however, is not the only one responsible. The promises of the companies, their slogans of yesterday and their publicity of responsible activity of today, work in that same logic. As an example, you can bring back the Texaco in the Texaco/Chevron case, whose slogan was "bringing muscles and machinery to a territory untouched by civilization" (documentary film *Crude* 2009: 21), and the current website of *El Peñasquito-Goldcorp*, which enumerates the multiple benefits to the community, the approach and promotion of education with respect to children and the care of the environment that the activity of the opencast mine claims to consider as essential and, therefore, obeys according to Mexican law.[5] Both the idea that civilization would come with oil exploitation, and the idea that school visits or Christmas programs can counteract the eviction of traditional ways of life and the diseases and deaths that pollution and displacement bring, seems not only strange, but offensive. Therefore, it cannot be explained that an international organization such as the United Nations, in a relevant document on indigenous communities in Guatemala – remember that this country was the location of the case referred to in Chapter 4 of *Indigenous Women of Lote 8* – and in relation to the violation of rights that takes place in the context of the extractive industries, it has ruled on the companies and their responsibility in these terms:

> Private companies have played an inevitable influence on the current situation of conflict that projects in the traditional indigenous territories of Guatemala are going through. For this same reason, these companies also have *a certain degree of responsibility* in relation to the disrespect of the rights of the indigenous peoples affected in specific cases, independently of the obligations that correspond to the State.[6]
>
> (italics mine)

The companies, the second largest group of sovereigns in the Latin American economic context – after the local elites in the state government – also enjoy, in this sense, the aforementioned exception. It is recognized the "inevitable influence" they have had in the grave conflicts that are experienced in Guatemala – and the region – but nevertheless, they are attributed only "a certain degree of responsibility" ("*un cierto grado de responsabilidad*") regarding human rights violations. How can this contradiction be understood? Agamben has his answer, but he does not help us to think about new schemes of responsibility.

His reflections, however, do inspire criminological thinking that can motivate explanations and – to this we aspire here – conceptual lines of work to think about a field of crime that opens an integral way of thinking about attributions and responsibilities in the face of false promises – unfulfilled and even harmful. The attribution of maldevelopment to specific actors, as indicated in previous chapters, and each time more explicitly, is a primarily conceptual task in terms of restructuring thinking about the subject, to be able to advance in practices and discourses that materialize the idea of this reality. Beyond the law, as Agamben dreamed, it is possible. But first, through the mechanisms of the economy, culture and law, it is necessary to forge a sustainable framework of personal and collective achievements that permeate and nourish even international relations and meshes.

Development and maldevelopment

It is necessary, in the first place, to remember why this concept has been taken up and what is understood here by development (in extenso, in Chapter 1). Development is the great internal and external promise on which deregulation programs, new investments, plants and installations of extractive industries come. For that reason, it is important to pay attention to that promise and understand what it consists of. For example, although for a long time the idea and measurement of development was associated with the notion of "economic growth" and this proposal was made by measuring the Gross Domestic Product index, today it is clear that this index does not reflect the growth of a country in terms of development, but reflects only the movement of the balance of payments of a state. This includes those flows of money, on the one hand, which are linked to activities that are negative for personal and national life, such as the production and sale of weapons and alarms related to the increase in the feeling of insecurity, the payment for the cleanup of polluted areas or the work of felling trees; all this implies a rise for the GDP while it means the generation of environmental liabilities for the future, for example. On the other hand, these measurements do not include in the study activities that make an improvement in the quality of life but do not imply a balance of payments, such as domestic work done by housewives, volunteering in social work spaces or improvements to multicultural education conditions, to give just a few examples.

On the other hand, it is clear today that democracy, or at least political growth, is directly linked to the possibility of improving the living conditions of the population. In this sense, it is important to understand development as communicative, technical and educational realization, in addition, of course, to the basic requirements of health, food, housing and work, to mention the most basic needs that must be improved in their effective conditions.

All this configures what could be called development. It could also be explained as the establishment of bases and mechanisms of realization based on an idea of integral security (security understood in terms of realization and nonviolence, as seen in Chapter 2), that is, of basic needs met. This is, in short, the task of the good governor mentioned by Foucault (see Chapter 5), who, unlike the sovereign, cares about his people and is concerned about generating the conditions that allow that good life.

From there to the idea of *Buen Vivir* (Good Living), there is only one step. *Buen Vivir* is a notion currently disseminated theoretically and even normatively in the Latin American context and that recovers notions and beliefs of the indigenous populations that had already developed their models of social and institutional life prior to the foreign imposition of modernity and its modern states. The study of *Buen Vivir*, besides, is based on traditional political philosophy with postmodern European notions, that is, we are facing theoretical and political developments that are taking place in Latin American countries based on local ancestral knowledge (Catrilef Santana et al. 2018).

Development, therefore, as mentioned earlier, is not only avoiding the negative (poverty, unemployment, hunger, disease), but also acting genuinely in search of the positive for a population. The promotion of its well-being, work, food, health, cultural realization within of its own collective worldview and political participation, for example – all this would come under the aim of development. In one way or another, we understand then that development implies the active and committed movement of state and private actors in the generation of positive living conditions. In this way, the state responsibility extends to not committing harmful acts via their agents and at the same time to preventing negative acts (previously prohibited by law and sanctioned by a penal code, for example), but also, it extends to promoting the realization of positive facts and conditions. The responsibility, therefore, in the case that "development" does not come to fruition in the promised way, falls via different paths to different actors. It is not enough to allege that it was not this actor who contaminated, or that the state did not give orders to kill anyone, or that resources do not suffice, in order to disengage from responsibility. If the political action and its aspirations have been raised in terms of development, and this not only does not materialize but in the attempt even maldevelopment conditions are generated, this implies the possibility of responsibility on the part the state and its agents because of *to do* and *not to do, to allow to do* and *not to prevent doing.*[7]

The formulation of a conceptual category of maldevelopment in the field of study of criminology is an indispensable and pending task. Thinking about this category means leaving the structuralist explanations here, because they could prevent the possibility of attributions. Possible ideas inspired by Marx's thought, as in the case of several works cited in previous chapters, and with which we share the rejection of the violence of economic orders that impede the realization of rights, also accompany this work only up to here, given that for those thoughts, probably, overcoming a superstructure is not possible in terms of visibility and work on specific areas and scenarios of violence and attribution, but can be thought of only – in broad strokes – as a result of a great revolution. And this academic proposal neither is, at all, revolutionary, nor does it arise in terms of confrontation or struggle. The work proposed here to visualize violence and its attribution to achieve prevention and reparation is far from any combative idea.

Liability does not necessarily mean imputation in terms of punishment, as will be seen later. That is to say, it is not the fall of a system or jail for every politician or businessmen that is proposed here, but the prevention, reduction and repair of the harmful effects of practices – regardless of the system – that are violent. It seeks to formulate forms of individual, social and institutional action, from the identification of processes that perpetuate regional maldevelopment, in order to avoid it, or at least mitigate it. This also means, finally, from now on moving away, to a certain extent, from Foucault's work, which has contributed greatly to the understanding of violence, confrontations and territorial defense, in terms of sovereign power. His study proposal was fundamental for the description and analysis of the reality on which we are working. However, it is opportune to go further, to make possible from this work a possibility of resistance to the strategies of power that for centuries have been marking the western European scenario, and that have extended until today the effect of their actions in contexts such as Latin America through practices, words and specific actors.

Background and horizon of a conceptual category of "crime of maldevelopment" in criminology

The link between visible and invisible violence and the concept of development and maldevelopment is direct. If development understood in an integral sense is the realization of basic needs to the highest possible level of its potential, then maldevelopment, because it implies the distorted implementation of such mechanisms and avoidable obstacles to the fulfillment of basic needs, turns out to be – purely – violence. And if the maldevelopment is violence, it must be imputable. This imputation, which may be carried out through different channels of attribution of responsibility, must be part of the work of research and study of criminology.

When the anthropologist Alberto Chirif resignedly said about the Baguazo case: *"There is guilt but not guilty"*,[8] he was referring precisely to this, a reaction against which is our aim here. The idea is to identify those "guilty" subjects, but not only as a merely indignant and symbolic denunciation. A path of systematic imputation eventually carries criminal, administrative and civil responsibility, but even more, at the same time it has to have a visible result and a useful sustainable effect in the political, economic, social and cultural spheres. In short, it is about overcoming the leitmotif of *"nadie fue"* (*"nobody was responsible"*) so typical of the idea of social injustice and of the damages accumulated generation after generation. It is necessary to understand that imputation and responsibility are essential as means to achieve the proposal of methods of prevention, sanction and, essentially, reparation of damages in an integral way. Only sustained prevention and effective reparation can heal the wounds generated by centuries of violence, and only in this way will the vicious circle between the structural, cultural and physical forms of violence, so typical of maldevelopment, be able to weaken its force of rotation and repetition.

Maldevelopment understood as violence is what calls for it to be treated within the field of criminology. This allows explaining other levels of subjective, institutional, social, economic and international interaction. And it allows, at the same time, nourishing criminological areas of work that have addressed the issue in its various facets before. To formulate a conceptual category of maldevelopment is to gather and, at the same time, to further, at least in a first intellectual attempt, those advances.

In the first part of this chapter, the articulation of fundamentally European and American works, taking them as a "toolbox" for the study of maldevelopment, provides an important work base with ideas that ran throughout the twentieth century and have even advanced over almost two decades of the twenty-first century and its challenges. It is quite impossible to carry out a comprehensive review of all these theoretical approaches. However, some works and thinkers who gave interpretations particularly useful for the objective of this book need to be presented. Therefore, the following pages will expose the most salient ideas of those theoretical proposals that explain important areas of the harmful links between economy, politics, resource management and the cultural patterns that justify these harmful links. This is a first step in the exposition of this new conceptual category of maldevelopment, which is not isolated from the previous work of numerous scholars, but learns from them and extends the utility of them in new mergers and uses.

On the other hand, the meeting of those vast fields of specialized study in Europe and the United States will be supplemented here by the presentation of authors and theories that were not developed in the Global North, but have been developed fundamentally since the last third of the twentieth century and in the first part of the twenty-first century in Latin America. Latin American criminology has made interesting contributions that tend to lie outside the range of theoretical proposals in other contexts, and which are essential to understanding the frameworks of economy, politics and violence from a Latin American perspective. The visions of some outstanding authors who have devoted part of their work to the explanation of crime in the Latin American context are central here. The theoretical tours from the South and for the South – reducing here for now the spectrum of work to the Latin American South – are, therefore, a second source from which the proposal of the conceptual category of the crime of maldevelopment is nourished.

A third field of work, which provides a base and inspiration for the proposal made here, is given by works still in progress relating to concepts also still in definition but already strong, such as "social harm", and the need to understand it as a subject of criminological studies.

Criminological background on the part of the Global North

In the framework of what I call Criminological Background on the part of the Global North, and following what was already suggested in a previous work (Böhm 2016), authors and ideas are briefly mentioned and fundamentally divided into six areas. It is clear that many more could be mentioned, and that even these areas have many subdivisions, and it is clear as well that there is no pretension of exhaustive exposition; the aim is to show in which way they can be used to explain different aspects of the violences that are subject of this study – there are already handbooks and dictionaries for their integral presentation and systematic explanation of definitions and conceptual frameworks, so this is not the purpose here. I have chosen theoretical and empirical criminological works that allow me to explain the form of attention that is given by the state and social scope to certain economic, political and cultural behaviors and activities that are extremely harmful, which even today are not sufficiently perceived as harmful or as criminal by mainstream scholars. As stated previously, there is no pretension of integrality in this revision. Rather, it should be read as significant and preexisting brushstrokes on the canvas on which the theoretical criminological work has to continue. The reference is to works on *white-collar crime and the criminality of the powerful*, to *macrocriminality*, and to *mass media studies in criminology*. Moreover, in relation to those who are affected by their actions, *green criminology* and specific ideas of *victimology* will be presented. Finally, special attention is given to the idea of the *crimes of globalization*, a new concept profoundly close to the concept of maldevelopment as a crime. These six approaches, briefly outlined, will be taken up again in the explanation of the crime of maldevelopment.

White-collar crime and the criminality of the powerful

The white-collar crime theory, taken with the studies on the criminality of the powerful, offers a first stream of study with a focus on the economic and power situation of criminal actors. Although this field could be explained extensively, including even the development of a special editorial series on this topic – to which this book pertains – let's focus on some specific aspects.[9]

As is well known, Sutherland (1983) stresses in his work on *white-collar crime* that illegalities committed by businessmen in the pursuit of their activities are not a goal per se, but merely a means to increase profit. "Honest" businessmen commit crimes "only" if it is necessary and not as their principal goal; they seem to be invisible to authorities and the damage they cause seems to be invisible as well. Everything comes under the umbrella of their decent appearance, because they are "well-respected" and "well-connected" members of society (Spapens 2014: 224, 228). In fact, there are no sharply delimited fields of activity: legal and illegal, corporate activity and organized crime, perpetrator and bystander – there is true symbiosis and exchange between them (Huisman 2008, 2010; Fernández Steinko 2008: 38). This grey zone between legal and illegal activities is completely transferable from individual to transnational corporate actors and their activities. Looking at the eight cases studied earlier (Chapters 3 and 4), for example, it was clear that, on the one hand, individual criminal acts were difficult to identify. This happened on the occasion of the fraudulent situation claimed by the Mapuche people against Endesa in the Chilean *Ralco* case, of the diseases and deaths that occurred because of toxic water and environment even years later that the company ceased activity in the cases *Texaco/Chevron* and *Valle de Siria* in Ecuador and Honduras, respectively. This was also the case in the collective rape of *indigenous women of Lote 8* in Guatemala, which was committed in the context of a mining project, and also in relation to the threats, injuries and homicides committed on the battlefield of the Argentinean and Brazilian rural regions because of economic land speculation, as in the *MOCASE* and

Matopiba cases. Finally, it was explicit in the case of the death of 34 people in the massacre known as the *Baguazo* in Peru. These are all individual behaviors and effects which are not easy to attribute to a legal person such as a corporation or institution. This is why it is so often heard that corporations do business; they do not commit crimes.

On the other hand, highly visible legal corporations, entrepreneurs and political actors with important investments or interests in the respective countries have been directly related to the grievous harm that has been caused. The companies Goldcorp, Endesa, Frisco, Chevron-Texaco, Hudbay, (and also Home Ministers, Energy Ministers and even Presidents, in some cases) were directly related to these results. The corporations are seen as "related" to the "problem", at most. As the UN document stated, "They have a certain responsibility".[10] However, this link does not seem to be strong enough to hold any of the corporations to account. What is crucial here is that individual acts are not easy to distinguish (Spapens 2014: 227) and causality is not easy to prove: in sum, big companies are not perceived as criminal.

Even grievous harm is not perceived as "criminal" (Hillyard & Tombs 2015) if it is not defined by the Criminal Code and if there is no visible individual harm to be causally explained and claimed (Albrecht 2007).

What is more, large companies usually have complex decision-making and management structures as well as a strong economic and political position in the country or countries where they carry out their business, as was the situation in all the cases analyzed in this study. This circumstance, added to the aforementioned reality that specific politicians are usually immediately related and recognized as involved in the adoption of specific political measures and decisions, may be analyzed from the perspective of the criminality of the powerful (Pearce 1976; Scheerer 1993; Barak 2015). According to this concept, the structural conditions for committing criminal acts in a systematic way are shaped by economic actors, economic relationships and powerful networks and structural institutional conditions (e.g. cultural or religious) which remain unchecked because of the state-routinized crime and crime control through the "decriminalization and deregulation of the powerful's production of harmful behavior", the "non-indictment of obvious criminal offenses" and "the discursive rationalization by ideologues for and defenders of the prevailing political and economic arrangements" (Barak 2017: 62). In the cases of *Ralco, Texaco/ Chevron, Valle de Siria* and *Indigenous Women of Lote 8*, the companies Endesa, Texaco, Goldcorp and CGN/Hudbay possessed an integral decision-making power and control in place. This encompassed not only their facilities, but also the people working and living in the area: depending on the case, medical assistance in their own centers, for example, was a better way of showing that "people care", whereas the health situation of workers and affected people had long been considered a "private" matter beyond state control. Here, we should think about the fact that if a transnational corporation replaces or displaces state intervention, the effectiveness and protection of rights is displaced as well (for an

African example, see Hönke 2010). Even more, in the cases *Salaverna* and *El Peñasquito*, the economic and political level and the relevance of the project led to the complete removal of the towns to other places, the destruction of the old towns and the construction of the new ones carried out exclusively by the companies Frisco and Goldcorp, respectively.

Let us remember the context once again. Viewed from an institutional perspective, as has been seen, Latin American democracies are often characterized by corruption, opacity in the functioning of bureaucratic proceedings, foreign-oriented conservative groups uninterested in the development of the low-class population, lack of respect for their own native people ("lack of solidarity", Ruggiero 2001: 141), violence by the state and against the state and political violence carried out as "protection" for these transactions, among other historically repeated and even currently common practices (for the political context, see Chapter 1). The need for and interest in economic development led the local political interests and the foreign economic interests to a common understanding. Besides, inequality is often accepted as historically conditioned and almost as normal *(cultural violence)*; only political and economic actors belonging to the selected strong sectors are those who are usually in the position of running businesses with foreign actors at corporate levels. Because of these factors, it is not difficult to understand that damage caused in the course of big business in the framework of deregulation of economic rules, and the violation of fundamental rights will not easily be brought to the judicial system. If businessmen, politicians and judges belong to a similar socioeconomic sector (and they usually do) with similar attitudes, it is not surprising that the harm caused by some of them will be neither condemned nor judged by the others. Powerful actors, in Latin America, are those who decide what is to be prosecuted or not prosecuted (such as the Chilean executive avoiding the prosecution of fraud practices by Endesa in the *Ralco* case), what is to be prohibited or not prohibited (as the Mexican, Peruvian or Argentinean legislation opening the possibility of destructive practices by the investors in forms that had previously been prohibited, as was the situation in the cases *Valle de Siria*, *Baguazo* and *MOCASE*); the powerful actors (including international actors) also decide where a new polluting industry or open-pit mine is to be opened (as in the *Salaverna*, *El Peñasquito* and *Texaco/Chevron* cases) or where land must be taken from indigenous people (see *Baguazo*, *Texaco/Chevron* and *Matopiba* as the most significant cases in this respect).[11] For this reason, because of the lack of interest in prosecution, and because of the economic benefit for many of these powerful actors (through legal or illegal means), social harm and human rights violations caused by corporate business are not seen as crime by the mass media, the public or even by governmental and judicial spheres, but rather as an inevitable side effect (externality) of progress and development – which, by the way, never materializes. Self-regulatory practices may be demanded, and the compliance with some rules can even be part of the visible image of some corporations (Cufré et al. 2018), but this does usually not lead to more responsibility or to less harm in society (Aguirre Alvarez 2018). This explanation can be better understood with the already-seen counterexample of a case of non-approval of a specific economic development on the part of the government. In Ecuador, the change in the presidency in 2007 gave a crucial new perspective to the *Texaco/Chevron* case. Whereas before 2007, Ecuadorian regimes friendly to neoliberal and foreign investments neglected the impact of the damaging activities carried out by Chevron, the left-wing, socially oriented regime that assumed the presidency that year paid attention to the victims' demands and publicly stated that foreign actors would not be allowed to take advantage of the local population in the future. The fact that years later, the same President Correa was violating the rights of indigenous populations and human rights activists in oil areas (see Chapter 2 for an explanation of this "brown progressivism"), does not change the fact – quite the contrary! it confirms it – that the good or bad relations between political and economic actors – the powerful – has an immediate effect on the respect or violation of the rights of the population. Without cooperation between those actors, the exploitation and violation of individual and social rights would not be possible.

Macrocriminality

The concept of *macrocriminality* (Jäger 1989) refers to a political structure involved in the commission of crimes. It refers, essentially, to the state apparatus and to activities conforming to the system and matched to the framework inside the structure of the organization, of the power apparatus or of another context of collective action (Jäger 1989: 11). In this sense, although the original idea linked macrocriminality to violent dictatorial regimes, the concept is useful when we rethink the role of the state in the continuous acceptance of human rights violations in the business methods of transnational corporations in currently democratic Latin American countries, and even more, when we think about the release of new economic measures which openly violate fundamental rights at the individual or collective level. The state, social structures, and government interest facilitate a criminogenic scenario with their insistence on development programs which are, indeed, paths of ever-greater non-satisfaction of needs.

State-corporate crime (Kramer et al. 2002), that is, crime specifically related to the interaction between political and corporate actors and interests, including corruption practices, judicial and administrative favors, fraudulent tenders and others, in this sense, is distinct. In the *Ralco* case, the company Endesa was not sued by the Office of Protection of Indigenous People (CONADI) because the government was afraid of Endesa's possible reaction and of losing investments in the case of criminal proceedings with charges of fraud. This means that whereas one office of the Executive (CONADI) was protecting the people and trying to act against Endesa, other offices, at the same hierarchical level (Energy Office) or even superior to it (Vice-President's Office), were protecting the project (see Namuncura 1999: 26). This could be understood as a "cooperation problem" (Spapens 2014: 228), or it could be understood as a state that takes active part in damaging structures, because the giant state structure and interrelationships are the ideal framework for the continuity of the economic plan promoted internationally. Harm in these cases is closely related to deep structures. In this sense,

> in order to provide a more detailed and deep evaluation of the mechanisms, actors and processes that allow for state-corporate harm to unfold, it is necessary to go beyond the description of the manifestation itself in trying to understand the macro structures (political economy, state nature, etc.) and global processes that frame and drive such manifestations.
>
> (Zaitch & Gutiérrez Gómez 2015: 389)

Because of the interest in development, governments take harmful decisions and allow, by omission, harmful activities on the part of large economic actors. Omission is always a possibility in macrocriminality (Alpaca Pérez 2013); however, with respect to the economic policies and the relation to economic actors acting in their own country, omission becomes the central mechanism of action. And this happens, without a doubt, with another fact, which is quite different from the original concept of macrocriminality: the organization (Contrafatto et al. 2018). The implicit permission is by no means organized, because different offices and agents of the state intervene in different instances and moments of the economic undertaking. Macrocriminality, in this case, thus becomes a form of *unorganized macrocriminality* – which does not mean that it is any less harmful, of course. This implicit permission is, in many cases, the same as authorization for rights violations. In this sense, even though macrocriminality was developed as a category for the explanation of severe human rights violations and crimes perpetrated in the context of nonlegal regimes (Ambos 2005: 51), if the structural conditions are repeated to such an extent in democratic times that fundamental needs are systematically not satisfied, and the state and its functionaries allow the harmful activities of third parties, the idea of *macrocriminality by omission* reveals itself as useful (Contrafatto et al. 2018), and this will be one of the main distinctive features of the crime of maldevelopment.

Mass media studies in criminology

Mass media studies present a third approach to this subject, one that is useful for criminological analysis. Social indifference and institutional impunity may be at least partly explained according to the higher or lower presence of a given piece of news in the mass media, and according to the specific construction of public opinion targeted by the report (Lee 2005: 129). Therefore, this approach offers conceptual components related to the visibility or invisibility of illegal activities and their consequences (see Jewkes 2015: Chapter 1). Cultural violence, of course, is the main expression of violence involved here.

In Latin America, large mass media corporations are usually part of economic groups connected to other industries apart from the media, or are related to governmental actors. For this reason, conflicts related to big companies are only partly shown or reported in order to avoid the formation of negative public opinion (Lee 2005: 133, 148), and because the questioning of the neoliberal economic system by the mainstream media is quite impossible (Pauls et al. 2015: 268–269). In this way, the audience's degree of empathy with conflicts and their protagonists is strictly managed. In the *Ralco* case, it was apparent that the conservative mass media represented the conflict from the perspective of the government, framing the Mapuche population as violent and fundamentalist, and presenting harsh criticisms to the environmental protection discourse, whereas the progressive media put the focus on the difficulties experienced by the indigenous communities and the detrimental impact of current economic processes (Namuncura 1999: epilogue).[12] In the same vein, the theory of Peruvian President Alan García, which he called "the gardener's dog", was given space in the main conservative media, *El Comercio*, forming with this comparison a social idea of indigenous people as the enemy and a lazy culture responsible for the national economic difficulties (see Chapter 4).

The strategies of "omission" *(Auslassung)*, "abbreviation and fragmentation" *(Verkürzung und Fragmentierung)* and of "episodic framing" *(episodische Einrahmung)* by a news release in order to construct reports in the "correct" way are common domestic mechanisms of the mass media (Lee 2005: 135). In the same sense, the "de-historization" *(deshistorización)* and "criminalization of reality" *(criminalización de la realidad)* are strategies that have been as well (Rodríguez 2011). However, these strategies are also central to broadcasting information abroad. Only big groups have the possibility of coming into contact with other important actors of international media businesses. For this reason, only part-news, or even conflicting perspectives (Pauls et al. 2015: 273) are translated and broadcast in foreign countries. The problem is that because of the lack of language skills or the impossibility of getting in contact with local alternative sources of information and social networks, the international mass media's information is not easy to draw on. Economic and political actors, for this reason, promote and take advantage of these filter systems in transnational information flows. In this way, further, mainstream mass media support unequal economic standards and social harm (Seaga Shaw 2011: 173, 165). In the *Chevron* case, Steve Donziger, the North American lawyer who led the victims' claim in Ecuador and United States, has made canny use of the mass media, for instance by attracting political and public attention through the arrangement of interviews in principal programs and magazines, inviting celebrities to support the claim and publishing material later, even in *Vanity Fair*.[13] It is remarkable here, however, that Donziger's economic and experienced position is not usual in human rights issues. His New York law firm was in the position to finance the media campaign, and because of that, the information published was sometimes even partial in the other direction – and this has caused several problems in the judicial processes as well; in fact, the way in which Donziger managed the mass media confirms that his good economic position and his professional status were the key elements in arousing interest on the part of the media, in Ecuador and abroad. The victims, indigenous people without economic resources of their own, could never have received that much attention. The findings of a quantitative study on international media reports of environmental disasters has shown, in this sense, that in the coverage of the oil spill in the Gulf of Mexico in 2010, "only 4 percent of the total reporting on risk made reference to vulnerable populations; the rest focused on marine life, oil companies, and capital protection" (Pauls et al. 2015: 276). Similarly, in a prior work, Wilkins (1987: 101) explained that in prestige media reports, the citizens who had been directly affected by the Bhopal disaster were the less quoted sources (the more cited ones being institutional and corporate spokespersons). Victims and the violence suffered, even when mass media inform us about conflicts, remain invisible.

With regard to the media, the approach of Abudara Bini[14] is particularly interesting in that it explains that the images on television and the need for commercialization of news, which are actually commodities more than a service provided by the corporate mass media, do not allow the persistent or integral following of some realities when these occur in "slow motion", that is, when there are no instant, quick pictures or new headlines from day to day. In the *Valle de Siria* case, for example, it was seen that some diseases and deaths occurred years after the mine had been deactivated. The news about what is happening right now is not capable of showing and reporting the death that takes place in slow motion, the invisible death of those who are affected with toxic metals now that are not going to kill them until years in the future. They are dying, but this is not a picture for the media, because they are still alive. In this sense, the media, like criminal law, do not see the violence, and when they do see it, it is too late.

Green criminology

The invisibility of these cases, further, is probably related to the characteristics of the immediately affected subjects. These subjects are distant populations on the one hand, and the environment on the other. The perspective of *green criminology* has already explained some central aspects in terms of the environment as object of the damaging activity. Originally, these studies were concerned with crimes related to fauna, flora and the environment. Over the past few years, however, they have provided interesting results on the severe impact of those crimes on the life and rights of the most marginalized segments of the world's population and the conflicts of interest related to natural resources such as minerals, water, oil and gas as well as to surfaces ideal for the production of energy (rivers, wind) and primary food (grains, soy) (Jarrell & Ozymy 2014; Brisman et al. 2015; Hall 2014: 103; Walters 2006), and in particular, on the life and rights of indigenous people (Boekhout van Solinge & Kuijpers 2013: 202; Brisman et al. 2015: 2;

Carrasco & Fernández 2009). Furthermore, this subdiscipline adds an innovative look at infractions committed by complex offenders against widely dispersed victim groups and spatial areas – which often remain diffuse (White & South 2013; Spapens 2014: 224). The impact, however, may be easily seen, as it is the case of physical consequences in the use of pesticides in rural areas near to small villages (Eleisegui 2013, and see also the documentary *Misiones de Tiza* 2014).

Economically, Latin American countries are poorer than western European or North American countries. However, the former have many natural resources, as has been shown in the cases described here. Because of these factors, foreign investments bring huge capital flow and numerous problematic projects (Ebus & Kuijpers 2015, for extractive industries McGregor 2009) which are interesting for governments and local business groups in Latin America, even if they are carried out in ways that may be harmful to the population. This is the afore-mentioned state-corporate crime (Kramer et al. 2002), but it extends to include environmental harm (for a review, see Brisman & South 2015). In cases in which an environmental impact study is required before the start of an exploi-tation project or for the evaluation of a new economic policy by the state, it is common that the results are not impartial, because even scientific and academic institutions might be involved for their own interests or well-founded fears; and in the case that they are impartial, they are often considered an affront to the corporation or to the government. In many other cases, as seen explicitly in the case of *Valle de Siria*, the environmental license for a mining project is granted independently of any environmental impact study (Mayoral et al. 2018).

These conflicts between interests in resources and the lack of protection have been specifically seen in the cases by talking about water for hydroelectric dams (the *Ralco* case), oil for petroleum (the *Texaco/Chevron* and *Baguazo* cases), silver and gold (the *Salaverna*, *El Peñasquisto* and *Indigenous Women of Lote 8* cases) and plenty of land and territories for large new projects by agrarian industries (the *MOCASE* and *Matopiba* cases).

The harm caused is, however, not only environmental. The environment is life for indigenous people such as the Mapuche in the *Ralco* case or the Awa-jún in the *Baguazo* case, to mention only two. In both cases, the impact on the environment was a concrete threat to the population. In the first case, the con-struction of the dam caused the displacement of the people from its territory and, for example, the waterlogging of their ancestral area, cemeteries included, which for them represented the waterlogging of their identity. In the *Baguazo* case, the loss of territory was in principle just a threat which in that instance did not materialize precisely because of the extremely violent massacre that took place between indigenous demonstrators and policemen after the protest of the Awajún. Their future was threatened and today, almost ten years later, the threat is still there, because new permits are again being processed by the min-ing company Afrodita. The perspective is not good. In this case, the concept of horizon scanning (White & South 2013) can be useful as a possible instru-ment to be applied not only with respect to the environment, but also to the affected populations. Green criminology, as the work of Lorenzo Natali (2016) has also shown through the potentialities of the visually qualitative approach and the contact with the affected people at a narrative level, is interested in the environment *because* people are living there. The connection of these proposals with the inherent meaning of the environment for the indigenous people in Latin America could take the analysis to even further levels in the context of maldevelopment.

Victimology

From the whole and extensive study field of victimology (for a general review, see Fattah 2010), three ideas will be stressed here as especially useful for the explanation of cases of economic projects, violence and permanently non-satisfied needs in Latin America.[15]

The isolation of vulnerable individuals has an impact on the risk of being affected by a criminal act and on the possibility of being helped. Acts committed against them can easily be hidden by the offender and thus, they often remain invisible to third parties. In the Latin American context, indigenous people (the *Ralco, Baguazo* and *Indigenous Women of Lote 8* cases), rural populations (the *Texaco/Chevron, MOCASE* and *Matopiba* cases) and people of remote little villages (the *Salaverna, El Peñasquito* and *Valle de Siria* cases) are often isolated from urban areas, or at least they are poorly connected to urban areas and institutional actors. This situation makes them more vulnerable and "available" for business interests, because the lack of access to information and to justice actors is an obstacle to obtaining official information on the conflict situation or for asking for the protection of their rights. In the *Ralco* case, the elders of the Mapuche-Pehuenche communities of Ralco, for example, had to undergo a strenuous, daylong journey in various local vehicles and buses, through many villages, before they reached the capital city of Santiago de Chile to inform CONADI about the activities of the firm Endesa in their home region (Namuncura 1999: 9), which had remained unknown to many authorities until that time.

A second relevant aspect is *how* a person or a group of people may interact with the offender or eventual offender before, during and after the commission of the crime, which defines the degree of involuntary collaboration that the victim could have given to the future author of the crime (see Fattah 2010: 47, 51, on ordinary violent crime). In the cases introduced here, the fact that the corporations are transnational has a particular impact on the communication opportunities: on the one hand, foreign actors are usually perceived as more trustworthy than local actors, but, on the other hand, the communication level is not always good. The idea of working for a transnational corporation has given Ecuadorians (the *Chevron* case), Mexicans (the *Salaverna* and *El Peñasquisto* cases) and Hondurans (the *Valle de Siria* case) the hope of better working conditions. In all cases, the individuals had been marginalized by their own state (and in the *Ralco* case, even historically persecuted by the state). This was the situation in the *Chevron* case, because the promise to the local population was the opportunity to be trained and employed in the corporation, for example, but these promises were not fulfilled. If the people refused to work under inadequate labor conditions, the state would respond with physical violence (the *Baguazo* case).

In the *Ralco* case, the promise of the corporation was not for improved labor conditions, but of better land and living conditions for the Mapuche-Pehuenche population, which was not fulfilled either. In this case, the involuntary collaboration of the victims consisted in the participation in individual or small groups' conversations with representatives of the firm instead of maintaining the community voice. The isolation mentioned earlier, combined with the firm's strategy of dividing the community, increased the chances of victimization. It has already been well expressed:

> Human rights violations are often preceded by stepwise invasions of the victim's territory. [. . .] Some large-scale victimizations cannot be achieved without gradual preparation of both the victim population and the victimizers' social environment. Stepwise victimization becomes possible if the institutions of formal social control – police and courts – do not control the victimization of people regardless of group, but actively, one-sidedly, serve the powerful.
>
> (Kirchhof 2010: 114)

For this reason, access to not only governmental channels, but also academic research findings and specialists is crucial in order to give the communities a voice (Jarrell & Ozymy 2014: 254).

A proper analysis of this interrelationship offers information for the construction of victimization patterns and, therefore, the design of alarm signals and prevention systems. The interrelationship between the population affected by new economic projects and industrial plants and the (future) offender is often very close and harmful. Socially, large parts of the population in Latin American countries do not have meaningful access to education, minority groups are often displaced and ignored and informal jobs are a common situation among large segments of the population, among other issues. Communities with low education levels, with no other employment options, and with a close relationship to nature but not to "papers" or bureaucratic matters cannot really evaluate and make a proper decision about whether they will really have new jobs or whether the company will respect their environment and their fundamental sources of food and water (soil and rivers), as was explicit in all the cases analyzed here.

These ideas lead to the third path to be discussed here, this time with a broader perspective in the sense of the relation of these collectives with the social and civil position they occupy in their countries. Following Fattah, but applying their concepts to the Latin American situation, some authors (Costanzo et al.

2018) suggest that living in certain areas (near natural resources, for example) can be considered a "risk activity", and that there is, in addition, further structural and cultural exposure in the cases of rural and indigenous communities. From these two examples alone, we can say that a combined strategy, better precautions, should be possible between the proposals of green criminology and the ordinary practices of crime prevention. Horizon scanning, again, is a possible means to register risk situations, given that the previous conditions have already been sufficiently characterized both in theory and empirically.

The whole picture puts these sectors, actual victims or potential victims, in an unfavorable situation with respect not only to the national actors, but to international actors as well (see also Viano 1990: xiv–xv). If they knew these companies would later use physical force to quash protests and to avoid claims of environmental damage, they would probably reject the project even more decisively. But this is often not the case. And when this is the case and the people protest even before the firm has begun its development, they are suppressed by police and military means and even, in some cases, condemned as terrorists (the *Ralco* case) (see Villegas 2009; Richards 2010).

Crimes of globalization

The new concept of Crimes of Globalization was presented by Friedrichs in 2007 as an "emerging hybrid form" of white-collar crimes (2007a: 165) and developed quickly as an interesting field of study (Rothe et al. 2008). It was probably established as a conceptual field of work for criminology through the recent work by Friedrichs and Rothe, which explains the various features and fields of the new category (Friedrichs & Rothe 2015). Starting from the idea that "globalization has important political and cultural dimensions" (Friedrichs 2007a: 168), the economic aspect prevails and the focus of the study is set on international financial institutions such as the World Bank, and the impact that several financing regulations, requirements and preferences have in the world. The background and the interest of Friedrichs and Rothe is close to the interest and questions treated by the present study of the crime of maldevelopment, in the sense that interdisciplinary and international research is needed, and especially in the fact that crimes of the powerful are also a kind of subgroup of white-collar crime.

The impact of the international financing institutions according to their concept (already in Friedrichs 2007b) is also fundamentally seen in the Global South – that is, the negative impact – and they also sustain that the approach should open the view to forms of activity which would not be considered criminal from an ordinary perspective. This, it could be said, is clearly an inheritance from Sutherland's original proposal. The new approach, however, goes much further because the framework is no longer national, not even regional, but global. In this sense, again, the familiarity with the crime of maldevelopment is clear.

Two points must nevertheless be indicated as quite different in the two approaches: crimes of globalization are centered in financing institutions at the international level, and analyze therefore capital flows. What is exactly done with those money flows, and their immediate impact on the local population or the interaction between institutions and national and local actors, remain in the background – or it is at least not the primary goal of the research. For this reason, it is argued here that whereas the crimes of globalization as a category are thought of as global, maldevelopment is studied primarily as the interaction between global and local interrelations and actors; maldevelopment – as the name shows – is the study of the impact and result of practices on the affected region. Global policies can have an impact on microphysical spaces and on individuals and local communities which interact with such economic and political policies. For this reason, the crime of maldevelopment should actually be seen as a combination of global and local – hence, *glocal*.

The link between international finances and financing institutions and extractive industries, on the one hand, and on the imposition of extremely difficult economic conditions on states of the Global South, such as external debt, for example, on the other hand, is the main subject of study for Friedrich and Rothe. Violence, however, as such and as a breeding ground for the emergence of countless other forms of violence, both visible and invisible, is not addressed as a priority. And this is a central difference, because the in-depth study of violence leads to the study of violations of human rights in democratic times as a main element in the concept of maldevelopment as a crime. Human rights are, indeed, considered as a consequence of crimes of globalization that requires more research (Friedrichs & Rothe 2015: 24s).

From these considerations, it is, therefore, possible to conclude that both concepts are closely related and the complementarity of the approaches can be of use for the reciprocal improvement and support of these studies.

Criminological background on the part of the Global South

While in the early twentieth century, criminology in Latin America was still strongly guided by the state of European criminological knowledge in the late nineteenth century, in the course of the twentieth century, Latin America strengthened its foundations for its own criminology. This process was largely driven by the critical thoughts that political exiles found in academies like the Italian, the German or the French, for example, in the 1960s and 1970s, and which they then brought with them or transmitted from those places with a strong burden of renewal and criticism of authoritarian state spaces and of the reproductive penal system of inequalities. With this imprint, then, Latin American criminology was installed as a clearly critical criminology, strongly inspired by Marxist ideas and its new studies. It was particularly focused on the explanation of the more or less violent oppressions and injustices that both under dictatorships and, later, with the arrival of neoliberal measures during the subsequent democracies, marked the forms of the penal system so directly linked to the prevailing economic systems at the national and international levels. While it is true that in Latin America there have been other voices of criminology (Del Olmo 1999; Marteau 2003; Elbert 2012b: 59 ss., 165 ss.), here we will put the emphasis on the critical perspective, because this is the one that has been genuinely concerned with recontextualizing North American and European ideas and proposals in the reality of the region. For this reason, this critical criminology is the only one that can be considered truly Latin American (and not merely imported or copied) (Anitua 2005: 418 ss.). For the purposes of this work, there are three authors who provide key elements of study, on which this proposal of a conceptual category of crime of maldevelopment intends to advance. They are Lolita Aniyar de Castro, Carlos Elbert and Eugenio Raúl Zaffaroni. Of course, many other authors have dealt with connected themes, but it is these three who have marked milestones of reflection that have greatly nurtured this study.

Lolita Aniyar de Castro and the political engagement of criminology

The idea of social damage, along with a way of thinking about criminology according to which criminology does not remain in academic thinking but is directly linked to the political space, characterized the work of Lola (Lolita, as she was called) Aniyar de Castro to the point that she took on the challenge of turning her theoretical and normative ideas into action when she worked in the capacity of the governor of Zulia, in Venezuela.

Her work is particularly relevant here because she did not focus her attention on regulations, but specifically on the results of certain actions, on the institutions that generated them, and especially on the victims who suffered them, without succumbing to the temptation of simple proposals of resentment or harsher punitiveness for the offenders. As she herself said (Aniyar de Castro 2010: 55 ss.), her work was perhaps the first to present a book on victimology (inspired by previous authors, of course), giving the conflictive relationship between offender and victim a relevance that criminal law does not usually grant (Aniyar de Castro 1969, 2010: 55 ss.). This relationship and the claim that the study should pay attention to both actors, offender and victim, as well as to all institutions that before, during and after that conflict intervene between them, was undoubtedly inspired by her broad, integrative approach in terms of balance and complementarity between security, freedom and equality (Aniyar de Castro 2010). For her, this was the framework for any idea of a desirable society. Her work, in this way, exceeded the purely criminological or criminal field, in the strictest sense, and advocated the necessary consideration of these disciplines, and criminal policy, as spaces for political action and social transformation (Anitua 2005: 420). The total conviction that human rights could be realized only in a context in which that security, freedom and equality were integral brings us to the central idea of this work on maldevelopment. The visible and invisible violence that is fueled by deregulated economic activity in the

Latin American context shows a biased vision of security, reduced to physical security and forgetting the security of the fulfillment of basic needs. Besides, violence in Latin America also demonstrates an elitist vision of the freedom thought in terms of individual and economic freedom, and not freedom as a space for the realization of individual and social rights, and evidence, finally, that the idea of equality is plainly neglected in the region.

This explicit dedication of her work to the realization of the human rights of all, without the exclusion of anyone, and to the defense of the democratic space as a political framework that enables such realization, led Lolita Aniyar de Castro to be critical of the restrictions on freedom that were introduced by Hugo Chávez's government, and this criticism has generated countercriticism by those who identified with the strong socialist approach that Chávez represented (Torres Luzardo 2014). Her opposition was consistent with her life work in pursuit of respect for human rights and the reduction of conflict situations that could impede the realization of rights. The scaling of the walls that have historically marked, in the field of criminology, the idea that *acting in the protection of rights of some* automatically means *to be against others*, is undoubtedly one of the great merits of her work, which was devoted to individuals as human beings and to the protection of the rights of all.

With this inspiration, the work proposed here does not intend to promote confrontational or vindictive theses, but to prop up the possible spaces of cooperation, having as an absolute goal the reduction of social damages that are the effect and cause of violence.

Carlos Elbert and the criminological approach to globalization and exclusion

Professor Carlos Elbert, also a criminal chamber judge at the time, has dedicated his work to criminology in an integral way, as did Aniyar de Castro, so his proposals have not been locked into the concepts and logic of crime and punishment. Elbert has worked out, in a prominent way difficult to find in other authors of law and criminology, the links between crime on a small scale and large scale and the national, regional and international neoliberal capitalist economic order (Elbert 2012a, 2012b, 2016). His work is characterized by historical material of high rigor. When he discusses thinkers or governments, what he offers is often a truly specialized work of history, and this allows him, when speaking of today, to offer a kind of genealogy, a history of the present situation of penal institutions and criminal policy, which can be understood only if it is placed in a certain historical moment and geographic space. From the marginal neighborhoods found in Buenos Aires at the beginning of the twentieth century (Elbert 2012b: 59 ss.) to the situation of Latin American external debt at the beginning of the twenty-first century (Elbert 2016: 135 ss.), nothing escapes his analytical and critical historical work. Two axes that run through his analysis are globalization and exclusion. He explains the first – globalization – with all the warnings of the case that Elbert himself always offers – as the economic and institutional mechanisms that dissolve states' position of power as service providers and replace them with economic actors as decision-makers and designers of policies and acts (Elbert 2016: 99 ss.); the second – exclusion – is explained by Elbert as the visible result of the state's withdrawal in terms of unemployment, housing instability, decrease in education and health levels experienced by a majority that is less and less accepted by the market, and which is increasingly concentrated in the urban centers, leaving the rural area with the consequent increase of unsatisfied basic needs, despair and conflict (Elbert 2012b: 177 ss.).

Hence, Elbert's description and economic analysis in terms of national orders, and regarding the generation of these orders starting from the role that Latin America has historically had in the international context – specifically, in its relations with Europe and the United States – are in the same vein as the theses raised in the present work. The eight cases described in Chapters 3 and 4 provided concrete examples of measures emanating from a global order, and of situations of exclusion generated by those measures or undertakings. In this sense, Elbert's Latin American vision also supports, from its contributions of historical data and economic figures, the diagnosis made here. Where there are differences, however, it is in the subject of his work – fundamentally dedicated to the visible effects in the urban areas – and in the scope he gives to it, of descriptive purpose, but – to my understanding – without pretending to design strategies that can overcome the situation. On several occasions, Elbert analyzes the deficiencies of the region with respect to development and growth. Responsibility, however, seems – as is often the case – to be dissolved for him in the mechanisms of macroeconomics and international pressures.

Eugenio Raúl Zaffaroni and mass crimes in authoritarian and democratic times

In the same line of critical and realistic work of the previous scholars, in the sense of combining the data and contexts of the Latin American reality in explanatory theoretical works, and integrating research of the European and North American academy but generating knowledge and constructing proposals from and for Latin America, the work of Eugenio Raúl Zaffaroni must be mentioned. This author, in particular, has also devoted part of his work in recent years to the explanation of mass crimes, traditionally alien to the field of Latin American criminology (Zaffaroni 2011: 447 ss., 2012a); moreover, it has advanced the idea of social damage, studying the relevance of activities that have a negative impact on the environment, and through it, on human beings and human rights, their culture and their identities (Zaffaroni 2012b). In this way, his work also provides an important background and study base that must be incorporated when studying the crime of maldevelopment. Street crime and the crime of the apparatus of political and economic power are comparable for Zaffaroni as far as their dimensions are concerned. He comes to this conclusion as it not only records the damage in the individual sense, but also proposes a consideration of the damage generated by the state from the large amount of damage that occurs daily, and "drip by drip" ("*por goteo*") is generated in the hands of a selective criminal system, which acts against the individuals of marginal collectives (Zaffaroni 2015: 62). On the other hand, he considers the state to be an agent of the great damages that the act of a politician or a company can generate at one time. Zaffaroni was awarded the Stockholm Criminology Prize in 2009 (the same year John Hagan was awarded as well) in acknowledgment of his work on State Crime as a study subject for criminology. His idea is based on the concept of macrocriminality analyzed in previous paragraphs, but goes further, and does so in the same sense in which in this work is also intended to go "further". Zaffaroni analyzes macrocriminality related to the use of the neutralization techniques of Sykes and Matza as mechanisms for the negligent state attitude with regard to its violation of rights (2012a: 87). He focuses on the need to explain mass crimes as related not only to dictatorships and armed conflicts, but also to the current versions of human rights violations in democratic times. He explains how that functioning, whether through massive physical violence – authoritarian regimes – or invisible – as in current democracies and the systematic selection of the penal system and the urban marginalization – can be thought of in terms of criminological categories (Zaffaroni et al. 2000: 6 ss., Zaffaroni 2011: 171 ss., also Gómez Urso 2012).

In this sense, as in the work of Aniyar de Castro and Elbert, Zaffaroni's proposal is absolutely regional and disruptive. None of the three, despite their studies and research in "*the first world*", were willing to copy discourses pleasing to the criminologies and knowledge of the mainstream, or in economic terms, of the establishment, and all of them simply refused to apply foreign theories to explain local situations.

Just as at some point it was done with white-collar crime and in another instance with macrocriminality, the processes of which Zaffaroni speaks, in the same sense in which we have also presented here processes of visible and invisible violence and its direct link with political and economic decisions, can be understood as a category with its own characteristics in the region. In our case, we propose that the crime of maldevelopment should not be considered merely as a conceptual category, but rather as a basis for the future design of accountability, reparation and prevention strategies in an integral sense.

Social harm as a subject of study

All the approaches and authors reviewed in the previous paragraphs are somehow gathered in spaces of shared dialogue that begin to take place between criminologists who risk more and more, to question the limits of the discipline, in their desire to develop a field of research that is socially useful and politically engaged. The tension between intellectual skepticism and political engagement (Cohen 2013) should be overcome.

As seen earlier, the most damaging acts are not always identified as crimes in national penal codes, and if they are, specific cases and forms of prosecution have in many cases rendered them useless for large-scale damage caused by structures that follow extremely complex rules of interaction. For these reasons, only a focus on the social damage (criminal offenses, violation of human rights or whatever label they have been given) can give a dimension of the real harm caused (see the terminological discussion in Hillyard & Tombs 2015; Rivera Beiras 2014: 253) and the required accountability.

Thus, in a recent work published in Barcelona, the need to expand categories and to compromise the legal order with solutions of a political nature is discussed, as it had been already said by Aniyar de Castro, but brought to the field of conflicts and to the economic violence of today. In that work, Luigi Ferrajoli, in his contribution entitled "Criminology, global crimes and criminal law: The epistemological debate in contemporary criminology" (2014), comes closer to the discussion about criminology and penal systems with respect to mass crimes. He is talking about mass crimes in the sense of international crimes, but the point is exactly this: these considerations are applicable also to severe social harm, irrespective of the concrete system that supports or causes it:

> Only by adopting the autonomous and external point of view of critical criminology – the one that refers to the "social damage" [. . .] – can we investigate and even see the existence of crimes that are not foreseen as crimes by any penal order and, in the opposite direction, the existence of prohibited offences that are not crimes but only the result of selective filters adopted by the different legal systems. What unites these very serious crimes, and what a criminology not subordinated to the constituted powers cannot continue to exclude from the subject of study itself, are certain elements common to all of them. These elements, which a critical criminology has the obligation to find out, are: beyond its terrible social damages, its character of mass crimes, its impunity and its substantial acceptance by our public opinions in spite of the atrocities that present.
>
> (Ferrajoli 2014: 84)

This fragment reveals that structural violence is at the center – or should be – of current criminology studies. It is not the criminal code or the criminal disposition which establishes what is a crime and what is not. It is the harm caused that should guide the study. It is not only the severe social harm that should be studied, but also, says Ferrajoli, the elements these mass crimes have in common: structural and cultural violence, we could say. The massive way they are perpetrated, and their impunity, are issues intrinsically related to structural violence, and the acceptance by the public is fundamentally related to cultural violence, as seen in the last chapters.

In fact, that discussion mentioned this need of broader approaches from beyond the criminological authors and definitions. Rivera Beiras said:

> Maybe we have to go back to Galtung's original concept of structural vio-
> lence (. . .) If we take this kind of structural violence concept, we can agree
> that we need a host of different types of knowledge to try to think, to study
> and to fight again.
>
> (Morrison et al. 2014: 222)

These discussions offer reflection keys to thinking about the violations of rights perpetrated during authoritarian governments of the more or less recent past in Latin America, violations whose effects have perpetuated until the present in the circularity of regional violence. They also allow us to consider the visible and invisible social damage in the current economic activity of deregulated national and transnational capitals, particularly when they are active at a regional level.

I have mentioned elsewhere[16] that if you think about the scope of crime not only in terms of the penal code, and not only in terms of the criminal-legal system, the thematic spectrum expands. That is what all the lines presented in the previous paragraphs have been doing. In Europe, in North America, and in Latin America, and excellently also in other contexts such as Oceania, links to the advances made in the framework of green criminology and restorative justice have been forged. In one way or another, these spaces were worked in terms of conflict, harm and violence, and it has been accepted, from the first stir generated by Sutherland to the last discussions on the FTA, that crime belongs to these spaces.

For this reason, we consider that these discursive and practical spaces are the ones that must be addressed by criminology in order to reach processes of violation of rights historically invisible to the penal system, and that are responsible for the maldevelopment of entire regions. Multifactorial transnational approaches are needed (Fernández Steinko 2013a: 21; Friedrichs & Rothe 2015: 3). The field of the crime of maldevelopment, understood as a work proposal that interrelates conflict, harm and violence, its criminological study and its implication for criminal study, could generate fissures in that crystallized and perpetual nonthinking that constantly reiterates that crime is committed by the poor and justice is imposed by the enlightened strata of society. And not only would it create fissures, but also, it would begin to build on the other side of those fissures, in a reconstructive resistance of economic, cultural and legal peace.

We share, to paraphrase Friedrichs, that there is a "need for new types of regulatory and justice system entities" to respond effectively to maldevelopment as a crime "in an increasingly postmodern, globalized world" (Friedrichs 2007a: 176). Therefore, a new conceptual category that brings together these diverse perspectives and that offers a basis and proposals to advance with epistemic, theoretical, normative and practical approaches seems to be more than justified.

The crime of maldevelopment

It is difficult to propose a definition of the crime of maldevelopment, given the intrinsic complexity of the concept. Any definition would necessarily be restrictive. However, given that scientific work must provide elements of systematization of realities and ideas about these realities, the task of systematization will be offered here, but in a different format. For now, the definition remains pending. However, the concept can be explained from its essential elements and its own characteristics, and when it is the case, its definition will be used by comparison or distinction with respect to preexisting conceptual categories in order to sufficiently clarify its particularity.

The characteristics of the crime of maldevelopment can be outlined in the following way – raised ex profeso with reiterated formulae in order to facilitate its discussion and review in a systematic way. Each formulation is based on the developments raised on these pages, so they should be understood as a result of everything discussed throughout the preceding chapters.

The crime of maldevelopment is the *cause and result of violence* in its expressions of cultural, structural and physical violence, and is the cause and result of its vicious circle dynamics.

The crime of maldevelopment is an *aggravated form of white-collar crime*, both because of the seriousness of the damage generated – at the level of violation of human rights – and because of the opacity of the structure and functioning of today's companies and capitals.

The crime of maldevelopment is an *aggravated form of criminality by the powerful*, because the actors involved are not only figures in search of an increase in economic or political power, but also the strategic and geopolitical position of transnational corporations and states implies that the greatest economic power is the power over resources that are economically scarce but vital for populations, and that political power extends to the promotion of physical violence.

The crime of maldevelopment is the *democratic and unorganized form, usually by omission, of macrocriminality*, because it is not based on state structures without rule of law and with legal authorization for the violation of rights, but is based on the indifference or nonintervention by the state concerning the protection and realization of rights of the population in the face of threats and injuries produced by private actors or even by state policies in the broad sense, or by state actors with practices that are formally identified as crimes, but not prosecuted.

The crime of maldevelopment is *legitimized by the international, national and local action of interest groups* that transcend national information spheres and participate in the dissemination of economic discourses of the Global North, thus promoting the justification of contextual conditions of the Global South, which sustains and deepens social distances toward the interior of the societies of the region.

The crime of maldevelopment is the *current and real form of merging environmental damage, the depletion of natural resources and the obstruction of potential in meeting the basic needs of groups of rural populations in the Global South* in favor of the flow of resources to the Global North.

The crime of maldevelopment is the *current and real form of fusion between social precarization, labor and educational deprivation and the obstruction of potentialities in satisfying the basic needs of urban groups in the Global South* in favor of the intensification of financial and technological resources and information in the Global North.

The crime of maldevelopment *hinders the satisfaction of basic needs immediately and mediately, both collectively and individually* among historically vulnerable population groups, *hinders the satisfaction of basic needs in a mediate way in the local society* in general, and *hinders the satisfaction of basic needs over the long term in the world population* as a whole.

The crime of maldevelopment is of a *glocal nature* because it arises from *global conditions* but is developed only in relation to *local conditions,* so that the actors are international, transnational and local alike in their interconnections and circumstances.

The crime of maldevelopment *develops at different speeds in a synchronic and diachronic manner* according to its expression through physical, structural or cultural violence, and according to the moments when each of these violences manifests itself. The crime of maldevelopment *unfolds in different spaces in a synchronic and diachronic manner* according to the actors involved in the different nodes of communications, systems and structures.

The crime of maldevelopment *causes local, national and international social harm* because of the lack of balance generated between the realization of freedom, security and equality understood in an integral manner, and hence, it damages democracy.

The crime of maldevelopment as such is *not punishable under the criminal code* because it transcends the national order and crosses innumerable legal infractions and legal decisions – practices and discursive – transcends the traditional logic of crime (offender–victim and impartial state) and its realization is not attributable in traditional terms of penal law. Typified crimes may be part of the crime of maldevelopment, but the crime of maldevelopment as a conceptual category and of political design of prevention and reparation goes beyond them.

A new concept as an incentive to think about old problems with new approaches

As a challenge to the criminological work that begins here, this new category implies dissolving the differences between the Global North and South and their speech. Joint work has been strengthened around common concepts and ideas such as social damage, and the internationality of violence, for example. Academic work should not continue to reproduce the gap generated at the economic and geopolitical level (Valdes Riesco 2017).

However, we should not lose sight of regional realities. The critical international vision looks principally to mechanisms and actors, sovereigns, who have their thrones in the Global North, as do the financial institutions to which Friedrichs and Rothe (2015), for example, devote their study when speaking of the crimes of globalization. The analysis that places the emphasis on the social damage generated by the various forms of harmful activities will probably be more strongly anchored in the reality of the Global South, being able to approach it, describing it and living it as the main recipient of the negative results of experiences and experiments of international and transnational economic policy.

This can also be explained in other, more specific, terms. The criminality of the powerful, white-collar crime and the crimes of globalization are examples of conceptualizations that have as their main concern the offender figure and its characteristics and activities. Speaking of the crime of maldevelopment, instead, places the emphasis on the results, on the severe social damage – maldevelopment – generated by different mechanisms in which those powerful criminals, white-collar criminals and globalization criminals are, of course, involved. However, they are actors only in the framework of communications, systems and structures in which other actors also participate, such as the affected groups, civil society and its apathy, the media and their news, the churches and their doctrines, and the academies and their theories. All these actors can play an essential part when evaluating the avoidability of a certain activity or measure that entails the obstruction of basic needs. All these actors are also essential parts of what is considered here to be the category of maldevelopment because all these actors occupy different roles and places in those communications, systems and structures. And they can be held accountable for the way they perform in those spaces of action. This responsibility, as explained, should not necessarily be understood in terms of criminal imputation, of course.

No sovereigns should be allowed, nor should exceptions be allowed. But this is easier said than done. That is why it is considered important to continue with the development of a category such as the crime of maldevelopment. New concepts bring new perspectives and, hence, renewed approaches to old issues and problems.

The conceptual category of the crime of maldevelopment involves thinking in integral forms about violence and the ways of avoiding it, so that the *Bad Living* generated by maldevelopment in the regions of the Global South can stop its vicious circle and be redirected toward constructive sustainable development that is imbued with the culture and practices of *Buen Vivir*. And this should happen not only in the Global South, but also in the Global North as well.

This explains the basis of this proposal and its main content. It remains only to go onward, to work on the realization of the potentiality that the proposal contains. But this will be a topic for some final words, which will be, in reality, words to start the next task.

Notes

1 For other possible interpretations, see Böhm (2011b).
2 (CIDH), *Informe de la Comisión Interamericana de Derechos Humanos sobre Pueblos Indígenas, comunidades afrodescendientes y recursos naturales* (OEA/Ser.I./V/II. Doc. 47/15, 31/12/2015).
3 See the official announcement on the website *Câmara Notícias – Câmara dos Deputados*, August 17, 2017 (available:http://www2.camara.leg.br/camaranoticias/noticias/agropecuaria/539298-agricultura-aprova-criacao-da-agencia-de-desenvolvimento-do-matopiba.html).
4 Speech by former President Alan García, June 7, 2009.
5 See the company website *Goldcorp – El Peñasquito* (www.goldcorp.com/English/portfolio/operations/penasquito/default.aspx)
6 UN, A/HRC/16/xx, *Observaciones sobre la situación de los derechos de los pueblos indígenas de Guatemala en relación con los proyectos extractivos, y otro tipo de proyectos, en sus territorios tradicionales, Informe del Relator Especial de Naciones Unidas sobre los derechos de los pueblos indígenas*, March 4, 2011, p. 18.
7 For a proposal in the sphere of international criminal law according to the concept of "aiding and abetting" (by financing activities that violate human rights), see Böhm (2011a). On the related idea of *Gewaltökonomie*, see Albrecht (2007), and on dirty economies, see Ruggiero (1997). In all these cases, the relation between economy and crime is given in interconnection with armed conflicts and dictatorial regimes; the analysis leads to the thinking of categories in the field of international crimes and their mechanisms of attribution. In the sphere of dictatorial regimes, the complicity between (national and international) economic actors and military forces gain in importance and should be considered as a central element in transitional processes and justice mechanisms (Böhm 2015).
8 Cfr. Interview with Prof. Alberto Chirif (Paucar Albino 2017).
9 For broader analysis and diverse perspectives, see the already traditional Pontell & Geis (2007); Simpson & Weisburd (2009), and for approaches from the European perspective Erp et al. (2015); Fernández Steinko (2013b). Especially on crimes of the powerful and the diverse areas approached (crimes of globalization, corporate crimes, environmental crimes, financial crimes and state and state-corporate crimes), see Barak (2015). For a timely review, analysis and innovative proposal on financial crimes, see Barak (2017).
10 UN, A/HRC/16/xx, *supra* note 6.
11 See, in a similar sense, the analysis on the immiseration of indigenous people through state-controlled labor and financial (mis-)appropriation conditions that are systematically fraudulent, racialized and in breach of human rights in Australia (and the United States) by Cunneen (2015).
12 In the documentary film *Apaga y vámonos* (2005), the influence of the media in the perception of the public is illustrative as well. See scenes at 26' 45" and 43' 20".
13 See the article "Jungle Law", in *Vanity Fair*, April 7, 2007 (available: www.vanityfair.com/news/2007/05/texaco200705).
14 This approach was presented by Marco Abudara Bini as a paper in a seminar on "Transnational Corporations and Human Rights" for undergraduate students that I held at the University of Buenos Aires.
15 For the use of victimology for the fundamental study of complex institutional crimes, see Cohen (1993). In the same vein, Aniyar de Castro (2010: 267 ss.), Zaffaroni (2012a).
16 Böhm, María Laura. 2018. "Presentación de la nueva sección sobre 'Empresas, actividades lesivas y Derechos Humanos'" *Revista de Derecho Penal y Criminología*.

References

Agamben, Giorgio. 2002. *Homo Sacer. Die souveräne Macht und das nackte Leben*, Frankfurt a.M.: Suhrkamp.

Agamben, Giorgio. 2004. *Ausnahmezustand*, Frankfurt a.M.: Suhrkamp.

Agamben, Giorgio. 2006. *Mittel ohne Zweck*, Zürich/Berlin: Diaphanes.

Aguirre Alvarez, Agostina Magalí. 2018. "La influencia de la Responsabilidad Social Empresarial en el desarrollo del conflicto del Cerrejón 'Minería Responsable' y la comunidad Wayuu en Colombia por el Proyecto de Expansión Iiwo'uyaa". *Revista de Derecho Penal y Criminología* Argentina. (in edition).

Albrecht, Hans-Jörg. 2007. "Internationale Kriminalität, Gewaltökonomie und Menschenrechtsverbrechen: Antworten des Strafrechts". *Internationale Politik und Gesellschaft* 2, 153–169.

Alpaca Pérez, Alfredo. 2013. "Macrocriminalidad y Derecho Penal Internacional". En *Cuaderno de Trabajo del CICAJ N.°3 Nueva serie*, Departamento Académico de Derecho, Centro de Investigación, Capacitación y Asesoría Jurídica (CICAJ), Pontificia Universidad Católica del Perú.

Ambos, Kai. 2005. *La parte general del derecho penal internacional*. Montevideo: Konrad-Adenauer-Stiftung E.V.

Anitua, Gabriel Ignacio. 2005. *Historias de los pensamientos criminológicos*, Buenos Aires: Editores del Puerto, 1ª reimp.

Aniyar de Castro, Lola. 1969. *Victimología*. Maracaibo: Centro de investigaciones criminológicas de la Universidad de Zulía.

Aniyar de Castro, Lola. 2010. *Criminología de los Derechos Humanos. Criminología axiológica como política criminal*, Buenos Aires: Editores del Puerto.

Barak, Gregg (ed.). 2015. *The Routledge International Handbook of the Crimes of the Powerful*. Cornwall: Routledge.

Barak, Gregg. 2017. *Unchecked Corporate Power: Why the Crimes of Multinational Corporations Are Routinized Away and What We Can Do about It*. London/New York: Routledge.

Boekhout van Solinge, Tim/Kuijpers, Karlijn. 2013. "The Amazon Rainforest: A Green Criminological Perspective". In: South, Nigel/Brisman, Avi (eds.). *Routledge International Handbook of Green Criminology*, London/New York: Routledge, 199–213.

Böhm, María Laura. 2011a. "Political Violence, International Crimes, and Transnational Corporations in Latin America". In: He, Bingsong/Liu, Yanping (eds.). *New Philosophy of Crime and Punishment in the Era of Globalization*, Beijing: Beijing University, 344.

Böhm, María Laura. 2011b. *Der 'Gefährder' und das 'Gefährdungsrecht': Eine rechtssoziologische Analyse am Beispiel der Urteile des Bundesverfassungsgericht über die nachträgliche Sicherungsverwahrung und die akustische Wohnraumüberwachung*, Göttingen: Göttingen Universitätsverlag.

Böhm, María Laura. 2015. "Los crímenes de Estado, la complicidad civil y el sistema punitivo". *En Letra. Derecho Penal*, Año 1, Nro. 1, 8–18.

Böhm, María Laura. 2016. "Transnational: Corporations, Human Rights Violations and Structural Violence in Latin America: A Criminological Approach". *Kriminologisches Journal: Sonderheft Lateinamerika* 4 (Germany), 272–293.

Brisman, Avi/South, Nigel. 2015. "State-Corporate Environmental Harms and Paradoxical Interventions: Thoughts in Honour of Stanley Cohen". In: Sollund, Ragnhild A. (ed.). *Green Harms and Crimes: Critical Criminology in a Changing World*, Basingstoke: Palgrave Macmillan, 27–42.

Brisman, Avi/South, Nigel/White, Rob. 2015. "Toward a Criminology of Environment-Conflict Relationships". In: id. (ed.). *Environmental Crime and Social Conflict: Contemporary and Emerging Issues*, Farnham, UK: Ashgate, 1–38.

Carrasco, Anita/Fernández, Eduardo. 2009. "Estrategias de resistencia indígena frente al desarrollo minero. La comunidad de Likantatay ante un posible traslado forzoso". *Estudios Atacameños* 38, 75–92.

Catrilef Santana, Ángela/Zubeldía Cascón, Florencia/Lobato, María Elicia/Pizá, Esteban. 2018. "Pueblos indígenas. Herramientas conceptuales". *Revista de Derecho Penal y Criminología* Argentina. (in edition).

Cohen, Stanley. 1993. "Human Rights and Crimes of the State: The Culture of Denial". *Australia & New Zealand Journal of Criminology* 26, 97–115.

Cohen, Stanley. 2013. "Escepticismo intelectual y compromiso político. La criminología radical" *Delito y Sociedad* 3 (4–5), 3–31.

Contrafatto, Silvia/Guevara, Micaela/Hinojosa, Laura/Loperfido, Manuela. 2018. "Macrocriminalidad. Herramientas conceptuales". *Revista de Derecho Penal y Criminología* Argentina. (in edition).

Costanzo, Leandro/Mannará, Federico/Álvarez Icaza R., Julia/Anativia, Julio. 2018. "Victimología. Herramientas conceptuales". *Revista de Derecho Penal y Criminología*. (in edition).

Cufré, Denise/Raskovsky, Rodrigo/Lascano, Sofía/Botero, Santiago. 2018. "Autorregulación empresarial. Herramientas conceptuales". *Revista de Derecho Penal y Criminología* Argentina. (in edition).

Cunneen, Chris. 2015. "The Race to Defraud: State Crime and the Immiseration of Indigenous People". In: Chambliss, William J./Moloney, Christopher J. (eds.). *State Crime: Critical Concepts in Criminology, Vol. 2: Varieties of State Crimes*, Abingdon, UK: Routledge, 658–671.

Del Olmo, Rosa. 1999 (4th ed.). *América Latina y su criminología*. México D.F.: Siglo XXI.

Ebus, Bram/Kuijpers, Karlijn. 2015. "The State-Corporate Tandem Cycling towards Collision: State-Corporate Harm and the Resource Frontiers of Brazil and Colombia". In: Brisman, Avi/South, Nigel/White, Rob (eds.). *Environmental Crime and Social Conflict: Contemporary and Emerging Issues*, Farnham, UK: Ashgate, 125–152.

Elbert, Carlos Alberto. 2012a. *Criminología, ciencia y cambio social*, Buenos Aires: Eudeba.

Elbert, Carlos Alberto. 2012b (5th ed.). *Manual básico de criminología*, Buenos Aires: Eudeba.

Elbert, Carlos Alberto. 2016. *Criminología Latinoamericana. Identidad, realidad social y Estado*. México D.F.: Res Pública.

Eleisegui, Patricio. 2013. *Envenenados: una bomba química nos extermina en silencio*. Buenos Aires: Wu Wei.

Erp, Judith van/Huisman, Wim/Vande Walle, Gudrun (eds.). 2015. *The Routledge Handbook of White-Collar and Corporate Crime in Europe*. Cornwall: Routledge.

Fattah, Ezzat A. 2010. "The Evolution of a Young, Promising Discipline: Sixty Years of Victimology, a Retrospective and Prospective Look". In: Shoham, Shlomo G./Knepper, Paul/Kett, Martin (eds.). *International Handbook of Victimology*, Boca Raton/London/New York: CRC Press, 43–94.

Fernández Steinko, Armando. 2008. *Las pistas falsas del crimen organizado: Finanzas paralelas y orden internacional*, Madrid: Catarata.

Fernández Steinko, Armando. 2013a. "Una visión de conjunto de la delincuencia contemporánea". In: Fernández Steinko, Armando (ed.). *Delincuencia, Finanzas y Globalización*, Madrid: Centro de Investigaciones Sociológicas, 15–129.

Fernández Steinko, Armando (ed.). 2013b. *Delincuencia, Finanzas y Globalización*, Madrid: Centro de Investigaciones Sociológicas.

Ferrajoli, Luigi. 2014. "Criminología, crímenes globales y derecho penal. El debate epistemológico en la criminología contemporánea". In: Rivera Beiras, I. (ed.). *Delitos de los Estados, de los Mercados y daño social*, Barcelona: Anthropos, 81–96.

Friedrichs, David O. 2007a. "White-Collar Crime in a Postmodern, Globalized World". In: Pontell, Henry N./Geis, Gilbert (eds.). *International Handbook of White-Collar and Corporate Crime*, New York: Springer, 163–176.

Friedrichs, David O. 2007b. "Transnational Crime and Global Criminology: Definitional, Typological, and Contextual Conundrums". *Social Justice* 34 (2), 4–18.

Friedrichs, David O./Rothe, Dawn L. 2015. *Crimes of Globalization*. London: Routledge.

Gómez Urso, Facundo. 2012. *La selectividad policial*. Buenos Aires: Di Plácido.

Hall, Matthew. 2014. "Victims of Environmental Crime: Routes for Recognition, Restitution and Redress". In: Spapens, Toine/White, Rob/Kluin, Marieke (eds.). *Environmental Crime and Its Victims: Perspectives within Green Criminology*, Aldershot: Ashgate, 103–118.

Harari, Yuval Noah. 2014. *Sapiens: A Brief History of Humankind*, London: Penguin Vintage.

Hillyard, Paddy/Tombs, Steve. 2015. "From 'Crime' to Social Harm?" In: Chambliss, William J./Moloney, Christopher J. (eds.). *State Crime: Critical Concepts in Criminology, Vol. 1: An Introduction to the Field of State Crime Research*, London/New York: Routledge, 229–247.

Hönke, Jana. 2010. "New Political Topographies: Mining Companies and Indirect Discharge in Southern Katanga (DRC)". *Politique africaine* 4 (120), 105–127.

Huisman, Wim. 2008. "Corporations and International Crimes". In: Smeulers, A./Haveman, R. (eds.). *Supranational Criminology: Towards a Criminology of International Crimes*, Antwerpen et al.: Intersentia, 181.

Huisman, Wim. 2010. *Business as Usual? Corporate Involvement in International Crimes*. The Hague: Eleven International Publishing.

Jäger, Herbert. 1989. *Makrokriminalität. Studien zur Kriminologie kollektiver Gewalt*, Frankfurt a.M.: Suhrkamp.

Jarrell, Melissa/Ozymy, Joshua. 2014. "Communities as Victims of Environmental Crime: Lessons from the Field". In: Spapens, Toine/White, Rob/Kluin/Marieke (eds.). *Environmental Crime and Its Victims: Perspectives within Green Criminology*, London: Routledge, 249–261.

Jewkes, Yvonne. 2015 (3rd ed.). *Media and Crime: Key Approaches to Criminology*, Thousand Oaks, CA: Sage.

Kirchhof, Gerd Ferdinand. 2010. "History and a Theoretical Structure of Victimology". In: Shoham, Shlomo G./Knepper, Paul/Kett/Martin (eds.). *International Handbook of Victimology*, Boca Raton/London/New York: CRC Press, 96–123.

Kramer, Ronald C./Michalowski, Raymond J./Kauzlarich, David. 2002. "The Origins and Development of the Concept and Theory of State-Corporate Crime". *Crime & Delinquency* 48 (2), 263–282.

Lee, Chul. 2005. *(Latente) soziale Probleme und Massenmedien*, Herzbolheim: Centaurus Verlag.

Marteau, Juan Félix. 2003. *Las palabras del orden. Proyecto republican y cuestión criminal en Argentina (Buenos Aires: 1880–1930)*. Buenos Aires: Editores del Puerto.

Mayoral, Pilar/Ojeda, Axel/Dworesky, Micaela. 2018. "Medio ambiente. Herramientas conceptuales". *Revista de Derecho Penal y Criminología*. (in edition).

McGregor, Michael A. 2009. "Ending Corporate Impunity: How to Really Curb the Pillaging of Natural Resources". *Case Western Reserve Journal of International Law* 42, 469–497.

Morrison, Wayne/Zaffaroni, Eugenio Raúl/Bergalli, Roberto. 2014. "Diálogos sobre criminología, genocidio y daño social con Wayne Morrison, Eugenio Raúl Zaffaroni y Roberto Bergalli". In: Rivera Beiras, Iñaki (ed.). *Delitos de los Estados, de los Mercados y daño social*, Barcelona: Anthropos.

Namuncura, Domingo. 1999. *Ralco: represa o pobreza?*. Santiago de Chile: Lom.

Natali, Lorenzo. 2016. *A Visual Approach for Green Criminology: Exploring the Social Perception of Environmental Harm*. London: Palgrave Macmillan.

Paucar Albino, Jorge. 2017. "Experto en temas amazónicos advierte que las causas del Baguazo se mantienen". Interview with Prof. Alberto Chirif *Lamula.pe*, June 5. https://

redaccion.lamula.pe/2017/06/05/baguazo-2009-bagua-conflicto-peru-alan-garcia-causasa niversario-pueblos-indigenas/jorgepaucar/

Pauls, Nels/Zagorski, Kim/Ferguson, D. Chris. 2015. "On Harm and Mediated Space: The BP Oil Spill in the Age of Globalisation". In: Brisman, Avi/South, Nigel/White, Rob (eds.). *Environmental Crime and Social Conflict: Contemporary and Emerging Issues*, Farnham: Ashgate. 265–283.

Pearce, Frank. 1976. *Crimes of the Powerful: Marxism, Crime and Deviance*, London: Pluto Press.

Pontell, Henry N./Geis, Gilbert (eds.). 2007. *International Handbook of White-Collar and Corporate Crime*, New York: Springer.

Richards, Patricia. 2010. "Of Indians and Terrorists: How the State and Local Elites Construct the Mapuche in Neoliberal Multicultural Chile". *Journal of Latin American Studies* 42, 59–90.

Rivera Beiras, Iñaki. 2014. "Retomando el concepto de violencia estructural. La memoria, el daño social y el derecho a la Resistencia como herramientas de trabajo". In: Rivera Beiras, Iñaki (ed.). *Delitos de los Estados, de los Mercados y daño social*, Barcelona: Anthropos, 253–279.

Rodríguez, Esteban. 2011. "¿Será justicia? La administración de justicia en los mass media: deshistorización y criminalización de la realidad en el periodismo contemporáneo". In: Gutiérrez, Mariano (ed.). *Populismo punitivo y justicia expresiva*, Buenos Aires: Di Plácido, 281–323.

Rothe, Dawn L./Mullins, Christopher W./Sandstrom, Kent. 2008. "The Rwandan Genocide: International Finance Policies and Human Rights". *Social Justice* 35 (3), 66–86.

Ruggiero, Vincenzo. 1997. "Criminals and Service Providers: Cross-National Dirty Economies". *Crime, Law & Social Change* 28, 27–38.

Ruggiero, Vincenzo. 2001. *Crime and Markets: Essays in Anti-Criminology*. Oxford: OUP.

Scheerer, Sebastian. 1993 (3rd ed.). "Kriminalität der Mächtigen". In: Kaiser, Günther et al. (eds.). *Kleines kriminologische Wörterbuch*, Heidelberg: C.F. Müller, 246–249.

Seaga Shaw, Ibrahim. 2011. *Human Rights Journalism: Advances in Reporting Distant Humanitarian Interventions*, London: Palgrave Macmillan.

Simpson, Sally S./Weisburd, David (eds.). 2009. *The Criminology of White-Collar Crime*. New York: Springer.

Spapens, Toine. 2014. "Invisible Victims: The Problem of Policing Environmental Crime". In: Spapens, Toine/White, Rob/Kluin, Marieke (eds.). *Environmental Crime and Its Victims: Perspectives within Green Criminology*, Farnham, UK: Ashgate, 221–236.

Sutherland, Edwin. 1983. *White Collar Crime: The Uncut Version*, New Haven, CT: Yale University Press.

Torres Luzardo, Roberto. 2014. "Lolita Aniyar de Castro: 'En Venezuela no hay estado de derecho desde hace mucho tiempo'". *LuzAdN*. March 10. www.agenciadenoticias.luz. edu.ve/index.php?option=com_content&task=view&id=5018&Itemid=186

Valdes Riesco, Amalia. 2017. *Can the Subaltern Speak in Criminology? Analysing the Production of Knowledge on Crimes of the Powerful in the 21st Century through Latin American Post-Colonial Lenses*, Unpublished paper (work in process, Master Thesis, University of Manchester)

Viano, Emilio C. 1990. "Victimology: A New Focus of Research and Practice". In: id. (ed.). *The Victimology Handbook. Research Findings, Treatment, and Public Policy*, New York: Garland Publishing, xi–xxiii.

Villegas, Myrna. 2009. "El Mapuche como enemigo en el Derecho (Penal). Consideraciones desde la biopolítica y el derecho penal del enemigo". *Portal Iberoamericano de las Ciencias Penales*. www.cienciaspenales.net

Walters, Reece. 2006. "Crime, Bio-Agriculture and the Exploitation of Hunger". *British Journal of Criminology* 46, 26–45.

White, Rob/South, Nigel. 2013. "The Future of Green Criminology: Horizon Scanning and Climate Change". Paper presented at the American Society of Criminology Conference, Atlanta, November. https://asc41.com/Annual_Meeting/2013/Presidential%20Papers/White,%20Rob-South,%20Nigel.pdf

Wilkins, Lee. 1987. *Shared Vulnerability: The Media and American Perceptions of the Bhopal Disaster*, New York: Greenwood Press.

Zaffaroni, Eugenio Raúl. 2011. *La palabra de los muertos. Conferencias de criminología cautelar*, Buenos Aires: Ediar.

Zaffaroni, Eugenio Raúl. 2012a (2nd ed.). *Crímenes de masa*. Buenos Aires: Ediciones Madres de Plaza de Mayo.

Zaffaroni, Eugenio Raúl. 2012b. *La* Pachamama *y el humano*. Buenos Aires: Ediciones Madres de Plaza de Mayo.

Zaffaroni, Eugenio Raúl. 2015. *El derecho latinoamericano en la fase superior del colonialismo*. Buenos Aires: Ediciones Madres de Plaza de Mayo.

Zaffaroni, Eugenio/Alagia, Alejandro/Slokar, Alejandro. 2000. *Manual de Derecho penal. Parte general*, Buenos Aires: Ediar.

Zaitch, Damián/Gutiérrez Gómez, Laura. 2015. "Mining as State-Corporate Crime: The Case of AngloGold Ashanti in Colombia". In: Barak, Gregg (ed.). *The Routledge International Handbook of the Crimes of the Powerful*. Cornwall: Routledge, 386–397.

Filmography

Apaga y vámonos. 2005. Documentary film. Dir. Manel Mayol. Spain.

Crude: El estigma del petróleo. 2009. Documentary film. Dir. Joe Berlinger, EEUU.

La espera. 2014. Documentary. Dir. Fernando Vílchez Rodríguez. Perú. www.youtube.com/watch?v=pVkONDVbe-w

Misiones de Tiza. 2014. Documentary. Dir. Leandro E. Costanzo. Argentina. https://vimeo.com/90656569

Approaching the crime of maldevelopment – conclusion and starting point

A summary of the journey made throughout this book clarifies the link between deregulated economies and violence, and offers the basis for some brief conclusions, which are not conclusions as such, of course, but offer some advice for the next steps on the way to a more concrete definition, not only of the conceptual category of maldevelopment as a crime, but also of a network of possible mechanisms for its prevention and sanction, and for the work of reparation and construction toward the satisfaction of the needs of the victim or victimizable populations.

Chapter 1 explained the political economic context in which economic policies are implemented with a strong deregulatory tendency regarding certain industries, commercial relations and resources in the Latin American region. The economic and political dialogues that are currently defined at the international and global levels via local governments have been presented as well. The explanation of neo-extractivism and the financialization of nature led to the idea of economic exploitation in favor of certain areas to the detriment of basic life needs of populations in other areas of the globe. Thus, Chapter 2 explained further that if Galtung's concept of violence is used, understood as unmet basic needs because of avoidable obstacles of a structural nature and its legitimization through discourses, practices and institutions in the cultural order, it becomes possible to understand that the structural and cultural violence to which important portions of the Latin American population are subject is closely linked to those economic policies of an international and global order. That is to say that the fact that there are unmet basic needs is not a mere question of impossibility or unbalanced distribution of virtues and disadvantages in the land, but is the result of practices, discourses, activities and omissions on the part of specific actors in specific contexts. Therefore, the death of a child due to high levels of heavy metals in his body since his conception, which occurred years after the closure of an oil exploitation plant in the area where his parents live, is attributable to someone. It is not "the economy" or the "political order" that is responsible; these would be the sovereigns exempted from responsibility, sovereigns as omnipresent as they are invisible. Those who embody these sovereigns in each case are the actors that must be made visible and dethroned. There are people of flesh and blood who sign a legislative decree, who promote an economic theory from a university or put it into practice in a ministerial cabinet, give an eviction order, pay retired military to liberate an area, start up an oil well close to towns without access to sources of water other than those from a stream into which waste will be poured, or threaten the population that does not want to abandon its original town when it is above water reserves, and even rapes its women. They are people of flesh and blood who carry out these actions, but only because they know that they have the coverage of the mantle of the political, economic and cultural sovereign. In all cases, it is people of flesh and blood who, with these activities, not only commit acts that may or may not be classified in the criminal codes, but also actively participate in the meshes of the microphysics of power, as Foucault would say. They are small spiders that weave and renew the threads of these networks that continue to impede the realization of rights, and that even act directly in the opposite direction, leaving children without school, mothers without food, men without work, women without a uterus, identities extinct or a lethal environment for human life. All this is not "the economy", "neoliberalism" or "political power". The law does not see it, as Galtung explains (1969, 1996), because the law is blind to structural violence. Nor does the law see it, as Agamben states (2002: 39), because law and violence, through the exception, have become accomplices. For this reason, it is necessary to know the name not only of those who perform these acts, but also of those who suffer them. It is necessary to give them reality and life. In the exercises of description and analysis of circumstances carried out through the case studies of Chapter 3 (through a systematic advance of the instances of invisible violence, fundamentally, before and after certain economic activities and measures) and Chapter 4 (from the description of situations of visible physical violence and the political and economic circumstances before and after its manifestation), a first attempt was made to locate the large structures, to trace decisions and actions in precise space-time positions with consequences traceable with more or less detail. The circularity of these processes, analyzed later in Chapter 5, then aimed to show that the cases do not represent isolated situations, but rather that the conditions given historically, as long as they are not modified, will continue to recycle, reiterate and deepen the circles of violence between economy, politics and affected population in a way that prevents (as it has been doing for centuries) any possibility of genuine growth in terms of an increase in the quantity and quality of satisfaction in terms of basic needs. As long as the conflicts appear to be an anonymous fight over territories and exercise of invisible powers, there will be no cessation of violence. Invisible violence closely intertwined with visible violence as long as the instances are considered abstract events, unrelated to any possibility of attribution, will continue to define the poor future of one of the richest regions of the planet. For this reason, it is necessary to speak of maldevelopment and denounce it, to explain that this failed promise – once and again reiterated –not only is an economic and social concept, but also means, among other things, death, illness, hunger, despair and the loss of cultural identity for a large part of the Latin American population. It is a matter for criminological studies (Chapter 6). While the numbers of the regional macroeconomy, according to the state, fluctuate in cycles, the violence is repeated and deepened. Violence, at the pace of maldevelopment, becomes more and more visible in those border transformations between the structural, cultural and physical manifestations of long or brief, silent or thunderous processes, in which the possibility of realizing individual and collective potentialities is curtailed. The possibility of peace, and all its potentialities, is thus interrupted.

From this review of the previous chapters, it may perhaps be thought that offering a concept is, after all, possible. A first attempt would appear as follows: *The crime of maldevelopment is the set of communications and activities in the context of international, transnational, regional and national economic policies and projects that entail or have materialized the risk of hindering the satisfaction of basic needs at a collective level, and that participate, directly or indirectly, in the exercise of cultural, structural or physical violence that prevents the sustainable and integral development of a population in terms of economic, cultural and legal peace.*

Bearing in mind this concept, as broad as it is specific in terms of the elements it contains, which concentrate the characteristics indicated in the previous chapter, it can now be considered as conclusive ideas and a bridge, in fact, for future work, offering 12 guidelines for the approach in a broad sense; and five mechanisms for a strict approach to the crime of maldevelopment. The first correspond to the characteristics presented in the chapter, so those will be taken up again in order to clarify their explanatory potential. The last ones, the mechanisms, will be outlined here in a preliminary way, as a basis for discussion, design and construction of said mechanisms – in improved versions – as concrete tools of intervention with respect to the crime of maldevelopment.

Guidelines for an approach to the crime of maldevelopment

1 Given that the crime of maldevelopment is the cause and result of violence in its expressions of cultural, structural and physical violence, and is the cause and result of its vicious circle dynamics, it is necessary to develop a *broader idea of crime*, in the sense of harmful activities even without penal sanction. This broader idea implies also a necessary *interdisciplinary approach* by means of the study, description and intervention as regarding the crime of maldevelopment. The analysis must go beyond criminal law and even beyond the law itself. Knowledge and perspectives from the political, economic and social sciences as well as from technical areas are needed.

2 We have said that the crime of maldevelopment is an aggravated form of white-collar crime, because of both the seriousness of the damage generated – the level of violation of human rights – and the opacity of the structure and functioning of companies and capitals of today. For this reason, the

mechanisms used for the study and investigation of crimes considered under the conceptual umbrella of the white-collar crime will be useful for an approach to the crime of maldevelopment as well. However, new spheres must be thought over. At the domestic level, for example, the discussion on the criminal liability of juridical persons and criminal compliance are pondered respectively as hard and soft ways of approaching the white-collar crime committed in the framework of corporate activity. In the case of the crime of maldevelopment, given the amount of human rights violations that the harm causes and because of the internationally related origin of the harmful activities, both mechanisms – criminal responsibility of juridical persons and criminal compliance – should be raised at the international level as well. Thus, the discussion on the possibility of a binding treaty for corporations' obligation to respect human rights, or hard law, as well as the better enforcement of the UN "Ruggie" Principles[1], or soft law, must be necessarily contemplated. In all cases, the corporate perspective and approach should be taken into account, and the international economic interest in scarce resources, of course, considered too. The approach, in this sense, must be sufficiently realistic and have the capacity of coming into conversation with the economic and economic political actors.

3   Just because of the type of actors and activities involved, we have asserted that the crime of maldevelopment is an aggravated form of criminality by the powerful, because the actors involved are not only figures in search of an increase in economic or political power, but also the strategic and geopolitical position of transnational corporations and states implies that the greatest economic power is over resources that are economically scarce but vital for populations, and that political power extends to the promotion of armed conflict. Therefore, this aggravated form of criminality of the powerful requires, as to the issues at stake – water, food, fuel as vital necessities – and to the actors involved – international financing institutions, economically regional actors, transnational economic groups – the *implementation of an interdisciplinary approach at the highest level, involving the development of economic and technological engineering at international, regional and national levels,* for the understanding and checking of the processes of the crime of maldevelopment. The work of social, political and legal knowledge calls for reciprocal, interrelated work with new areas of study and intervention, such as environment technologies, the management of international organizations and the financial structure of investment, industry and trade at the international and transnational levels.

4   Because the crime of maldevelopment is the democratic, disorganized form of macrocriminality, usually by omission, the perspective of the democratic state must be exhaustively considered in the study and intervention. Given that in this case macrocriminality is related to the indifference or nonintervention on the part of the state in terms of the protection and realization of rights of the population in the face of threats and injuries engendered by

private actors or even by state policies in the broad sense, or by state actors with practices that are formally identified as crimes, but not prosecuted, the restrictions provided by the legislation in states bounded by the rule of law (Estados de Derecho) demand at least the *understanding of state functioning in order to establish concrete functions, duties and sanctions in case of infraction.* In this sense, to reverse macrocriminality by disorganization and omission in democratic states, at least three levels should be improved: *reinforcement of the regulation and enforcement of the duties of public officers, the articulation of the public offices, and the design of a transparency system by the accountability of public acts and decisions in each public unit before all other public offices and the society.* Almost all these measures are related to the knowledge and experience related to public administration and services. This means, again, that a criminal code is just one component of a much more complex, enormous apparatus of accountability levels.

5 The crime of maldevelopment is legitimized by the international, national and local action of interest groups that transcend national information spheres and participate in the broadcasting of economic discourses that generate and endorse the justification of violent contextual conditions of the Global South, which sustains and deepens social distances toward the interior of the societies of the region. This aspect, which is related to the mass media as a reality-performing power requires – at least – a threefold approach, which already exists in part but should be deepened and articulated. The distinction between information and opinion, which is difficult enough, should, however, be strengthened in the sense of *liability mechanisms* related to false information or the deliberate omission of essential information and of *study and monitoring of the cultural presence and impact of corporate mass media.* In this sense, also the design of *mechanisms of social responsibility for the media business* must yet be researched in depth and developed, in particular with regard to the cultural violence that may be exerted.

6 The crime of maldevelopment is the current and real form of merging environmental damage, the depletion of natural resources and the avoidance of potentials in meeting the basic needs of groups of rural populations in the Global South in favor of the flow of resources to the Global North. This characteristic of the crime of maldevelopment demands the *expansion of criminological research from the urban to the rural areas.* This expansion has, to a certain extent, been done by green criminology. It is now necessary to add to this approach the comprehensive study of environmental and human harm in relation to the structural, physical and cultural violence in rural areas. In this sense, the integration of the non-realization of basic needs at the individual and social levels requires a demand for other fields of knowledge. Social scientists and anthropologists, as well as economic and environmental scientists, are asked to take part in the study and support of the understanding of violence processes – from legal, physically violent land conflict to the poor health and interrupted school attendance of local

children. In addition, specific areas of the technological areas such as environmental and energy engineering, housing and infrastructure engineering, in areas where the extractive industries mean a direct impact on living conditions, should be considered along with the design and implementation in situ of specific public policies in the areas of health, food, education and work.

7 Because of the conception of the crime of maldevelopment as the current and real form of fusion between social precarization, labor and educational deprivation and the avoidance of potentialities in satisfying the basic needs of urban groups in the Global South in favor of the intensification of financial and technological resources and information in the Global North, it is necessary to adopt a *broader scope in the criminological field as regards the interrelations between the different expressions of violence in the urban spaces.* To the need for design and implementation of specific public policies as regard to work, education, food, health and housing conditions, the concrete link between physical violence at the collective level – as is the case in the most marginalized areas of *villas miseria, favelas* or *comunidades* in different Latin American countries – should be comprehensively approached, taking into account the role of public and private security forces and the forms of their connection with the population in these areas. Urban security, in the narrow sense of the term – physical and property security – is to be seen as closely defined by structural and cultural violence and its deep-running economic roots and, in particular, as entangled with violence processes in rural areas. Here again, therefore, criminological work will expand and enter into dialogue with other areas of public policy in general.

8 We have affirmed that the crime of maldevelopment hinders the satisfaction of basic needs directly and indirectly, both collectively and individually in historically vulnerable population groups. Besides this, it hinders the satisfaction of basic needs in a mediate way in the local society in general, and hinders the satisfaction of basic needs long term in the world population as a whole. This means that the different times for the development and visibility of the impact have an effect in different ways and instances on the diverse individuals and collectives of a population depending on the region in which these individuals and collectives are located. This complex scenario of superimposed affected individuals and groups requires, therefore, the *calculation and measurement of impact at all these diverse levels with respect to the immediate and mediate effects* of an economic political measure or a new industrial project, and in a broad framework of previsions and in the concrete area where immediate harm can be expected. Concrete tools for this measurement (horizon scanning) are to be suggested among the mechanisms for the approaching of the crime of maldevelopment. Here, it must be added that the different impact levels require, beyond concrete tools, the aforementioned study and training in interdisciplinary and international research and cooperation.

9   The crime of maldevelopment, it was explained, is of a *glocal nature* because it arises from *global conditions* but is developed only in relation to *local conditions*, so that the actors are international, transnational and local alike in their interconnections and circumstances. *The feature of glocality in the crime of maldevelopment stresses the challenge that imposes the individualization of involved actors in the meshes of the interrelations and activities in each case, at both the international and local level.* These actors may be physical individuals, corporations or institutional units. These actors may be settled in a state or in an international institution in the Global North as well as in a state office or a village in the Global South. Although the network of international, regional and national relations at economic, political, social and legal levels is always similar, in each concrete case the intervening actors and individuals are different – the judges intervening, the international financing office or the authorities signing an economic agreement, for example, are always different, as is the affected community, the local entrepreneur carrying out the outsourced activities of the multinational company or the school located near the mine. For this reason, an approach is necessary that takes into account general conditions and, at the same time, the specific circumstances and subjective facts of the concrete case. The position of the actors in the several superimposed communication systems and structures are of different hierarchies and of different meaning in each relationship. In order to gather the singularity of these roles, the invisible connections from the international actors to the local actors must be sufficiently captured. Corresponding mechanisms to this need will be suggested ahead.

10 That the crime of maldevelopment *develops at different speeds in a synchronic and diachronic manner* according to its expression through physical, structural or cultural violence, and according to the moments when each of these forms of violence manifest, lead to the need of an intense study of the manifestations of violence. It must be taken into account that cultural violence is inherent in slowly growing convictions and beliefs which accumulate and entangle with new perspectives in extremely slow movements at the collective level, whereas structural violence moves at a speed according to processes at the institutional and organizational level and moves faster than cultural violence in its progression. Last, physical violence can happen in less than one second. It takes a long time to remove discriminatory convictions; it takes less time to adopt protective legislation or the legislation of territorial norms embodying that discriminatory perspective, and it takes just a couple of seconds to shoot at a member of an indigenous community facing the police. At the same moment, three speeds of violence are evident, and they will repeat themselves on future occasions at different speeds (synchronic) and crystallized by different actors as well (diachronic). There are different "times" to be approached (Friedrichs & Rothe 2015: xxiv). Besides, the crime of maldevelopment *unfolds in different spaces in a synchronic*

and diachronic manner according to the actors involved in the different nodes of communications, systems and structures, which means that the speed of violence expressions (time perspective) must be considered along with the spatial perspective. At the same moment, the crime of maldevelopment can be taking place with respect to the same case in different places. This is what would happen in the following scenario: discriminatory convictions against rural people in the capital city of state A coexist with an institutional agreement signed in foreign state B between state A and state B for the reinforcement of agricultural business relations and the use of technological packages under better trade conditions, while at the same moment a peasant is being killed in the rural area of state A because of land conflicts generated by that expected expansion of the agricultural frontier, and a child is slowly dying because of the toxic substances that she has being consuming via polluted water in state A as a consequence of the toxic pesticides used for the culture of soy for export to state B. In short, it can be said that *the complex combination of time and space references offer the coordinates for the consideration of accountability*, as will be shown in the mechanism drafted ahead.

11 The crime of maldevelopment causes local, national and international social harm because of the lack of balance generated between the realization of freedom, security and equality understood in an integral manner, and hence, it damages democracy. Because of this impact, which is related to the results of deregulating policies that leaves in private hands the decisions and implementation of projects and practices that are damaging for the local population because of the withdrawal of the protective state presence, the aspect of the political impact in terms of a decrease in the realization of democracy must be considered and approached seriously. It may be that one of the most detrimental effects of the crime of maldevelopment is the weakening of political participation at individual and collective levels, which, in turn, conduces to the exclusion of important segments of the population from participative life and the limits to their potential to make decisions concerning their own lives. This need, hence, is related to the "economic democracy" (Chiriboga 1992). Unsatisfied basic needs, in this sense, are the visible consequence of that absence of the genuine attention of the state. The de-democratization of societies and public spaces as a result of these conditions, in the extreme case, facilitates the path for the emergence of nondemocratic regimes. The history of Latin America has plenty of examples in this sense. If the population and the state institutions are not sufficiently empowered in terms of democratic culture and institutional and economic conditions, the path from cultural to structural violence, and from structural to physical violence, ends by opening the door to violent regimes sustained by international and local interests. In this sense, the vicious circle between political and economic policies is an explanation of the crime of maldevelopment in its ultimate form, dictatorship, and the systematized and organized cultural, structural and physical violation of fundamental rights that a dictatorship

means. The political approach from a scientific and empirical perspective, therefore, is unavoidable as a supporting discipline for the measure and explanation of processes that could lead or enhance violent processes when they are still invisible to the ordinary eyes of a criminologist or penal lawyer.

12   After recalling all these features and the suggested guidelines for the general approach to the crime of maldevelopment, it remains only to reiterate – and hopefully it will be more clear now – that the crime of maldevelopment as such is *not punishable under the criminal code* because it transcends the national order and crosses innumerable legal infractions and legal decisions, transcends the traditional logic of crime (offender–victim and impartial state) and its realization is not attributable in traditional terms of penal law. For this reason, typified crimes may be part of the crime of maldevelopment, but the crime of maldevelopment as a conceptual category and as a base for political design of prevention and reparation, supersedes them. A broader approach should consider cooperative terms at first as well as mandatory terms later, in case of unsuccessful cooperation. The first approach, the cooperative one, must be developed and implemented with regard to all involved actors. The last one, the mandatory approach, must be developed and implemented as well.

Mechanisms for the approach to the crime of maldevelopment

Taking into account the aforementioned guidelines, there are some specific mechanisms that could be considered as first concrete proposals for study and intervention. They will be merely sketched here as suggestions for further analysis and, eventually, for their development and implementation. The idea in the following is to offer a concrete short list of mechanisms which, against the background of the crime of maldevelopment and of the aforementioned general guidelines, will allow us to think about tools – concrete tools – for immediate intervention in specific spaces that find themselves threatened or at risk of being directly affected in terms of maldevelopment.

It is necessary to be aware that it is *impossible* to think of a strategic program initiated and established in *all* affected regions *at the same time*. This would be plain nonsense. The proposal is much more to start with the concrete design of an articulated apparatus in order to test it and to put it into practice at first in specific pilot cases aiming to detect weaknesses and strengths in the field. This micro-level implementation of mechanisms following macro-level guidelines, that is, a bottom-up approach, it is here suggested, would be a realistic way to approach the crime of maldevelopment. It cannot be expected that a state change its economic policies all at once, that a corporation promptly stop production or that state agents change their convictions and habits overnight. However, it could be expected that the presence of academic and even political actors in new communication with local actors could gather information and

understand local processes in direct contact with the situation in order to pre-
pare a preliminary report on the observed situation, and to suggest subsequent
steps for the prevention and reparation of possible or committed violence. A
starting point in the field in order to retrace the path to the current instance and,
in so doing, to determine the degrees and forms of responsibility, and this for
the purpose of defining ways to decelerate the vicious circle of economic deregulation and violence, is needed. A systematic constructive progress is needed.
There is difficult, comprehensive and long-term work to do.

The five stepwise suggested mechanisms for this bottom-up approach to
the crime of maldevelopment based on a case-by-case progression, then, are as
follows:

1   *Static map of actors.* The design of this map should consider differences in
    hierarchy and position among the diverse internationally, regionally, nation-
    ally and locally superimposed levels. A model map or blank template would
    function as guide for the realization with specific data of each concrete map
    of actors in each concrete case. The identification of international, regional,
    national and local actors at the political, economic, public and community
    levels is to be captured in this static map. According to the time extent of
    each concrete conflict, it is probable that different maps of actors will be
    needed in order to sufficiently consider changes in the situation in the per-
    spective of time.

2   *Diagram of retrospective and prospective traceability according to related activities and
    harm.* As in the case of the map of actors, a blank sample must be designed
    as a model for the realization with concrete data in each specific case. This
    diagram, envisioned as a flow diagram in the sense that it will register activi-
    ties and links between all actors and the caused effects, will be constructed
    on the basis of two axes. The horizontal axis reflects the time perspective,
    which means the development of the conflict in time as well as the actors'
    interconnections along this timeline – in a synchronic and diachronic way.
    The vertical axis shows the intensity of harm – the higher along the axis, the
    more severe – also positioned on the timeline, of course. In this sense, the
    diagram will enable a graphic presentation of the activities in the past and
    the harm caused, activities at present and the harm in progress and possible
    future activities and the foreseeable damage they may cause. The retrospec-
    tive traceability would be complemented, in this manner, by a prospective
    traceability. This concept, related to the horizon scanning used by green
    criminology, would be implemented in terms of the prevision of future
    responsibilities in order to access the involved – in the future – actors and
    to start with the needed accountability alerts and actions.

3   *Table of responsibilities.* Although the responsibilities in the different areas
    and levels are usually provided by law and are well known to the obligated
    subjects, it is important in each case, taking into account the map of actors
    and the diagram of traceability, to work out a definition and description

of the specific responsibilities that correspond to each involved actor. This mechanism will promote the visibility of the conflict in a systematic way. A table with primary information about actors, duties and binding regulations at the economic, political, social, civil, penal or institutional level (of course, these categories require further development) would provide clarity and simplify communications and processes of demand for all actors involved in the conflict. With respect to the table of responsibilities, the same system of the design of a blank sample should be implemented as a model in order to guide the completion of the table with concrete names, positions, legislations or other binding norms. Not only duties but prohibitions are to be registered, because as shown before, actions and omissions are equally responsible for cultural, structural and physical violence. It may be added that it is not insignificant that a carefully prepared table of responsibilities would attract the attention of not only the involved actors, but also interested media, bystanders and corporate stakeholders, to list just a few. The effects of blame and embarrassment at the level of corporate and political image, in this way, would take on its own weight. The general population's empathy with the affected population would probably take new forms. This may sound trivial. However, the shorter the social distance is, the stronger the support for affected collectives.

4   *Plan of intervention and accountability.* According to the involved actors, the complexity of retrospective and prospective traceability, and the table of responsibilities – as well as the distinction between compliance or no-compliance of the various actors – the design of a plan of intervention and accountability should be possible. In some cases, the cooperative period could still be put into practice with the initiation and formulation of communication among different actors (e.g. political, economic, affected communities). The planning of cooperative steps in order to prevent, stop or redress harm at the different levels should be drafted taking into account all the data and information collected and registered in the previous steps, aiming to reach the least possible violent action and reaction, demanding realistic paths and seeking the best agreement that can be achieved, first at civil and collective levels without judicial intervention. In cases in which cooperative steps are not possible with respect to certain actors or situations, the resort to legal means and judicial action must be available and the appropriate response should be considered in the intervention plan as well. Civil, administrative and penal action, as well as demands from economic or social institutions, or even at the regional and international level in cases of severe violation of human rights, should be likewise triggered. A plan of intervention and accountability drafted on the foundation of specific data would constitute a platform for public and private action as well as for collective organization and even for the involvement of society at various levels.

5   *Proceeding protocol.* The most important function of this plan of intervention and accountability is to be the foundation for the preparation of specific

proceeding protocols for each state office, economic actor, social institution or affected collective in order to establish the next steps to be taken after the diagnosis and prognosis of responsibilities and accountabilities defined by the four prior mechanisms. Proceedings protocols are to be designed as a clear reference for concrete actions, with the indication of means and datelines specifically designed for each concrete case. Blank samples will be the guide in this step as well, but the real data and particular requirements according to the specific circumstances must be defined for each case. These proceeding protocols, further, should be inter-articulated and must effectively reflect the communication and contact between actors. The proceeding protocols, in this way, should be the expression of the steps that are possible and exigible for each actor (Costanzo 2015: 169 ss.). Given that the possibility of its fulfillment is the base of its design, there will be no excuse for noncompliance. This means that if the non-satisfaction of basic needs continues because the proceeding protocol steps have not been fulfilled, this is not unavoidable. Violence, in a concrete and specific way, will thereafter have specific responsible names, and visible actions and omissions will be able to be individualized and claimed.

These mechanisms of approach for concrete instances of violence and conflict are not the solution in a context of violence. However, they are a further step toward the visibilization of invisible violence and of responsibilities. All these steps, recalling the 12 guidelines for a broad – macro – approach of the crime of maldevelopment, are to be understood as a concretization of those guidelines. Interdisciplinary and international academic work and public offices, rural and urban complexities are to be considered in each new concrete step. This is, however, a first proposal in this sense. The in–depth development of guidelines and mechanisms, however, is a long-term task that is just starting.

The integrative approach to the crime of maldevelopment has eradicated the idea of sovereigns and landlords. The approach of the penal system, therefore, is present, but it acts in a distinct form. This is what is called the subversion of the role assigned to the criminal system. As a criminological proposal, the updated role of the criminal system in this framework must be specifically explained.

Subverting the submissive attitude of criminal law toward the sovereign

The objective to identify and investigate maldevelopment as a crime is related to the penal system. This is not a priority, but it is, of course, important. As seen in some cases, a civil mechanism or administrative measures will be the best reactions. For severe cases of obstruction of the fulfillment of basic needs – fundamental rights violations – however, the civil and the administrative legal order will probably not suffice. In cases in which the criminal system is called to action, its function should be oriented toward quite different goals than the usual retributive or even preventive ones. A penal system or a system of account-ability and sanctions must be oriented toward the non-repetition based on an integral intervention not only upon the responsible actors, but – especially! – on the criminogenic conditions of the individuals and populations most exposed to the current or future violence. The integral intervention should be oriented, therefore, toward not only the binomial prevention/retribution formula but also prevention/reparation/prevention, triggering a "virtuous circle" of mechanisms for economic, cultural and legal peace – or, which is the same thing, triggering a movement in the opposite direction of the vicious circle of violence and the deregulated promotion of (mal)development.

Taking these ideas into account, therefore, the whole logic of the penal sys-tem should be revised because its current form does not really fulfill current requirements (see, in this sense, also Wells 2001: 14 ss.). The penal system should have a different perspective for the investigation and sanction of actors involved in acts which could belong to the crime of maldevelopment. This system would involve investigations carried out in the field of action of the punitive system that I have called *rebel*. Its counterpart is the traditional punitive system, which I have called *submissive*, and which is the manifestation of a legislative, executive and judicial system obedient to the mandates of the police state that acts on and against the rights of many of its citizens; servant to and, to a certain extent, even the weapon of the sovereign power of which Foucault spoke. Their submission does not take away responsibility for their performance, much less diminish their violence. On the contrary, the submissive acceptance of unjust orders and the active participation in the perpetuation of those orders, on the one hand, and the repression of the disadvantaged, on the other, make of that submission a repudiable and imputable attitude. Criminal intervention in the first case is submissive to the vagaries and interests of a huge state, economic and political apparatus, selective from its origin and obsequious to the established order; it is an intervention that is often unthinking (Zaffaroni et al. 2000) and complacent toward those who exercise power from privileged spaces of the most varied spheres (political, economic, cultural). As explained elsewhere (Böhm 2016), the *permissive* attitude with respect to severe corporate harm and human rights vio-lations is directly proportional to the *punitive* attitude with respect to ordinary criminal violence of vulnerable and marginalized individuals. This can be easily seen with respect, on the one hand, to the reaction of the state to the affected communities, which became "offenders" in the eyes of the state. On the other hand, with respect to ordinary crime, this can be seen as not directly related to business projects, as in the state attitude against street crime, for example. The more favorable the support for big, economic transnational projects, the more intensive the criminalization of street crime and social protest against the social and economic gap will be. Looking at this complex situation, the idea of a *penal state* (Wacquant 2009; Müller 2012) as the other face of an economically *accom-modating state* becomes more than apparent.

In contrast, the punitive power that is involved when we speak of the investigation and eventual punishment of the crime of maldevelopment is a punitive rebel system. The sense given to criminal intervention in this case is one of rebellion against that established order, of subversion of long-held practices of selective exercise and repression of the penal system. It deals with the claim and recovery of the right to use the discourse and the legal system truly in favor of individual and fundamental rights. It could be said that it is a rebel system in the sense of Locke, a rebellion against the unjust judicial system, because it rejects that this judicial system (actor of the jurisdictional function of the state) protects the interests of the Leviathan and not those of the citizens; the rebel punitive system, thus, rebels against a state of things in which the logics and mechanisms of institutional adjustment silently continue in favor of the corporatized organs of the state, and of the structures and economic actors that are developed both with and within it and they flourish, perpetuating the violence now deeply rooted in social and institutional structures. This punitive rebel system understands political needs, as does the criminology that provides empirical and conceptual support for reality (see Chapter 6) and the subversion of sterile formal orders that go against the rights that supposedly should be protected. That criminal lawyers and criminologists should pay attention and even encourage themselves to break down barriers in order to advance in the investigation (understood now in a broad sense) of macrocriminality systems was revealed in a clear admonition of the Spanish professor Juan Carlos Carbonell Mateu before a large audience of criminal lawyers and academics in Brazil: "When it becomes more important to discuss the place of the *dolus* than the atrocities committed by dictatorial regimes, you are complicit".[2] And to this it could be added that the violations of fundamental rights that take place in the context of democratic governments can also lead to the category of complicity for those who refuse to investigate and discuss them constructively.

This punitive rebel system aspires to recompose equilibrium states where situations of structural imbalance have been generated and continue perpetuating. This goal is different from the goal of the submissive punitive system. Therefore, the purposes that are assigned to a system that acts against the crime of maldevelopment must also be thought of in a different way. I understand that the objectives of criminal intervention against the crime of maldevelopment – apart from the penal purposes if punishing the complicity that civil actors may have lent to military dictatorships, for example – are at least three, not mutually exclusive, but cumulative: visibility, dignification and restoration.

By judging acts understood as part of the crime of maldevelopment, we aspire to make *visible* the vast scope and number of victims, direct and indirect. Through entrepreneurial undertakings and past and current economic measures, physical violence, cultural violence and structural violence are inflicted both by state actors and by private actors. Physical violence is often in the eye of criminal investigation, although it is insufficient, but cultural and structural violence, invisible, is not. For this reason, this category makes possible the visualization through the research and sanction, and gives voice and image to victims and relatives of victims of that violence not perceived as such. The purpose of the investigations and possible sanctions is, therefore, also to create visibility for the existing relationships in the various areas of civil society, as a support and inescapable part of these structures and violence, for example through silence and judicial indifference, or perhaps through the economic benefit of business or financial actors, to mention just a few assumptions. In many cases, this invisible and silent action is what facilitates the continuity of the harmful activity or measure, so that institutions, despite being democratic, perpetuate and build on the benefits emanating from violent economic activities (Ruggiero 1997, 2007; Albrecht 2007; Huisman 2008, 2010).

Visibility necessarily entails *dignifying* the victims, their relatives and society as a whole. It is about the recovery of figure and voice through the identification of the facts and the subjects that generate these less studied forms of victimization. It is not about the punishment for the punishment itself, but about the narration of stories not yet narrated. If the penal sanction is loaded with symbolism in the submissive order, much more symbolism can be acquired within the framework of a rebellious punitive system. In the field of rebel punitive power, the symbolism is embodied in victims who recover their battered indigenous cultural dignity, in businessmen confronted with the fact that the economic benefit of their activity, related to structural violence, can bring about a concrete corporate loss of prestige. That is to say, giving voice to a victim takes away from the person of the political or economic actor – the representative of the sovereign – the monopoly of the audible voice which it has enjoyed until now.

To these two purposes, primarily intangible, is added the purpose of tangible and material result of the restoration, at the same level of importance as the previous ones. I use here the term "restoration" in a broad sense, to encompass both the concrete material compensation to individual victims and affected communities as well as the estimation and recovery of spaces, villages and – if possible – environmental surroundings and through symbolic reparation works, such as the installation of plaques and memorial sculptures, or the construction of health care spaces, educational centers, areas of study and training according to local needs, which in the short, medium and long term bring a tangible improvement in the level of satisfaction of basic needs and a certain autonomy in the existential conditions of the community or communities in question and in the areas in which the main affectations have occurred. It deals with the restoration of a multiplicity of damages, understood in economic, social and cultural terms.[3] In this sense, it can be said that negative general prevention would be an implied goal: it must be clear that it is not profitable to do business or collaborate in any way with relationships and structures that entail the use or perpetuation of violence.[4]

Therefore, the role of the penal system with respect to the crime of maldevelopment, although it is a conceptual category within the framework of criminology, is not the typical role of determining a criminal type, defining it and imposing a possible penalty. The penal system, understood in this way, is just one mechanism, and not even the most important one, among many others that, based on this theoretical proposal, can begin to be considered in a joint manner.

A call for discussion, exchange and transformative work

If violence is understood as the absence of peace, and if it is understood that construction for peace should also be mobilized from knowledge, research and teaching, this work in the introduction of the crime of maldevelopment as a conceptual category of criminology can be thought of as a contribution in this sense. Think of conflicts not as spaces of confrontation, but as platforms for the establishment of dialogue, with the aim of being an academy that contributes to the cessation of structural violence under which large segments of the populations of the Global South still live. In this sense, even understanding that the conflict has not yet ceased, it is interesting to open up for future exploration the idea of transition, and to incorporate, in this way, the use of the concept of structural violence as a basis to construct positive peace (Sharp 2014: 4, 20 ss.) and overcome social harms and deficiencies accumulated over centuries of inequality.

Although this will be the subject of future research and specifications, first theoretical reflections, first guidelines and first sketches of approach mechanisms, inspired by the concepts and cases studied throughout this work, were presented here. The development and in-depth work of this map and its work route will undoubtedly require a lot of time, and significant effort on the part of academics from both the Global South and North.

In particular, a clear approach on the part of the academy is necessary to understand the real conditions of the powerful, political and economic actors which are protagonists in the crime of maldevelopment, and the real conditions of those in the territory, those who find or may be exposed to victimization with this form of violence. Deregulation is not going to be decided in a textbook, nor are territorial struggles to be fought in a classroom. This is clear. However, interdisciplinary and in-between actors' efforts can be made to ensure that voices are heard in relatively balanced conditions, and that the satisfaction of needs, therefore, whose refusal is linked to the violence of maldevelopment, is reduced through each conversation, program, measure, judicial decision or signed decree. From all these spaces, the approach must be attempted, and for this, the theoretical scaffolding with perspective of reality is essential.

Notes

1 The *Ruggie Principles* are embodied in a UN document released in 2011 that stresses the role and responsibility of states and corporations almost as unique subjects and decision-makers before and during the operation of transnational businesses, whereas victims groups are considered only in the third part of the document, which is related to measures to be taken after harm has been done, and even in this case, victims are not regarded

as central actors in agreements and compromises, but just as people who must be asked for their opinions in a nonbinding way. As a follow-up to the Global Compact project, the Ruggie Principles aspired to put more pressure on states and corporations and to better protect victims. In reality, unfortunately, the role of victims and potential victims of transnational business remains marginalized. This soft law document can be understood, on the one hand, as a (smooth) attempt to impose order on the transnational business world, especially with respect to activities in economically weaker countries; however, on the other hand, it is clear that international regulations and goals are not oriented toward constraining the economically stronger states by mandatory limiting norms which could mean a reduction in profits for those states and their largest companies. For this reason, a binding document is being considered as a necessary harder level also in the institutional framework of the UN. See the official information on the *Open-ended intergovernmental working group on transnational corporations and other business enterprises with respect to human rights.* https://www.ohchr.org/en/hrbodies/hrc/wgtranscorp/pages/igwgontnc.aspx.

2 Seminario del Instituto Brasilero de Ciencias Criminales (IBCCRIM), 2015, August. São Paulo.
3 For a comprehensive and detailed reading on justice based on the idea of reparation, see the work of Galain Palermo (2009).
4 On state-corporation cooperation, and the difficulties in investigating this link with respect to international crimes, see Huisman (2010).

References

Agamben, Giorgio. 2002. *Homo Sacer. Die souveräne Macht und das nackte Leben*, Frankfurt a.M.: Suhrkamp.

Albrecht, Hans-Jörg. 2007. "Internationale Kriminalität, Gewaltökonomie und Menschenrechtsverbrechen: Antworten des Strafrechts". *Internationale Politik und Gesellschaft* 2, 153–169.

Böhm, María Laura. 2016. "Transnational Corporations, Human Rights Violations and Structural Violence in Latin America: A Criminological Approach". *Kriminologisches Journal: Sonderheft Lateinamerika* 4, 272–293.

Chiriboga, V. Manuel. 1992. "Desarrollo agropecuario que necesitan América Latina y el Caribe: democracia económica y crecimiento con equidad". In: Asociación Latinoamericana de Organizaciones de Promoción (ed.). *América Latina: opciones estratégicas de desarrollo*, Caracas: Ed. Nueva Sociedad, 219–235.

Costanzo, Leandro. 2015. "Inclusión social, probation y política criminal democrática: Una conjugación posible". In: Ministerio Público de la Defensa (ed.). *Algunas propuestas para el ejercicio de la defensa durante la ejecución de la pena*, Buenos Aires: MPD, 171–207.

Friedrichs, David/Rothe, Dawn L. 2015. *Crimes of Globalization*. London: Routledge.

Galain Palermo, Pablo. 2009. *La reparación del daño como equivalente funcional de la pena*. Montevideo: Universidad Católica del Uruguay/Konrad Adenauer Stiftung.

Galtung, Johan. 1969. "Violence, Peace, and Peace Research". *Journal of Peace Research* 6 (3), 167–191.

Galtung, Johan. 1996. *Peace by Peaceful Means: Peace and Conflict, Development and Civilization*. London: Sage.

Huisman, Wim. 2008. "Corporations and International Crimes". In: Smeulers, A./Haveman, R. (eds.). *Supranational Criminology: Towards a Criminology of International Crimes*, Antwerpen et al.: Intersentia, 181–211.

Huisman, Wim. 2010. *Business as Usual? Corporate Involvement in International Crimes*. The Hague: Eleven International Publishing.

Müller, Markus-Michael. 2012. "The Rise of the Penal State in Latin America". *Contemporary Justice Review: Issues in Criminal, Social, and Restorative Justice* 15 (1), 57–76.

Pauls, Nels/Zagorski, Kim/Ferguson, D. Chris. 2015. "On Harm and Mediated Space: The BP Oil Spill in The Age of Globalisation". In: Brisman, Avi/South, Nigel/White, Rob (eds.). *Environmental Crime and Social Conflict. Contemporary and Emerging Issues*, Farnham: Ashgate, 265–283.

Ruggiero, Vincenzo. 1997. "Criminals and Service Providers: Cross-National Dirty Economies". *Crime, Law & Social Change* 28, 27–38.

Ruggiero, Vincenzo. 2007. "It's the Economy, Stupid! Classifying Power Crime". *International Journal of the Sociology of Law* 24 (4), 163–177.

Sharp, Dustin N. 2014. "Introduction". In: Sharp, D. N. (ed.). *Justice and Economic Violence in Transition*, New York: Springer, 1–26.

Wacquant, Loïc. 2009. "The Body, the Ghetto and the Penal State". *Qualitative Sociology* 32 (1), 101–129.

Wells, Celia. 2001 (2nd ed.). *Corporations and Criminal Responsibility*. New York: Oxford University Press.

Zaffaroni, Eugenio Raül/Alagia, Alejandro/Slokar, Alejandro. 2000. *Manual de Derecho penal. Parte general*, Buenos Aires: Ediar.

Index

abbreviation and fragmentation 195
accountability 181–185
actor position 57–58
Agamben, Giorgio 33, 171, 176, 180–182
agrarian economy 162–165
American Convention on Human Rights
    (ACHR) 96
Aniyar de Castro, Lolita 202–203, 205, 206
Argentina: medical attention 50–51;
    MOCASE case study 2, 67, 99–111, 121,
    153–154, 158, 160, 190, 192, 197, 198;
    United States support of dictatorships 31
authority 181–182
avoidability 54–55

Baguazo case study: aftermath 137–138;
    crime of maldevelopment 182–183, 188;
    free trade agreement with United States
    133–135; mass media representation 197;
    overview 2, 120, 133; physical violence
    135–137, 191; preexisting invisible
    violence 153–154; white-collar crime
    191, 192
bare life 171–172, 175
basic needs 6, 51–52, 58, 112, 154
biopolitics: economization and
    internationalization of 172–173;
    as fundamental technology
    of governmentality 170–171;
    governmentality and 166–167; norms
    and 169; sovereign power and 166–167
Bolivia 31
Brazil: Campos Lindos Agricultural Project
    164–165; Matopiba case study 2, 120,
    127–133, 153–154, 156, 158, 165, 191,
    192, 197, 198
Buen Vivir (Good Living) 22, 186, 210

Campos Lindos Agricultural Project 164–165
case studies: Baguazo case in Peru 2, 120,
    133–138, 153–154, 181–182, 188, 192,
    197; Indigenous Women of Lote 8 case
    in Guatemala 2, 120, 121–128, 153–154,
    158, 185, 190, 197, 198; Matopiba case in
    Brazil 2, 120, 127–133, 153–154, 156, 158,
    165, 191, 192, 197, 198; MOCASE case
    in Argentina 67, 99–111, 121, 153–154,
    158, 165, 190, 192, 197, 198; MOCASE
    case study 2; Ralco case in Chile 2, 67,
    87–98, 153–154, 158, 190, 192, 193–194,
    198; Salaverna and El Peñasquito cases in
    Mexico 2, 67, 68–77, 153–154, 158, 160,
    192, 197, 198; Texaco/Chevron case in
    Ecuador 2, 67, 78–87, 153–154, 158, 190,
    192–193, 195, 197, 198; Valle de Siria
    case in Honduras 2, 120–121, 138–142,
    153–154, 158, 190, 197, 198
Chile: Indigenous Law 87; Ralco case study
    2, 67, 87–98, 153–154, 190, 192, 193–194,
    195, 197, 198; United States support of
    dictatorships 31
China 13, 16
Chirif, Alberto 138, 160–161, 188
city medicine 168
collective action 24–25
crimes of globalization 156, 190, 200–201
criminalization of reality 195
criminal policy 27, 30–32, 57
cultural violence: in Argentina 104–105,
    110–111; in Chile after business
    activity 97–98; in Chile before business
    activity 89–91; concept of 43–45;
    development and 24; in Ecuador before
    business activity 79–80; in Ecuador
    during and after business activity

85–87; inequality and 192; in State of Zacatecas after business activity 77; in State of Zacatecas before business activity 70–71

death 169–171
de-historization 195
deregulation 5, 18–19, 26, 27–32, 33, 186
development 20–25, 58–59, 100, 139–140, 159, 176
domestic structural violence 6
Donziger, Steve 195–196
Durkheim, Émile 44

Ecuador: environmental framework of Constitution 23; Texaco/Chevron case study 2, 67, 78–87, 153–154, 158, 190, 192–193, 195, 197, 198
Elbert, Carlos 203–204, 205
energy industry 4
episodic framing 195
Europe 20, 27
European Union 156
exclusion 171–172, 203–204
extractive industries 2, 23, 120, 159, 164, 185, 201, 222

Ferrajoli, Luigi 206
form of relation 57–58
Foucault, Michel 30, 152, 166–168, 169, 173, 176, 186, 187
Free Economy and the Strong State, The (Gamble) 31
free trade agreements 18–20, 133–135, 162
Friedman, Milton 31

Galtung, Johan 5, 6, 8, 41–47, 51–58, 152, 157, 159, 171
Gamble, Andrew 31
globalization 100, 156, 172–173, 190, 200–201, 203–204
governmentality 166–167, 171, 173
green criminology 196–198
Guatemala, Indigenous Women of Lote 8 case study 2, 120, 121–128, 153–154, 185, 197, 198
Gudynas, Eduardo 22–24

Hagan, John 205
hegemon 5, 34
Honduras, Valle de Siria case study 2, 120–121, 138–142, 153–154, 158, 190, 197, 198

human rights 1–4, 21, 23, 40, 52, 58, 96, 109, 123, 158–159, 174, 183–185, 193–194, 199, 201–206, 219–220
hydrocarbon industry 4

inclusion 171–172
India 13
Indigenous Women of Lote 8 case study: especial situation in the face of the mining industry 122–123; mass media representation 197; overview 2, 120, 121; physical violence against women 123–125; preexisting invisible violence 153–154; sexual violence 125–126; victimology 198; violation of rights 185; white-collar crime 190
inequality 55, 192
Inter-American Commission of Human Rights, 96, 159
Inter-American Court of Human Rights 21, 23
international economic policies 5
invisible violence: concept of 3–4, 44–45; neoliberalism and 33; new forms of 154–157; preexisting 153–154; reconfiguration and deepened conditions of 160–162

labor force medicine 168
Latin America: agrarian economy in 162–165; Buen Vivir in 186; characterization of democracies 192; deregulation 5, 18–19, 26, 27–32; development 20–25; environmental harm 197–198; free trade agreements 18–19; global relationships 34; historical perspective of invisible structures of violence in 45–51; impact of state actors and international economies at social domestic level 25–27; infrastructure 16; interrelationship between Europe and 14–15; interrelationship between United States and 14–15; mass media corporations 195; natural resources of region 16, 17–18, 23; neoliberalism 21–22, 26; political and economic features of current 13–27; sovereign violence in 174–176; structural and physical violent relationships between local and foreign actors 55–57
laws 168–170, 181–182, 202

macrocriminality 2, 193–194
maldevelopment: attribution to specific actors 185; background and horizon of

crime of maldevelopment in criminology
188–208; conceptual category 6–7,
180–181, 187; crime of 208–209;
criminological background on the
part of the Global North 189–201;
criminological background on the
part of the Global South 201–205;
development and 176, 186–188;
guidelines for an approach to the
crime of 219–225; mechanisms for the
approach to the crime of 225–228
Mapuche people 32–33, 87–98, 151–152, 199
Marx, Karl 187
mass crimes 204–205
mass media studies 194–196
Matopiba case study: crimes of globalization
156; economic development 127–130;
mass media representation 197; overview 2,
120, 127; physical violence 131–133, 158;
preexisting invisible violence 153–154;
resistance against state actors 165; structural
and physical negative impact 130–131;
victimology 198; white-collar crime 191,
192
measure 57–58
medical attention 50–51
Mexico, Salaverna and El Peñasquito case
studies 2, 67, 68–77, 153–154, 158, 160,
192, 197, 198
mining industry 4
MOCASE case study: cultural violence in
region 104–105, 110–111; mass media
representation 197; overview 2, 67, 99–100,
121; physical violence 107–110, 158;
preexisting invisible violence 153–154;
relevance of specific business area/activity
101–104; resistance against state actors 165;
structural violence in region 105–107;
victimology 198; white-collar crime 190,
192
most favored nation status 19

national treatment 19
neoliberalism 26, 27–32, 33
neutralization techniques 20, 83, 205
non-satisfaction 52–53
norms 168–170

obstacles 53–54
omission 81, 109, 194, 195, 208, 220–221
organizational obstacles 53–54

Pehuenche people 87–98, 199
personal violence 42

Peru: Baguazo case study 2, 120, 133–138,
153–154, 181–182, 188, 192, 197; free trade
agreements with United States 133–135
physical obstacles 53–54
physical violence: in Argentina 107–110;
in Brazil 127; categories of 157–160;
in Chile after business activity 96–97;
development and 24; in Ecuador
during and after business activity
84–85; interrelationship between cultural
violence and 43–45; interrelationship
between structural violence and 42–45;
in Peru 135–137; in State of Zacatecas
during and after business activity
76–77; structural violent relationships
between local and foreign actors and
2–3, 56–57; use on part of corporations/
businessmen/entrepreneurs in protection
facilities/ investments 157–158; use on
part of individuals and communities
affected by economic projects 157; use
on part of individuals working with/
in relation with newly arrived facilities
159; use on part of the state in defense
of established order 158–159; against
women 123–126
"Poor Laws" 168
protection of prior investments 19

Ralco case study: business/people/economic
situation in area "during" and "after"
94–95; cultural violence in region "after"
97–98; cultural violence in region
"before" 89–91; green criminology 197;
macrocriminality 193–194; mass media
representation 195; overview 2, 67, 87–88;
physical violence in region "after" 96–97;
preexisting invisible violence 153–154;
relevance of specific business area/activity
88; structural violence in region "before"
91–94; structural violence in region
"during" and "after" 95–96; victimology
198; white-collar crime 190, 192
reregulation 5, 139–140
responsibility 183–185
Rivera Beiras, Iñaki 52, 60, 206–207
rule of law 33
Russia 13

Sack, Fritz 172
Salaverna and El Peñasquito case studies:
business/people/economic situation
in area "during" and "after" 72–73;
crime of maldevelopment 160; cultural

violence in region "after" 77; cultural violence in region "before" 70; mass media representation 197; overview 2, 67, 68; physical violence 158; physical violence in region "during" and "after" 76–77; preexisting invisible violence 153–154; relevance of specific business area/activity 68–70; structural violence in region "before" 71–72; structural violence in region "during" and "after" 73–76; victimology 198; white-collar crime 192
Schmitt, Carl 165
security 29
sexual violence 125–126, 157
social distance 44, 77, 90, 221
Social Division of Labour, The (Durkheim) 44
social medicine 168
sovereign power: authority and 181–182; governmentality and 166–168; as interstate power 173; in Latin America 165–176; protected territories of 174–176; subverting the submissive attitude of criminal law toward 228–232
state medicine 168
state of emergency 181–182
Stenson, Kevin 30
structural violence: in Argentina 105–107; in Chile before business activity 91–94; in Chile during and after business activity 95–96; concept of 5–6; development and 24; domestic 6; in Ecuador before business activity 79–80; in Ecuador during and after business activity 81–84; international conditions and 34; interrelationship between cultural violence and 43–45; interrelationship between physical violence and 42–45; physical violent relationships between local and foreign actors and 2–3, 55–57; in State of Zacatecas before business activity 71–72; in State of Zacatecas during and after business activity 73–76
supranational courts 19–20
sustainable development 22
Svampa, Maristella 24, 122, 159, 175

territory 174–176
Texaco/Chevron case study: business/people/economic situation in area "during" and "after" 80–81; cultural violence in region "before" 79–80; cultural violence in region "during" and "after" 85–87; green criminology 197; mass media representation 195; overview 2, 67, 78; physical violence 158; physical violence in region "during" and "after" 84–85; preexisting invisible violence 153–154; relevance of specific business area/activity 78–79; structural violence in region "before" 79–80; structural violence in region "during" and "after" 81–84; victimology 198; white-collar crime 190, 192–193
transnational business activities 4

United States 13, 20, 27, 31, 133–135, 138
Uruguay 31

Valle de Siria case study: mass media representation 197; overview 2, 120–121, 138–139; physical diseases and death from poisoning 140–141; physical violence 158; preexisting invisible violence 153–154; promise of project 139–140; victimology 198; white-collar crime 190
victimology 198–200, 202
violence: development and 24; forms of 3–4, 42–45; invisible structures of violence in Latin America 45–57; maldevelopment understood as 188; visibilization and action against invisible 57–59; see also cultural violence; invisible violence; physical violence; sexual violence; structural violence; visible violence
visible violence: concept of 3–4; neoliberalism and 33; new forms of 157–160

Wacquant, Loïc 28
white-collar crime 2, 190–193

Yunus, Muhammad 24

Zaffaroni, Eugenio Rául 204–205